A Brief Inquiry into the Meaning of Sin and Faith

John Rawls

A BRIEF INQUIRY INTO THE MEANING OF SIN AND FAITH

WITH "ON MY RELIGION"

Edited by Thomas Nagel

With commentaries by Joshua Cohen and Thomas Nagel, and by Robert Merrihew Adams

HARVARD UNIVERSITY PRESS
Cambridge, Massachusetts, and London, England

First Harvard University Press paperback edition, 2010

Library of Congress Cataloging-in-Publication Data

Rawls, John, 1921–2002.
A brief inquiry into the meaning of sin and faith :
with "on my religion" /
John Rawls ; edited by Thomas Nagel.
p.   cm.
Includes bibliographical references and index.
ISBN 978-0-674-03331-3 (cloth : alk. paper)
ISBN 978-0-674-04753-2 (pbk.)
1. Philosophical theology.   2. Philosophy and religion.
3. Sin.   4. Faith.
5. Rawls, John, 1921–2002—Religion.
I. Nagel, Thomas.   II. Title.
BT40.R39 2009
230—dc22   2008033809

Contents

A Brief Inquiry into the Meaning of Sin and Faith

Introduction

Joshua Cohen and Thomas Nagel

1. When John Rawls died in 2002, there was found among his files a short statement entitled "On My Religion," the second of the two texts included in this volume. He had apparently written it in the 1990s,[1] not for publication but perhaps for the interest of family and friends—though he did not distribute it. Rawls describes the history of his religious beliefs and attitudes toward religion, and refers to a period during his last two years as an undergraduate at Princeton (1941–42) when he "became deeply concerned with theology and its doctrines," and considered attending a seminary to study for the Episcopal priesthood. But he decided to enlist in the army instead, "as so many of my friends and classmates were doing." By June of 1945, he had abandoned his orthodox Christian beliefs. With characteristic tentativeness and a disclaimer of self-knowledge, Rawls speculates that his beliefs changed because of his experiences in the war and his reflections on the moral significance of the Holocaust. When he

---

1. The version published here comes from a file created on his computer in 1997.

returned to Princeton in 1946, it was to pursue a doctorate in philosophy.

Friends of Rawls knew that before the war he had considered the priesthood, but they did not know of any surviving writings that expressed his religious views from that period, and "On My Religion" does not mention any. Not long after Rawls's death, however, Professor Eric Gregory of the Princeton religion department made the startling discovery that just such a document, the more substantial of the two texts included here, was on deposit in the Princeton library. *A Brief Inquiry into the Meaning of Sin and Faith: An Interpretation Based on the Concept of Community* is Rawls's senior thesis, submitted to the philosophy department in December 1942, just before the accelerated completion of his bachelor's degree.[2] Gregory came upon it while idly browsing the catalogue for senior theses by famous Princeton graduates, but when he ordered a copy and read it, he immediately recognized its importance and decided to write about it.[3]

Gregory has discovered that the two readers of the thesis were Walter Stace and Theodore M. Greene, and that they gave it a grade of 98 out of 100. Rawls also thanks the Reformation historian E. Harris

---

2. In a brief, unpublished autobiographical essay, Rawls says that he graduated from Princeton a semester early, "all study and examinations having been completed by the Christmas break in December [1942]," but he does not refer to the thesis. In a biographical chapter of his book on Rawls, based on taped interviews with Rawls in summer 1993, Thomas Pogge mentions the thesis. He says only that it was on a religious subject, and that it grew out of a course on human evil that Rawls had taken in spring 1942, with Norman Malcolm. The reading list included Plato, Augustine, Philip Leon, Reinhold Niebuhr, and Bishop Butler. All but Butler play a significant role in the thesis. See Pogge, *John Rawls: His Life and Theory of Justice* (New York: Oxford University Press, 2007), p. 11.

3. The result is his illuminating essay, "Before the Original Position: The Neo-Orthodox Theology of the Young John Rawls," *Journal of Religious Ethics* 35.2 (2007): 179–206.

Harbison at one point in a footnote. But it has not been possible to identify Rawls's adviser. (Stace was his adviser for the Ph.D. thesis.)

In 2006 Gregory approached John Rawls's widow, Margaret Rawls, with the suggestion that the thesis be published. This presented Mrs. Rawls and her fellow literary executor, T. M. Scanlon, with a difficult decision. Another copy of the thesis had remained in Rawls's possession, the one he got back from the two faculty readers with their initialed comments in the margins. On deposit in the Rawls archive at the Harvard library, it had not yet attracted attention. Now copies were made and circulated to several friends and former students of Rawls.

The period of Rawls's final illness and the years since his death have seen the publication of several works brought to completion with the help of others, but they are all books to which he had given his approval. This was entirely different: a youthful work written under pressure of time to meet a college requirement, meant only for the eyes of two faculty members, and expressing views that he had long since abandoned. It seemed clear that Rawls had never imagined that the thesis might one day be published, and that if the question had been put to him, he would certainly have refused. That was a serious reason against publication, and in favor of leaving the thesis accessible only by the much more limited and cumbersome route of consultation through the Princeton and Harvard libraries.

Another question was whether, apart from what Rawls would have wished, publishing the thesis would be a disservice to him, in light of its unevenness and occasional lack of polish. While there was some difference of opinion over how much weight should be given to the generally acknowledged hypothetical truth that Rawls would not, if asked, have consented to its publication, it seemed significantly less than the decisive weight owed to an actual refusal of consent. And this made it necessary for us to consider more directly whether publication would be consistent with our obligations of loyalty to Rawls and our respect for his memory.

A favorable answer to this question comes from the character of the thesis itself. To read it is a moving experience: the thesis is an extraordinary work for a 21-year-old, animated by youthful passion and powerful ethical conviction, often vividly expressed, and informed by erudition and deep philosophical reflection. Though the quality is not uniform (Chapters Two and Three are weaker than the rest), the intellectual force and the moral and spiritual motivation that made Rawls who he is are already there. The thesis was written in the middle of the war that Rawls was about to join as a combatant, and this somber background is palpable through his reflections on Fascism and Nazism. Given the estimable intellectual and personal qualities the thesis displays, making it more widely available cannot be regarded as a disservice to his memory.

If publication is not on balance contrary to Rawls's interest, then it can be justified if it benefits a wider public, and that seems clearly true. Apart from its purely biographical importance, the thesis is a remarkable resource for understanding the development of his thought. Although it can in no sense be presented as a publication of John Rawls, it seems permissible to bring it out as a publication by others of an important piece of writing by John Rawls—comparable to the publication of letters by a writer that shed light on his published work.

An alternative was to make the thesis available on the Harvard philosophy department website, but it seemed preferable to bring it out in book form, together with "On My Religion," and to include some commentary both on its relation to Rawls's later work and, more important, on its theological content and background. The latter is the particular concern of Robert Adams's essay in this volume.

After extended deliberation the literary executors concluded that publication was warranted, and Harvard University Press accepted the proposal. This book is the result.

2. Those who have studied Rawls's work, and even more, those who knew him personally, are aware of a deeply religious temperament that informed his life and writings, whatever may have been his beliefs. He says, for example, that political philosophy aims at a defense of reasonable faith, in particular reasonable faith in the possibility of a just constitutional democracy;[4] he says that the recognition of this possibility shapes our attitude "toward the world as a whole";[5] he suggests that if a reasonably just society is not possible, one might appropriately wonder whether "it is worthwhile for human beings to live on earth";[6] and he concludes *A Theory of Justice* with powerfully moving remarks about how the original position enables us to see the social world and our place in it *sub specie aeternitatis*.[7] These and kindred reflections express an aspiration to a comprehensive outlook on the world, which is an element of what we mean by a religious temperament.

Religion and religious conviction are also important as themes within Rawls's political philosophy. For example, his case for the first principle of justice—that of equal basic liberties—aims to "generalize the principle of religious toleration."[8] More broadly, his theory of

4. John Rawls, *Political Liberalism* [hereafter *PL*] (New York: Columbia University Press, 1993; paperback edition, 1996), p. 172.

5. *PL*, p. 128.

6. Ibid., p. lxxii; John Rawls, *The Law of Peoples, with "The Idea of Public Reason Revisited"* [hereafter *LP*] (Cambridge, Mass.: Harvard University Press, 1999), p. 128.

7. John Rawls, *A Theory of Justice* [hereafter *TJ*] (Cambridge, Mass.: Harvard University Press, 1971; revised edition, 1999), p. 514 (all page references will be to the revised edition).

8. *TJ*, p. 180, n. 6; also p. 181.

justice is in part a response to the problem of how political legitimacy can be achieved despite religious conflict, and how, among citizens of different religious confessions, political justification can proceed without reference to religious conviction. And these concerns lie at the heart of Rawls's account of political liberalism, whose fundamental question he states as follows: "How is it possible for those affirming a religious doctrine that is based on religious authority, for example, the Church or the Bible, also to hold a reasonable political conception that supports a just democratic regime?"[9] For these reasons, Rawls's own attitudes toward religion and their development over time are of extraordinary interest, both personally and for the understanding of his thought.

The texts published here are relevant to such understanding in two different ways. First, they display the profound engagement with and knowledge of religion that form the background of Rawls's later views on the importance of separating religion and politics. Unlike many liberals, Rawls was not the product of a secular culture. Though his Episcopalian upbringing was, as he says, only conventionally religious, everything changed during his last two years at Princeton. He developed the religious convictions so vividly expressed in the thesis, which conveys a strong sense of the reality of sin, faith, and the divine presence, and which has as its first "fundamental presupposition" that "there is a being whom Christians call God and who has revealed Himself in Christ Jesus" (111).[10] Rawls's repeated emphasis through-

9. This comes from the Introduction to the paperback edition of *Political Liberalism*, where Rawls explains that the first edition had failed to "identify explicitly the philosophical issue it addresses" because it had spoken too generically about "reasonable religious, philosophical, and moral doctrines," and had not identified the particular concern with religious doctrines and religious authority. See *PL*, paperback ed., p. xxxix.

10. Page references to the thesis and to "On My Religion" are given in parentheses in the text.

out his mature work on the importance in the lives of the faithful of religious convictions—he describes them as "non-negotiable" and as "binding absolutely"[11]—and the need for a theory of justice to take them seriously drew on his personal experience of religious faith.

Second, the moral and social convictions that the thesis expresses in religious form are related in complex and illuminating ways to the central ideas of Rawls's later writings on moral and political theory. His notions of sin, faith, and community are simultaneously moral and theological, and despite fundamental differences they prefigure the moral outlook found in *A Theory of Justice.* The main points of contact are these: (1) endorsement of a morality defined by interpersonal relations rather than by pursuit of the highest good; (2) insistence on the importance of the separateness of persons, so that the moral community or community of faith is a relation among distinct individuals; (3) rejection of the concept of society as a contract or bargain among egoistic individuals; (4) condemnation of inequality based on exclusion and hierarchy; (5) rejection of the idea of merit.

The most conspicuous discontinuity with the later work is the absence from the thesis of a political as contrasted with a purely moral conception of society. Ideas about rights, law, constitutions, and democracy play no role in the thesis. More pointedly, there is no suggestion that conflicts of value and conviction are inevitable even among reasonable persons, nor is there any suggestion that we must put aside some of our most fundamental convictions to work out principles of justice—ideas that play a central role in justice as fairness and political liberalism. Instead of seeing a conception of justice in part as a response to disagreements that are inevitable even under favorable social and political conditions, Rawls here says that the "chief prob-

11. See *PL,* p. 311, and *TJ,* p. 182. It should be said that both phrases are used to characterize moral views and obligations as well as specifically religious commitments and obligations.

lem of politics is to work out some scheme of social arrangements which can so harness human sin as to make the natural correlates of community and personality possible." In theology, ethics, and politics alike, the problem is "one of controlling and ridding the world of sin" (127–128).[12]

Our discussion will begin with these philosophical continuities and discontinuities, and then we will return to Rawls's mature views on politics, religion, and public reason.

3. In the thesis, Rawls presents his own ethical views in opposition to a position he calls naturalism. By "naturalism" he does not mean what goes by that name in present-day philosophical discourse, namely the position that all of reality can be completely described in the terms of natural science. This could not very well be what he means, since he finds naturalism to be exemplified by Plato, Aristotle, Augustine, and Aquinas, among others. "Naturalism as we understand it," he says, "is not materialism, but is any view which constructs the cosmos in naturalistic terms" (119). In presenting his account Rawls distinguishes two kinds of relations—natural and personal—and one can best understand what he means by the "natural" by contrasting it with the personal.

The natural world is extended in space and contains objects, including the bodies of persons. Things in the natural world interact in various ways. All kinds of objects can interact causally, but persons also enter into psychological relations of perception, desire, aversion, and so forth, with other objects. It is this category of relations between persons and objects—particularly the relations of perception and appetite—that Rawls calls "natural."

12. See, more generally, the brief discussion of implications for political theory at 126–128.

There is also, however, a very different system of relations among the persons in the world. Distinct from natural relations between persons and objects, these relations are essentially interpersonal, or communal, and are marked by mutuality of regard:

> The relation between the "I" and the "thou" is therefore personal, that between the "I" as desiring and the thing desired such as food and drink is natural, while the relation between any two things is causal, such as the relation between the food and drink and the table upon which it rests. (114)

This is fairly rough-and-ready, but one understands what Rawls means. The I-thou relation is not a relation of a person to an object in the world, but a recognition of a unique other self as a person with powers of personality comparable to one's own:

> A personal relation is characterized by a "thou" over on the "other" side. A natural relation has as its "beyond" a "that" or an "it", i.e., some object. The fact that a "thou" stands over against us and not an object changes the entire atmosphere of the relation. There is no man who acts the same way to objects as he does to persons. In personal relations we are conscious that we are related to "others" who resemble ourselves. (115)

Thus personal relations, unlike natural ones, are active on both sides, and the activity of the other, of the "thou", includes both judging and self-revelation.[13]

Drawing on this natural-personal distinction, Rawls criticizes a group of ethical views he calls naturalistic, which treat all relations as natural, and suppose the aim of ethics is to identify the proper object of human striving and desire. These systems disagree about what that object is (happiness, the form of the good, God) and what human beings require in order to achieve the exalted object (knowledge, educa-

---

13. Rawls lists eight features of personal relations at 115–118.

tion and habituation, or God's saving grace). But all are founded on the desire for an object, not on interpersonal relations. Naturalism, the thesis argues, reduces spiritual life to "the level of desire and appetition" (107), as if "the whole universe, including God, can be naturalized" (157).

True Christian ethics is founded instead on a recognition of the independent reality and fundamental importance of personality and community (111–112). It concerns the appropriate relations of persons to one another; moreover, these personal relations form a nexus (116), so that our relation to any one person resonates in our relation to others, including God. "The universe is at its root a spiritual or personal one. . . . The world in its essence, is a community, a community of creator and created and has as its source, God" (112–113). Personal relations can be either positive or negative: they include hate as well as love, envy and egotistic pride as well as fellowship among persons in community. Ethics and religion should both be concerned not with the pursuit of the good but with establishing the proper form of interpersonal relations: community. "Proper ethics is not the relating of a person to some objective 'good' for which he should strive, but is the relating of person to person and finally to God" (114).

Taking up the historical framework of Anders Nygren, the thesis criticizes the infection of Christianity, through Augustine and Aquinas, by the naturalistic ethical conceptions of Plato and Aristotle, according to which ethics is concerned not with interpersonal relations but with the pursuit of the good by each individual separately. In its Hellenized form, Christianity treats God as the supreme object of desire. Rawls dismisses this as a theistic form of naturalism: "God is not just a satisfying object of supreme desirability. Nor can personality and community be explained in naturalistic terms. . . . All naturalistic thinkers have completely missed the spiritual and personal element which forms the deep inner core of the universe" (120).

The idea that ethics is fundamentally a matter of ensuring appropriate interpersonal relations rather than pursuing ultimately desirable ends has close affinities with Rawls's later view that principles of justice are not founded on an account of the good to be pursued but specify fair terms of cooperation among free and equal persons. Though the naturalism that Rawls criticizes in the thesis comprises both metaphysical and ethical claims, his opposition to its goal-directed structure foreshadows his later opposition to teleological conceptions of morality, whether utilitarian or perfectionist.

Although Rawls makes only two passing references to Kant in the thesis (181, 195), his conception strongly resembles the Kantian ideal that we should regard all persons as ends in themselves, and the totality of persons, human and divine, as a realm of ends. In Rawls's later writings, the claim that the right is prior to the good expresses an avowedly Kantian conception of morality based on certain relations among persons, rather than on the relation of action to an end, even an end common to all persons. The right is not what maximizes the good, but what manifests an equal respect for all persons as separate individuals.[14]

4. The moral importance of the separateness of persons, a fundamental theme of Rawls's work,[15] is strikingly anticipated in the moral and religious conception of community that lies at the heart of the thesis. Rawls proposes that the essential feature of human beings is our capacity for community,[16] that sin deforms our essential nature and destroys community, and that faith is the realization of our na-

14. See *TJ*, Section 6.

15. See *TJ*, Section 5.

16. Rawls's account of our nature as made for community is associated with his interpretation of the *imago Dei*. Human beings are created in the image of God, who is, as triune, essentially communal: one substance comprising three persons. See 121, 193, 206. In particular, the relations of perfect obedience and love between the Father and the Son provide "the model for any community."

ture through integration into community: our "openness" to God and other persons overcomes the terrible aloneness that is the consequence of sin (124, 214, 243–252). Though the term "community" may suggest otherwise, the human fellowship in which we realize our nature does not destroy the separateness of individual persons, but is founded on an affirmation of their distinctness. Here is a revealing passage:

> We reject mysticism because it seeks a union which excludes all particularity, and wants to overcome all distinctions. Since the universe is in its essence communal and personal, mysticism cannot be accepted. The Christian dogma of the resurrection of the body shows considerable profundity on this point. The doctrine means that we shall be resurrected in our full personality and particularity, and that salvation is the full restoration of the whole person, not the wiping away of particularity. Salvation integrates personality into community; it does not destroy personality to dissolve it into some mysterious and meaningless "One." (126)[17]

The importance of the separateness of persons is further expressed in the idea that we need bodies, and faces, in order to be able to communicate with and recognize one another (117–118, 152–156). It is also essential for understanding the significance of the Incarnation, whose importance is that it establishes a direct personal relation between us and God (118). Distancing himself from deism, Rawls emphasizes that natural religion or reason alone can tell us very little about God (154, 224), and that community with God requires that he reveal himself to us in person. Natural religion cannot tell us God's name, but revelation tells us that God's name is Christ, so that we can address him directly, as we address other persons by the names that they reveal to us and that single them out as distinct individuals (154).

The later, secular analogue of this conception of community as a

---

17. See, too, the criticisms of the notion of a "general will" at 127.

system of relations that upholds the moral importance of separate individuals is found in Rawls's opposition to aggregation, maximization, and interchangeability of persons in moral and political theory. "The reasoning which balances the gains and losses of different persons as if they were one person is excluded."[18] That is because morality requires a certain relation to each person as a distinct individual, rather than to the aggregate of persons. To be sure, essential elements of Rawls's account of individuals in liberal political morality are nowhere suggested in the thesis: for example, the idea that persons are self-authenticating sources of valid claims, with a capacity to form and to revise a conception of the good, and the capacity to take responsibility for their ends.[19] Still, Rawls's later insistence on the importance of the distinction between persons generalizes his claim in the thesis that personal relations are "I-thou" relations, and that the "thou" is not interchangeable (117).

5. The thesis does not offer much detail about the condition of fellowship and interpersonal openness that delivers us from sin and aloneness (206–213). In particular, it does not present a worked-out positive morality, either individual, social, or political. Perhaps a morality of rules or principles would be incompatible with the I-thou relations that form the community of faith, or with the ideal of Christian love, which "includes the totality of the person in its giving" (250). Nevertheless, the thesis makes some strong negative points that are consonant with Rawls's later views.

One of these is the attack on social contract theories, which the young Rawls understood as claiming that society is founded on a bargain among self-interested individuals (126, 227–229). "The idea of

18. *TJ*, p. 25.
19. See *PL*, pp. 29–34.

justice expressed in the political theories of Hobbes and Locke, the view of Adam Smith that we best serve our fellow-men by enlightened self interest, are all false views of community. Any society which explains itself in terms of mutual egoism is heading for certain destruction" (189).

In his later work Rawls is not a social contract theorist in this sense, since his account of justice as fairness uses the idea of a contract under the veil of ignorance principally as a device for representing the value of fairness and the equal freedom of moral persons. The well-ordered society of justice as fairness is not founded on a bargain; it is a social union in which institutions that express our social nature are valued as good in themselves. What attaches people to those institutions, according to the later Rawls, is not self-interest but an allegiance to principles of justice founded on respect for one another as equals. This respect is shown by a willingness to abide by principles that would be chosen under fair conditions in which individuals are assumed not to know their place in society or the particulars of their endowments or convictions.

The thesis also makes an important point against traditional social contract theories that was one of Rawls's reasons later on for developing his own distinctive version, with principles of justice chosen behind a veil of ignorance: namely that persons are not persons apart from the social world that forms and sustains them. Therefore we cannot understand society as a contract among individuals whose aspirations and identities exist independent of it. Oddly, Rawls has sometimes been accused of ignoring the essentially social nature of persons. But he never advocated the sort of individualism that he criticizes in the thesis; as he says in explaining why his contract view has a distinctive shape, "not only our final ends and hopes for ourselves but also our realized abilities and talents reflect, to a large degree, our personal history, opportunities, and social position. There is no way of knowing what we might have been had these things been different."[20]

Despite these similarities, however, the conception of community in the thesis is very different from justice as fairness. The thesis suggests that the problems of society could be overcome if human sin were brought under control. Sin is defined as the "repudiation of community." Egotism—the desire to dominate or exploit others—lies at the root of sin because it necessarily disfigures human relationships. The egotist worships himself and treats others as potential worshipers, all subservient, an audience for preening self-display. Egoism—understood as a concern with one's own interests and projects—can also turn sinful, particularly when it is enlisted by egotism in the exploitation of others. But Rawls strongly resists the idea that sin is the result of natural desires, even egoistic natural desires: nature is good (Chapter Two), the body is the spirit's temple, and the appetites are neither pro-social nor anti-social (186). All explanations of sin in terms other than the disfigurement of our own social nature— all efforts to blame "outside sources" (189–192), including our natural appetites—are variants on the Manichean heresy. The explanation of sin is not that we are overcome by appetites, or weak in the face of a world of temptation, but, simply and irreducibly, that the "spirit depraves itself" (192).

Rawls seems to have believed that appropriate relations of community can only emerge, and will emerge, if egotism (and with it, deformed egoism) is brought under control. That requires God's grace and efforts by the elect to bring others into a community of faith. A true community, he says, is "one integrated in faith under God. . . . It is the sin of one group which seeks to dominate another group that

20. Ibid., p. 270.

gives rise to the fear of communal dependence; but in community as such, and in the heavenly community, we have no such fear" (127).

The later Rawls was also concerned about egotism—more generally with the social damage wrought by a preoccupation with relative position. But he thought that a just society could forestall the damage by establishing "equality in the social bases of respect"[21]—specifically, by ensuring equal basic liberties, fair equality of opportunity, and, through the difference principle, treating "the distribution of natural abilities in some respects as a collective asset."[22] All of this could be achieved without conversion founded on grace or a community of faith. Moreover, in the social union of justice as fairness, citizens accept that conflicts of ultimate value are inevitable and that the most intractable conflicts are not egoistic or egotistic but are due to conflicting ideals. In Rawls's mature theory the conflicting interests and ideals that create the need for a specifically political conception of justice are not an expression of sin, but the consequence of human reason and judgment working under favorable conditions.[23]

6. Although this aspect of Rawls's later liberalism is absent from the thesis, the ideal of equality is very much present, expressed in particular in the close association between egotism and pride, the cardinal sin. Pride seems to be understood here not—as in Milton's depiction—as an aspiration to divinity and the root of rebellion against a divine order, but as a sense of superior worth to other persons, ex-

---

21. *TJ*, p. 478.

22. Ibid., p. 156.

23. Another significant passage: "The fact that all personal relations form . . . a nexus makes a separation between religion and ethics impossible. What on the surface appears as an action purely in the ethical sphere possesses religious significance because God is sovereign of the community, and no action can be severed from relation with Him . . . because God is the ultimate reference of community, all sin is sin in relation to God" (205–206).

pressed in a demand for servile admiration. So understood, pride fosters more familiar vices like selfishness and a refusal to share, because possessions are a badge of superiority. Selfishness and the desire to accumulate possessions are based not in a morally unrestrained appetitiveness, or in simple indifference to the fate of others, but in a sinful embrace of the deformed personal relations of superior and inferior. This is the pride of the capitalist, whose egoism reflects a deeper, more destructive egotism.

Pride also leads to the formation of closed groups, which express and reinforce a sense of group superiority. There have been religious, economic, and cultural closed groups, but now we are faced with a particularly virulent form of pride: "In Nazism we find that what condemns us or exalts us is what sort of blood we have in our veins. This last closed group is pride in its most demonic form" (197)— demonic because in its wholehearted embrace of exclusionary egotism, it turns the root of evil into its own good.

What Rawls says here about Nazism prefigures his remarks in *The Law of Peoples* that Nazism advances a "demonic conception of the world" and is in "some perverse sense" a religious view, offering salvation and redemption.[24] "Nazism is profound, but profound in the sense that the devil is profound. It is conscious of spirituality, but knows only the spirituality of egotism which leads to destruction" (218).

Pride is not, however, the monopoly of the demonic. It is pervasive, and particularly likely to infect the upright, the law-abiding, and the pious: "There is always a tendency to call the lower groups of society the worst sinners. The street-walkers, the beggars, the outcasts, the robbers and the drunkards are the usual scapegoats. The real sinners, however, are those who pride themselves on being otherwise" (201).

24. *LP,* p. 20.

7. This brings us to a particularly striking continuity between the thesis and Rawls's later views: the rejection of merit. One of the most famous and controversial claims of *A Theory of Justice* is that a just social order should not aim to distribute benefits according to desert.[25] Rawls is concerned there not to reject the idea of moral worth or merit entirely, but to deny its suitability as a basis for determining distributive shares, or any of the other entitlements of persons in a well-ordered society. But it is not hard to detect a general sense that the factors usually thought to confer deservingness are not enough under our control to be the source of moral claims: "Even the willingness to make an effort, to try, and so to be deserving in the ordinary sense is itself dependent on happy family and social circumstances."[26]

This view comes powerfully to mind when in the thesis we encounter Rawls's opposition to Pelagian and semi-Pelagian doctrines (170–174, 229–230). He sides with Augustine in denying that we can earn salvation by our own merit—by freely choosing virtue, or by works of any kind:

> There is no merit before God. Nor should there be merit before Him. True community does not count the merits of its members. Merit is a concept rooted in sin, and well disposed of. (241)

This is a theological claim, associated with an interpretation of divine grace. But consider the following passage:

> The human person, once perceiving that the Revelation of the Word is a condemnation of the self, casts away all thoughts of his own merit. . . . The more he examines his life, the more he looks into himself with complete honesty, the more clearly he perceives that what he has is a

25. See *TJ*, Section 48. For further discussion see John Rawls, *Justice as Fairness: A Restatement*, ed. Erin Kelly (Cambridge, Mass.: Harvard University Press, 2001), pp. 72–73.

26. *TJ*, p. 64; cf. p. 274.

gift. Suppose he was an upright man in the eyes of society, then he will now say to himself: "So you were an educated man, yes, but who paid for your education; so you were a good man and upright, yes, but who taught you your good manners and so provided you with good fortune that you did not need to steal; so you were a man of a loving disposition and not like the hard-hearted, yes, but who raised you in a good family, who showed you care and affection when you were young so that you would grow up to appreciate kindness—must you not admit that what you have, you have received? Then be thankful and cease your boasting." (240)

These reflections, though linked here to revelation, can be given a purely secular significance, and they lead directly to the moral sensibility that underlies the difference principle.

Rawls strikingly associates Pelagian ideas of election by merit with the individualist contractarianism that he consistently rejects. Both views treat our relations—either with God or with others in the community—as a kind of bargain, and thus assume, at the root of those relations, a determinate individuality, antecedent to community. This "bargain basis" makes genuine community impossible (227–230).

8. As we have said, the ideas of pluralism and good-faith conflict among reasonable people are essential to Rawls's liberalism, but absent from the thesis. Its ideal of community implies a degree of harmony and a universality of interpersonal regard that would make politics unnecessary, and perhaps justice as well—for both are concerned with collective decision in the face of conflicts of interest and conviction. In Rawls's published work, by contrast, it is the inevitability of competing interests and doctrinal disagreements, even among people of good will, that drives the search for justice and legitimacy. We cannot pursue a just society merely by eliminating sin, because justice is not a response to sin, nor to egotism, nor indeed a remedy for any human failing at all.

The recognition of the political as presenting a distinct moral problem is therefore a decisive break in Rawls's development, and it would be interesting to know when and how it occurred. Rawls says in the Introduction to *Political Liberalism* (1993) that *A Theory of Justice* (1971) did not draw a distinction "between moral and political philosophy";[27] but he was concerned from early on with the special moral problems of political society. As early as his doctoral dissertation (submitted in 1950, and addressed to the role of reason in ethical argument), his philosophical work was animated by a sense of the political that is not evident in the undergraduate thesis. Thus he says in the dissertation that a "democratic conception of government . . . views the law as the outcome of public discussions as to what rules can be voluntarily consented to as binding upon the government and the citizens." For this reason, he continues, "rational discussion . . . constitutes an essential precondition of reasonable law," and an investigation of the "rational foundation of ethical principles" serves as "an addition to democratic theory, as well as to ethical philosophy."[28] The close association here of issues of philosophical ethics with concerns about public argument in a democracy marks a sharp departure from the view in the thesis, and looks forward to the idea that justice as fairness is "the most appropriate moral basis for a democratic society."[29]

Yet while Rawls came to see that a just society could not be a community "integrated in faith under God," his personal knowledge and experience of religion were important for the formation of his later

27. *PL*, p. xvii.

28. John Rawls, *A Study in the Grounds of Ethical Knowledge: Considered with Reference to Judgments on the Moral Worth of Character* (Ph.D. diss., Princeton University, 1950), pp. 7–8. Available from UMI Dissertation Services, Ann Arbor, Michigan.

29. *TJ*, p. xviii.

views, in particular his views about the kind of public reasoning that we could reasonably expect in a democratic society. Rawls's liberalism, unlike that of many liberals who know very little about religion, is founded on a vivid sense of the importance of religious faith and an understanding of the difference between genuine and merely conventional religion. He knows what he is talking about when he says that the Reformation "introduces into people's conceptions of their good a transcendent element not admitting of compromise"; that "this element forces either mortal conflict moderated only by circumstance and exhaustion, or equal liberty of conscience and freedom of thought"; and that political thought needs to understand "the absolute depth of that irreconcilable latent conflict."[30]

By insisting on the importance of a terrain of political justification that is consistent with such ultimate commitments but does not depend on them, Rawls was not devaluing religion. On the contrary. The importance of liberty and of separating the state from religion is that they make possible the commitment of all members of a pluralistic society to common political institutions and a shared enterprise of public justification, despite their ultimate disagreements about the nature of the world, the ends of life, and the path to salvation. Such disagreement, he emphasizes, is not a disaster, but the natural consequence of reason's exercise under free conditions.

"On My Religion" may describe the first stage of Rawls's change of view: his study of the history of the Inquisition in the early years after the war. His rejection of orthodox Christianity went hand in hand with his rejection of its long history of using "political power to establish its hegemony and to oppress other religions" (264). But he remained intent throughout his career on showing that toleration did

30. *PL,* p. 28.

not depend on religious skepticism—that it was compatible with faith in the fullest sense and could be embraced by people of faith.

In developing a specifically political form of liberalism, Rawls responds to the complaint that a liberal political outlook is simply the political department of a comprehensively liberal philosophy of life—secular, skeptical, dismissive of the idea of a moral order antecedent to human will—and therefore hostile to citizens of faith. Rawls disagrees; he believes that there are different routes, none preferred, that citizens may take to endorsing common political principles: "In endorsing a constitutional democratic regime, a religious doctrine may say that such are the limits God sets to our liberty; a nonreligious doctrine will express itself otherwise."[31] What we learn from "the history of religion and philosophy" is that "there are many reasonable ways in which the wider realm of values can be understood so as to be either congruent with, or supportive of, or else not in conflict with, the values appropriate to the special domain of the political as specified by a political conception of justice."[32]

Here, Rawls's discussion in "On My Religion" of Bodin's views on toleration is instructive. Bodin, he says, "was not someone who, like Spinoza, came to toleration after rejecting or changing his religious faith." Instead, Bodin endorsed toleration on religious grounds, as a Catholic, and not only for political reasons; moreover, Bodin suggested that an admissible religion must affirm "toleration as part of a religious doctrine and distinct from political ideas" (266–267).

In his latest writings, Rawls attempted to formulate his views on political justification in a concept of public reason. He meant by this a common space of political argument that could be inhabited with comparable ease by reasonable adherents of different religious con-

---

31. "The Idea of Public Reason Revisited," in *LP*, p. 151.

32. *PL*, p. 140.

fessions and moral positions, and that was not itself dependent on a comprehensive philosophical or religious view. Like all of his work, this proposal has attracted strong opposition. But its motivation, like the motivation of his liberalism in general, does not come from devaluing religion, but from an understanding of its ultimate importance.

Rawls tells us that "of the many texts I have read on religion few have struck me as much as Bodin's views as expressed in his *Colloquium of the Seven*" (266). At the end of the *Colloquium,* the seven participants in the dialogue—Catholic, Jew, Lutheran, Calvinist, Muslim, philosophical naturalist, and skeptic—end their conversation and "embrace each other in mutual love." But their "remarkable harmony" is not founded on conversion, much less on a shared secularism. Instead, we are told that "afterwards they held no other conversation about religions, although each defended his own religion with the supreme sanctity of his life."[33]

33. Jean Bodin, *Colloquium of the Seven about Secrets of the Sublime,* trans. Marion Leathers Daniels Kuntz (Princeton: Princeton University Press, 1975), p. 471.

The Theological Ethics of the Young Rawls and Its Background

Robert Merrihew Adams

My aim in this essay is to illuminate the content of the senior thesis that John Rawls wrote as an undergraduate at Princeton in the fall of 1942, and his use of the authors to whom he refers. The scope of the thesis is wider than might be suggested by the title, *A Brief Inquiry into the Meaning of Sin and Faith*. At the heart of the theory is a contrast between what Rawls calls "naturalism" and a "proper ethics" that is focused on personal relationships and community. In section 2 I will discuss the concepts (notably, those of egoism and egotism) in terms of which this contrast is framed; in section 3 I will examine Rawls's critique of naturalism; and in section 4 I will look at the conceptions of values and ends that emerge in the critique. Community is the end that Rawls values most. His account of it leaves far too many questions unanswered, but I try in section 5 to bring out as clearly as possible the views about community that are expressed in the thesis. Rawls's concepts of egoism and egotism help to structure his account of moral and religious evil, or sin, which is my topic in section 6. Closely related to the account of sin, and in my opinion the most impressive part of Rawls's senior thesis, integrating many of its themes, is his account of conversion, the transition from sin to faith, which I will examine in section 7.

What will be most striking to many about this undergraduate essay by one who is widely regarded as the most significant moral philosopher of his generation is the unmistakably theological character of the ethical theory it presents. It states flatly that "there can be no separation between religion and ethics" (114). A form of Protestant Christianity is affirmed in the thesis, without serious discussion of other religious alternatives. Section 8 of my essay is focused on what the thesis says about God.

I begin, in section 1, with some observations about the historical setting in which Rawls wrote his undergraduate thesis.

1. 1942 and Neo-Orthodoxy

The cultural and intellectual background of the thesis Rawls wrote in 1942 was quite different from that of the moral and political philosophy he published in later years. Indeed, some of the authors mentioned in the thesis may be unfamiliar to readers of the later work. The index of *A Theory of Justice* (1971) contains no entries for any of the authors that the bibliography of the undergraduate thesis lists as "chief sources" for Rawls's own view. One of them, Philip Leon, who seems to me to have had as much influence on the thesis as any other, is all but forgotten now. The movement that has come to be known as "analytical philosophy" already had a significant history in Europe by 1942, but it was not widely established in America, and not yet dominant in the Princeton philosophy department. It hardly casts a shadow on the pages of Rawls's senior thesis, even though his work on the topic began in a class taught by the ardent Wittgensteinian Norman Malcolm.

The thesis was clearly influenced, however, by the best-known Protestant theological movement of its time. Rawls wrote it during the heyday of neo-orthodoxy. The label "neo-orthodox" was applied to a rather disparate group of Protestant theologians working in Europe and North America during several decades following the end of the First World War. The movement lost its agenda-setting position during the social and cultural transformations of the 1960s and 1970s, although the most famous neo-orthodox theologian, Karl Barth, has never ceased to have a following.

The term "neo-orthodox" obviously suggests a revival or renewal of orthodoxy—orthodoxy with a new twist. Typical neo-orthodox theologians, having become disillusioned with the "liberal" or modernizing form of Protestant theology in which they had been educated, sought to reappropriate aspects of an older orthodoxy—specifically including, in Barth's case, the "orthodoxy" of Protestant theologians of the seventeenth and eighteenth centuries. As the prefix "neo" suggests, they remained indebted in some ways to the liberal theology of their teachers, while at the same time engaging in vigorous polemic against them.

Neo-orthodox theology claimed a biblical basis, but rejected "fundamentalism" or literalism in the interpretation of the Bible. As one of the first neo-orthodox theologians, Emil Brunner, put it,

> What I said of God incarnate is true of the revelation in the Bible; to be a real revelation it must be veiled. . . . The words of Scripture are human; that is, God makes use of human and, therefore, frail and fallible words of men who are liable to err. But men and their words are the means through which God speaks to men and in men. Only through a serious misunderstanding will genuine faith find satisfaction in the theory of verbal inspiration of the Bible. . . . He who identifies the letters and words of the Scriptures with the word of God has never truly understood the word of God; he does not know what constitutes revelation.[1]

One of the major projects of neo-orthodoxy was developing less literalist, but no less serious, ways of interpreting the Bible as a vehicle of God's self-revelation.

1. Emil Brunner, *The Theology of Crisis* (New York: Charles Scribner's Sons, 1929), p. 19.

An earlier label for the neo-orthodox movement was "the theology of crisis." "Crisis" is intended in this context in two senses. It refers on the one hand to the crisis of European civilization that was widely thought to have been precipitated, or revealed, by World War I.[2] On the other hand, it refers to God's *judgment* (*krisis* in the Greek of St. Paul's letter to the Romans). In his commentary on Romans, in which the theology of crisis first burst upon the Protestant scene in 1918, Barth speaks of

> the fact that the whole concrete world is ambiguous and under KRISIS [judgment] . . . If . . . God were . . . an object among other objects, if He were Himself subject to the KRISIS, He would then obviously not be God, and the true God would have to be sought in the Origin of the KRISIS. . . . The true God, Himself removed from all concretion, is the Origin of the KRISIS of every concrete thing, the Judge, the negation of this world in which is included also the god of human logic. It is of this true God we speak—of the Judge of the world of which He forms no part.[3]

The transcendence of God—God's complete otherness, Barth says— is one of the main themes of neo-orthodox theology.[4]

Barth's conception of *krisis* connects knowledge of the transcendent God with recognition of negativities in human life.

> The vast distinction between God and man is their veritable union. . . . All 'law', all human being and having and doing, the whole course of this world and its inevitability, are a sign-post, a parable, a possibility, an expectation. For this reason they are always deprivation and dissatisfaction, a void and a longing. But once this is recognized there appears above them all the faithfulness of God, who forgives by condemn-

2. Ibid., pp. 1ff.

3. Karl Barth, *The Epistle to the Romans,* translated from the sixth edition by Edwyn C. Hoskyns (London: Oxford University Press, 1933), p. 82. Barth completely rewrote the book for the second edition in 1921, and it is that rewritten form that appears in later editions and in the English translation.

4. Barth, *The Epistle to the Romans,* p. 115.

ing, gives life by killing, and utters His 'Yes' when nothing but His 'No' is audible. In Jesus God is known to be the unknown God. In the light of this KRISIS also the deepest unity of men with men is apprehended.[5]

I have no reason to believe that the young Rawls had read Barth. And the form of relation between human beings and God that Barth seems to set before us in this passage looks different from that favored by Rawls in his senior thesis.[6] Nevertheless, the idea of a God who utters a "Yes" by making a "No" audible finds an echo in Rawls's account of conversion;[7] it is a neo-orthodox theme.

In the preface to his senior thesis Rawls says he thinks that Brunner is the theologian from whom he has learned the most (108). Brunner's theology was no duplicate of Barth's; and although he agreed with Barth that knowledge of God depends on God's self-revelation, they had a furious public falling out in the 1930s over natural theology, which Brunner would not reject as thoroughly as Barth did.[8] Brunner's work was less influential in Europe than Barth's, and attracts relatively little attention today (less, perhaps, than it deserves).

5. Ibid., p. 114. The idea of a divine affirmation that is uttered when only a "No" is audible is developed at greater length, and in a different form, in Paul Tillich, *The Courage to Be* (New Haven: Yale University Press, 1952).

6. I find it natural to read "a void and a longing" in the passage just quoted as expressing a form of the Platonic eros piety that Rawls rejected in his senior thesis. By 1942 Barth himself might well have opposed his earlier book on this point.

7. "Out of the feeling of being dissolved," Rawls says, "there thus grows this perception of givenness, of the bounteous mercy and love of God which gives even in the face of denial, and the understanding of dependence upon God" (238).

8. The primary texts, *Nature and Grace* by Brunner and *No* by Barth, have been published together in English translation, under the title *Natural Theology*, by Peter Fraenkel (London: The Centenary Press, 1946). See also John W. Hart, *Karl Barth vs. Emil Brunner: The Formation and Dissolution of a Theological Alliance, 1916–1936* (New York: Peter Lang, 2001).

But Brunner was many people's introduction to neo-orthodox theology, particularly in America. He had an American audience before Barth did, and his work may still have been better known in America than Barth's in 1942.

There were some advantages to reading Brunner. One of them is that he wrote in a more accessible style than Barth did. Moreover, I would say that the theology is more thoroughly integrated with ethics in Brunner's writings of the period than in the most important of Barth's works that were available in English in 1942. For Rawls, among others, that would have been an advantage. As Rawls notes, Brunner's enthusiastic personalism also appealed very strongly to him. He might well have preferred Brunner to Barth even if he had read Barth.

Brunner helped himself to gain an American audience by lecturing in America in the 1920s and 1930s, as Barth would not do until 1962. Brunner's visibility in Princeton in particular was enhanced by his presence as a celebrity visiting professor at Princeton Theological Seminary during the academic year 1938–39, just before Rawls came to Princeton as an undergraduate. Although Rawls may not have heard Brunner in person, Brunner's ideas would certainly have been "in the air" at Princeton, and it would be surprising if any student with the interests of the young Rawls didn't talk with people at Princeton who had heard Brunner speak at the Seminary. So although Rawls cites three of Brunner's books in the thesis, Brunner's influence may have reached him through oral as well as printed sources.

It is tempting to describe Rawls's undergraduate thesis as an essay in neo-orthodox theology.[9] I have vacillated about that. Such vacilla-

9. It is described in that way in Eric Gregory's valuable essay, "Before the Original Position: The Neo-Orthodox Theology of the Young John Rawls," *Journal of Religious Ethics* 35 (2007): 179–206. I am grateful to Gregory for helpful correspondence.

tion is encouraged by the looseness of neo-orthodoxy as a category; it covers such a range of different views that an ascription of neo-orthodoxy offers little precise information. Sometimes the term "neo-orthodoxy" refers to a fairly well defined movement or school of thought, of which Barth was the main leader and Brunner a prime exemplar, despite his disagreements with Barth. Often, however (perhaps indeed more often), the term has been used to refer to something more like an intellectual climate which most Protestant theologians, from the 1920s to the 1960s, except the most conservative and the most modernist, inhaled to some extent.

Those who have spoken of Reinhold Niebuhr and Paul Tillich, for instance, as neo-orthodox theologians, as many have, were presumably thinking of neo-orthodoxy as an intellectual climate rather than a tightly unified movement or school. For Tillich was regarded as much less orthodox than Barth and Brunner, and Niebuhr did not share their preoccupations with theological methodology and the epistemology of religious belief. Indeed, Niebuhr himself said, with regard to the continental neo-orthodox theologians, that he thought he belonged "more to the liberal tradition than to theirs."[10]

To the extent that there was a theological climate called "neo-orthodox," it is fair to say that Rawls's senior thesis is a neo-orthodox document, for it certainly took shape in that climate. If we think of neo-orthodoxy as a movement or school of thought, on the other hand, it is more questionable to classify the thesis as a piece of neo-orthodox theology, for Rawls gives in it little evidence of allegiance to such a movement.

The theological work of Barth and Brunner in the 1920s and 1930s was intensely polemical, and the concept of the theology of crisis, or

10. In a letter of 13 March 1943 to John Bennett, quoted in Richard Wightman Fox, *Reinhold Niebuhr: A Biography* (San Francisco: Harper & Row, 1985), p. 214.

neo-orthodoxy, as a movement was formed in a polemical context, defined by opposition to theological liberalism on the left and to fundamentalism on the right. Eventually, bitter polemic broke out even between Barth and Brunner. Rawls's senior thesis seems rather innocent in relation to these polemics. He appropriates ideas from Brunner, but shows little interest in the controversies in which Brunner was engaged and, indeed, little knowledge of them. Rawls comes close to many neo-orthodox writers when he says it is one of his main aims "to attack a specific Christian problem . . . using the concepts which are derived from Biblical thought," rather than from "the Greek tradition" (107–108) (by which, like many who said such things, he meant in effect the Platonic tradition). And his conception of the Word of God as God's act of self-revelation (which I discuss in section 8) is very similar to views of Brunner and Barth. But Rawls's references to the Bible itself seem methodologically quite unself-conscious, and the battles about the authority and interpretation of the Bible that were raging in American Protestantism at the time are hardly addressed in the senior thesis.

Rawls did agree on many points with Brunner, who was a central figure in the neo-orthodox movement. But Brunner's work, like that of Niebuhr and Anders Nygren, who exemplified neo-orthodoxy as a theological climate, seems to have been treated by Rawls as grist for his own mill. His preoccupations, as I will argue in subsequent sections, were different from theirs. I believe his senior thesis project was primarily one of working out a religious and ethical position for himself. He was not participating in a polemical movement in theology, was not fighting loyally in its battles, and may not even have informed himself very fully about those battles.

The thesis can certainly be classified as an essay in theology. As to genre, however, it is equally an essay in ethical theory. Most precisely, then, it is an essay in theological ethical theory. And though its ethical theory is theological, its theological presuppositions are less fully developed than its ethical conclusions. The thesis is written from an explicitly Christian point of view, but it contains only a fragment of Christian theology. In marked divergence from the famously christocentric character that Brunner's theology largely shares with Barth's, Rawls's thesis contains no developed christology, no articulated doctrine of "the person and work of Christ." Indeed, the ethical theory of the thesis does not seem strongly connected with any christological view.

The primary object of evaluation in this first of Rawls's ethical theories is not actions but states of mind. He proposes no criteria of right action, but criticizes and commends attitudes and motives. This is not an unusual focus for a Protestant "inquiry into the meaning of sin and faith." In the thought of Luther and other Protestant Reformers, sin is primarily a state of mind, a complex of attitudes and motives, rather than a straightforwardly voluntary act or a pattern of action. Conceptions of sin as primarily a state rather than a particular deed were characteristic of broadly neo-orthodox theologians, but can also be found in liberal Protestantism.[11] In keeping with this, evaluation of attitudes and motives has held a central place in Protestant ethical thinking. This focus is a classically Protestant feature of Rawls's senior thesis.

2. The Natural and the Personal

If Rawls is engaged in any polemic in his senior thesis, it is a polemic against "naturalism." The first in his list of two main aims of his thesis is "To enter a strong protest against a certain scheme of thought which

---

11. Notably, in the most famous prototype of liberal Protestant theology: Friedrich Schleiermacher, *The Christian Faith* (1830), trans. H. R. Mackintosh et al. (Edinburgh: T. & T. Clark, 1928), p. 273 (§66).

I have called naturalism." He immediately offers an explanation of the term:

> By naturalism I mean something far broader than is usually meant by the term. Naturalism is the universe in which all relations are natural and in which spiritual life is reduced to the level of desire and appetition.

He adds that naturalism in this sense has been so "prevalent in the West since Augustine" that his protest against it proposes "more or less of a 'revolution'" (107). Elsewhere he says of "naturalism,"

> We intend to use the word in a different sense than it is usually used. When we think of naturalism we are inclined to imagine a view resembling materialism and kindred philosophies. For us, however, naturalism is the type of thought which speaks of all relations in natural terms. (119)

Two main features of Rawls's conception of naturalism are adumbrated in these explanations. The first is that he conceives of naturalism primarily as a view about *relations*. Indeed, although he often speaks of "nature" or "the realm of nature," or of a universe or cosmos as "natural," his central use of "natural" seems to be in a sense in which it is not clear that anything but relationships can be natural. The second main point is that Rawls connects naturalism also with a certain view of *motivation*—as not rising above "desire and appetition." What we must next try to determine, therefore, is, first, what it is for a relation to be "natural," or spoken of as natural, and what sort of relations Rawls contrasts with natural relations; and, second, what counts for him as "desire and appetition," and what motives he regards as superior to them.

Rawls holds that "there are two types of relations, natural and personal" (112). It is in terms of the contrast between natural and personal relations that the type of ethics that he advocates is distinguished from the alternative that is his polemical target. His own outlook, he says,

> will be contrasted with another point of view which we shall call "natural ethics," which is the ethics of Plato and Aristotle, and to which we oppose the Christian or "communal" ethics. Proper ethics is not the relating of a person to some objective "good" for which he should strive, but is the relating of person to person and finally to God. (114)

Thus naturalism is the kind of ethics that Rawls ascribes to Plato and Aristotle, and he contrasts it with a "communal" ethics of personal relationships.

Such an opposition of the "natural" to the "personal"—or to the "spiritual," which Rawls regards as interchangeable with the personal (111)—was certainly not unprecedented. He could have found polarities expressed in these terms in both Brunner and Nygren, two of his main sources.[12] Neither Brunner nor Nygren, however, assigns a central theoretical or polemical role, as Rawls does, to a conception of "naturalism" defined in terms of relationships. In the end we must look, not to such precedents, but to what Rawls says about naturalism, for an understanding of what he meant by a term he said he was using in an unusual sense.

An initial statement suggests that Rawls conceives of the difference between natural and personal relations simply in terms of the nature of the terms of the relations. He says,

> In experience as we know it there are actually three types of relations: (a) personal and communal, (b) natural and (c) causal. The first type is

12. Emil Brunner, *Man in Revolt: A Christian Anthropology,* trans. Olive Wyon (London: Lutterworth Press, 1939), p. 364, speaking of relapsing "into the animal and natural sphere" if one neglects or ignores "the spiritual life for which [one] is destined." Anders Nygren, *Agape and Eros,* trans. Philip S. Watson, 1-volume edition (New York: Harper & Row, 1969), pp. 287–288, speaking of a conception of salvation that is "naturalistic" rather than framed "in personal or ethical terms"; see also ibid., p. 225.

between two persons, the second between a person and some object insofar as personality is involved in the relation, and the third is the relation between two objects. (114)

Unfortunately, it soon emerges that this is too simple for Rawls's theory. For he notes that there is a "type of relation in which the 'thou' is used as a thing," which "is an impersonalized personal relation . . . not in itself personal." Though it is obviously between two persons, it is not personal enough to meet the requirements of the kind of ethics that Rawls regards as "proper." It is indeed "one type of sin" (117), and endorsement of some instances of it is, I believe, one of the main things Rawls objects to in what he calls "naturalism."

His more extensive discussion of the difference between natural and personal relations in section II.2 of Chapter One is more subtle and more satisfying. One important point that emerges there is that in a relation that is personal in the intended sense, one relates to another person as a "thou," and the "thou" not only "gives, shares and loves," but also "it is this 'thou' which constitutes the judge in personal relations" (116). In other words, in fully personal relations, one is morally accountable to the other person; and personal relations are, at least in part, "moral relations," as Rawls calls them at one point (146), in a sense in which "moral" contrasts not with "immoral" but with "non-moral."

The second main feature of "naturalism," as noted above, is that it reduces human *motivation* to "desire" and "appetition." There are large problems of understanding on this point also. For both "desire" and "appetition" are often used to signify motives aiming at any sort of end whatever, including personal relations. There also exist narrower senses or uses of both—or at least of "desire" and "appetite," if not "appetition"—but I think there is no one precise narrow sense that is assigned to them in ordinary discourse. To understand Rawls's polemic against "naturalism" we need a reasonably precise understanding of what motives he assigns to the natural and the personal realms respectively, and what is the difference between them. Among other things, we may well wonder what the motives belonging to the personal realm are, if they are not desires or appetitions, and whether Rawls has a most general term that applies in both realms, to motives aiming at any end whatever.

Rawls seems not to have been altogether content with his treatment of these questions. Trying, in Chapter Five, to provide some illumination on an "obscure" point, he says,

> Our natural natures are frustrated, but as persons we are disappointed; appetitions are satisfied, as persons we are happy and joyful; impulses and instincts in a sense drive us forward, but personality longs; and whereas nature hunts, personality seeks. (220)

In the next paragraph, however, after saying more in a similar vein, he feels obliged to add: "The above discussion is obscure and vague, and for that reason we should not make too much of it" (221).

The questions are addressed with a somewhat more satisfying directness and clarity at the beginning of Chapter Four:

> In the following sections we shall use these definitions: (a) Natural relations mark off that sphere of experience in which a person desires, strives for, wants, or needs an object or a concrete process. The activity may be described as desiring, wanting, or striving for. (b) Personal relations mark off that sphere of experience in which one person seeks to establish a definite relation or a definite rapport between another person and himself. The activity cannot be described as desire or wanting or needing in the appetitional sense. The activity is not an urge or an impulse, but something different. It is the sharing of fellowship, of communion, of mutual presence; or it is giving, loving, and sharing; or it may be, as it most usually is, hating, envying, despising, priding oneself over the other and so on. (180)

These definitions offer a fairly clear distinction in terms of the *ends* aimed at by the motives. The motives belonging to the personal sphere aim at the establishment (or, presumably, the maintenance) of a personal relationship. The motives belonging to the natural sphere aim at something else, described as "an object or a concrete process." Similarly, Rawls says, "The criterion of appetition is that it seeks some *object,* something which is impersonal, objective and self-revealing by nature" (180). The definitions also contain material that may be intended to distinguish the two classes of motives in terms of their *modality;* but no such distinction seems to me very clearly provided here. We are told that the "natural" motives (as we may call them for short), or their "activity" or exercise, "may be described as desiring, wanting or striving for," and that the activity of the "personal" motives cannot be described in terms of that sort; but that is of little help if we are struggling to understand what modality is signified by the terms affirmed on the one side and denied on the other. And the positive terms suggested, for the personal sphere, in the last sentence of the quotation are also of little help. For it is far from clear why the "sharing" mentioned could not be an activity or an end of "striving." And while "loving," "hating," "envying," "despising," and "priding oneself" do indeed suggest an emotional modality rather different from the modality of desire and appetition, it also seems true that an emotional modality of loving and hating is found outside the realm of personal relations—for instance, in loving and hating certain foods or styles of music.

Rawls's definitions at the beginning of Chapter Four bear clear marks of the influence of *The Ethics of Power* by the British philosopher Philip Leon. The mention of "concrete process" is reminiscent of Leon's view, described by Rawls (150), that appetition seeks concrete processes. And the classification of "hating, envying, despising, priding oneself over the other and so on" as belonging to the sphere of personal relations is part of Leon's conception of egotism, which Rawls describes and accepts as his own (150–151). In his taxonomy of motives, in fact, Rawls is closer to Leon than to any other of his sources. A sketch of Leon's taxonomy, which is more sharply defined, may help us at least to frame the right questions about Rawls's taxonomy. Leon summarizes it very clearly and concisely:

> Appetition, or biological striving or the desire for processes or experiences as such in oneself and in others, yields the egoistic life or egoism, which includes altruism or alteregoism . . . Ambition is the desire for position (or relations), and for processes or experiences only as symbols of this. It seeks for . . . soleness or allness . . ., difference or separation, identity, supremacy, superiority, equality. It makes the egotistic or egotism . . . The moral desire or *nisus* is for right structures or situations (union, at-oneness, communication) embodying or expressing Goodness, and for processes only as ingredients in these. It makes the genuinely moral life and man or the good man.[13]

The main division of Leon's taxonomy of motives is thus a trichotomy of egoism, egotism, and the moral desire or *nisus*. Rawls's taxonomy differs from it in that its main partition is a dichotomy of motives belonging to the "natural" and "personal" spheres. Motives that aim at personal relations, good or bad, for their own sake are contrasted with all other end-directed motives. I think this is a point of originality in Rawls's treatment of these ideas. The importance of this difference should not be exaggerated, however. Both egotism and the moral *nisus* are conceived by Leon as taking states or situations of personal relationship as ends in themselves, and thus as belonging to what Rawls would call the personal sphere.[14] And Rawls, undoubtedly under the influence of Leon, divides the motives belonging to the personal sphere into two main classes, one egotistic and the other

13. Philip Leon, *The Ethics of Power: or The Problem of Evil* (London: George Allen & Unwin, 1935), pp. 23–24.

14. As regards egotism, this is clear from the definition of ambition quoted above. As regards the moral *nisus*, see, for instance, Leon, *The Ethics of Power*, p. 282.

aiming at community. "Personal relations," Rawls says, "are motivated by egotism or by fellowship and love" (118).

The prominent place assigned to egotism is an unusual feature of a taxonomy of motives, in which Rawls follows Leon. 'Egotism' is used here in a rather broad sense. It does not just signify conceit, or an excessively high opinion of oneself. For both Rawls and Leon, I would say, it signifies all sorts of lust for social position, or for the appearance of social position. Forms of egotism include pride, conceit, competitiveness, and lust for power. This last form was a particularly important topic for Leon, whose book was pretty clearly meant to have an anti-Fascist polemical point. Lust for any sort of social position is, of course, a desire for a sort of relationship between persons rather than for an individual process.

Rawls's use of "egoism" and "appetition," as well as "egotism," largely follows Leon's (cf. 150–151). However, he clearly does not follow Leon's use of "desire." For Rawls "desire" generally is distinctive of the "natural" sphere, whereas for Leon it belongs equally to egoism, egotism, and moral action. He uses it as a quite general term for end-directed motives of any sort, and says that it can "denote any urge, 'making for' or 'hormic drive.'"[15] The term that comes closest to fulfilling that general role in Rawls's senior thesis may be "seek." In a passage I have quoted, he self-consciously assigns it to the personal sphere (220); but in practice he applies it both there and in the natural sphere.[16]

In section I.3 of Chapter Four (180–182), Rawls classifies appetitions in four "categories," according to the type of object at which

15. Ibid., pp. 295–296.

16. For instance, in the personal sphere: "love seeks equality with the person to whom its givenness is directed" (207). In the natural sphere: "The criterion of appetition is that it seeks some *object*, something which is impersonal . . ." (180); this is not an exceptional case.

they aim. (a) "Concrete" appetitions are desires for bodily states or processes. (b) "Rational" appetitions include "the desire and longing for truth, for coherence or for necessity in the interpretation of experience." Rawls believes there are rational appetitions, but grants that a "pragmatist" might deny it. (c) "Aesthetic" appetition is "the desire to enjoy an object of beauty." Typically we would "enjoy it for its own sake." Professing ignorance of aesthetics, Rawls is somewhat agnostic about the actual existence of aesthetic appetition. Finally, (d) the "religious" appetition "is the appetition which seeks God as its object, or the Form of the Good, the Alone and so forth. It is the appetition directed to the highest object, to the source of all Beauty, Truth and Goodness." Doubts may well be raised as to whether this partition really covers all types of appetition. In particular, many desires for mental processes don't uncontroversially or obviously fall under any of Rawls's four categories.

Rawls regards appetitions of the first three types "as being legitimate, as being proper for man, and as forming the substance of natural activity in the natural sphere of our experience" (183). I count Rawls as substantially in agreement with Leon's view that the appetitional life is an indispensable basis of the moral life because "we cannot have the moral life without processes and the desire for processes," since "processes are life and the moral life is life."[17]

However, Rawls rejects the fourth category of appetition, the "religious" appetition. "Whether such an appetition exists," Rawls says, "I do not know; but if it does exist, it should not be allowed to exist. To have such an appetition is to sin." That is "because one of the forms of sin, as we shall see, is to turn a personal relation into a natural relation," and it is especially sinful "to do this misdeed in relation to God" (182).

17. Leon, *The Ethics of Power*, pp. 244–245.

Rawls rejects the religious appetition "as constituting the sinful extension of natural relations to a sphere where they do not apply" (183). The "extension" to which Rawls refers is no doubt the enlargement of the domain of natural relations that results in "the extended natural cosmos" that he discusses in Chapter Three and that perverts the merely natural into the natural*ism* that he attacks. Should we infer from the terms in which he rejects the religious appetition that the only illegitimate extension of natural relations that is involved in naturalism and the extended natural cosmos is their extension to our relation to God? It is hard to believe that Rawls meant that. His discussion of "the extended natural cosmos" is certainly less than cosmic in the range of topics it touches.[18] But he does recognize "impersonalized" relations between human beings, which he surely regards as an illegitimate "extension of natural relations."

Rawls's objection to extending natural relations cohabits uneasily with a recognition that in actual human life, interests in personal relationship are complexly and pervasively interwoven with appetitions. "In sensuality we seek," among other things, Rawls says, "community and fellowship" (150). In this reference to sensuality he presumably has sexual appetition in mind. He says that "the sexual appetition . . . is utterly unique because the object of the appetition is intimately bound up with another *person*." This way of putting it suggests that "the object of the appetition" is not identical with the other person. And indeed that, or a generalization of it, seems to be the main (though not fully articulate) thesis in this discussion of sexual relations. Rawls seems to be arguing that although there are mixtures, so to speak, of natural and personal motives, they do not ever form with each other an organic whole. In particular, he seems to mean to

18. As one of the official readers of the senior thesis, T. M. Greene, pointed out in a comment on Rawls's copy.

exclude the possibility of a single motive aiming at both a broadly moral personal relation and a physical sexual process as a more than merely instrumental part of the relation. However, the clearest argument he offers, from the phenomenon of prostitution, seems not to show that no single motive can be both sexual and personal, but only that a person *can* want sex without wanting a personal relationship that is more than sexual (187–188).

In any event, the senior thesis contains no systematic effort to explain where appetition is legitimate in human relations and where it is illegitimate. Rawls's systematic argument against illegitimate extension of natural relations deals only with relations with God. That will accordingly be our focus as we turn to consider Rawls's criticism of naturalism.

3. The Criticism of Naturalism

The main historical targets of Rawls's critique of "naturalism" are Plato and Augustine, whom he discusses at length in Chapter Three. I will focus on Augustine, as the discussion of Plato is less theological and, for reasons just stated, I believe the issue of illegitimate extension of "natural" relations is most fully engaged by Rawls at the theological level. His main objections against Augustine are made clear enough in a summary in the last paragraph of Chapter Three:

> The natural cosmos is marked by the following characteristics: (a) all relations are relations to objects; even God may be treated as an object; (b) appetitional desires are the energies of all relations, and all love is acquisitive, hence not love in the Christian sense; (c) grace (when the system is Christian) is likewise spoken of in terms of an object presented to the will as an object of desire; and (d) all natural systems lose communality, personality, and the true nature of God, and are therefore not really Christian but individualistic. (178)

The characteristics listed are four, but they indicate two main criticisms. The one most obviously linked with the idea of an illegitimate extension of natural relations is that "communality, personality and the true nature of God" are lost in a system such as Rawls ascribes to Augustine. This is in effect an accusation that Augustine has committed the sin of turning the relation of a human being to God into a "natural," impersonal relation.

It must be said that on this point Rawls's interpretation of Augustine is neither persuasive nor fair. Rawls does not actually use the terminology of "personal relationship" in discussing Augustine in Chapter Three of the thesis. The key term that he uses instead is "object." Sometimes he uses it in the well-established sense in which "object of" signifies a relation of something to an action or attitude. But sometimes he uses it in a sense defined early in the chapter, in which an "object" is something that "exists as the 'other' in what we have termed a natural relation" (160). And he does claim, evidently in this sense, that according to Augustine, God is to be loved as an "object" (175). Given the definition that Rawls is using, this is tantamount to claiming that in Augustine's view, love toward God should not be understood as seeking or participating in a personal relationship with God. Rawls gives little argument to support this interpretive claim. Augustine does not actually say that God is an object in the sense Rawls uses (nor does Rawls ascribe such a statement to him). In fact, I think it is quite clear (from his *Confessions,* for example) that Augustine does think of his relation to God as a personal, broadly moral relation—though he also sometimes uses impersonal models in speaking of it (as the Bible does too). In this respect, Rawls's historical argument is weak. However, that deficiency does not touch the systematic claim, in his own theoretical framework, that it is reasonable to object to any view that treats the relation of humans to God as wholly impersonal.

The other main criticism indicated in the summary at the end of Chapter Three is that in a wholly natural system of relations (and hence in Augustine's view, on Rawls's reading of it), all love, even love toward God, is acquisitive, and that cannot be true of Christian love. This criticism may be better grounded historically than systematically. I take it that what is meant by saying that Augustinian love toward God is "acquisitive" is that in it God is loved as *one's own* highest Good, and the relation to God is sought as good for oneself and able to make one happy. That is surely true of Augustine, who was profoundly influenced by the eudaemonistic framework of ancient Greek and Roman philosophical ethics. Whether Augustine thought that God is loved *only* as one's own good is more controversial, however. And if he did not, it may be less clear how far Rawls disagrees with him on the point. For in Chapters Four and Five of his thesis, as I will argue, Rawls holds that our salvation (and hence in some sense, surely, our good) depends on fellowship with God, and he seems to regard that as a consideration that can appropriately motivate us to some extent.

The historical framework for Rawls's critique of Augustine is largely borrowed from Anders Nygren. In particular, Rawls follows Nygren in accusing Augustine of taking over from Plato a conception of aspiration for the highest Good that is ill suited to Christianity. The debt to Nygren on this point is acknowledged (174n37). However, Rawls also departs from Nygren's views and arguments in important respects.

Nygren's *Agape and Eros,* first published in Swedish, in two parts, in 1930 and 1936, is the last century's most famous and influential study of Christian ideas of love. It is structured throughout by a contrast of two ideals of love; Nygren calls them Eros and Agape, and sees them as having archetypal protagonists in Plato and St. Paul, respectively. Not coincidentally, *eros* is the Greek word for love used in many significant contexts in Plato's dialogues, and *agap*e is the usual word for love in the Greek New Testament. But Nygren wisely declines to rest his historical analysis or his theological argument on such lexico-

graphical facts.[19] As a historian, he argues that many Christian thinkers have tried to synthesize Agape and Eros—thus compromising the
essence of Christianity, in Nygren's opinion. He sees such a synthesis
most notably in the conception of Christian love or charity (*caritas*)
developed by St. Augustine, and embraced by medieval theologians
following him. At the end of Nygren's narrative, Luther comes on the
scene to purify the Agape motif again.

Rawls's complaint that Augustine presents love toward God as acquisitive and egoistic is one of Nygren's arguments too. However,
Rawls's other main criticism, the one most deeply connected with his
polemic against "naturalism"—that human community with God is
lost in Augustine's view—is not one of Nygren's arguments. Though
Nygren does say that "Greek thought has no place for fellowship with
God in the strict sense of the term," he means this as a charge against
the *pure* Platonic form of the Eros motif. He does not level this charge
against the Augustinian *caritas* synthesis as he understands it. Indeed,
he explicitly (though not often) mentions "fellowship with God,"
rightly, as having a place in Augustine's theological views.[20]

Is Nygren's critique of Augustine solely based, then, on the charge
of egoism? Far from it. At least as important to Nygren is another argument that does not clearly play any part in Rawls's polemic against
"naturalism." Nygren was a Lutheran bishop and theologian, and his
book breathes the spirit of an early-twentieth-century Luther renaissance that was akin to neo-orthodoxy. The deepest motive of his argument, I believe, is Luther's conviction that salvation is by grace
alone, to which Nygren attempts to give ethical form in his delinea-
tion of the concept of Agape. For Nygren, "Agape is God's grace" and

19. Nygren, *Agape and Eros,* p. 33. In fact, I believe, *agape* and its cognate verb
agapan are simply the most general words for love in biblical Greek; see, e.g., the
"Septuagint" Greek translation of 2 Samuel 13:1.

20. Nygren, *Agape and Eros,* pp. 528–529.

"God's way to man," and in Agape "salvation is the work of Divine love"; whereas "Eros is man's effort" and "man's way to God," and in Eros "man's salvation is his own work."[21] In agreement with Plato's *Symposium*, Nygren conceives of Eros as an expression of *need*, so that God's love cannot be Eros, since God is not needy at all. In contrast, Agape is an expression of overflowing abundance, and therefore, at the most fundamental level, can only be God's love.[22]

From this conception of Agape Nygren draws the remarkable, and perhaps paradoxical, consequence that "in the life that is governed by Agape, the acting subject is not man himself," but God. In developing this conclusion Nygren embraces a strikingly impersonal model of the divine-human relation involved—a model that would hardly be at home in Rawls's rigorous personalism, although it is a biblical model. Nygren says, "God's Agape can be described by Paul quite realistically as a kind of 'pneumatic fluid', which is 'shed abroad in our hearts through the Holy Ghost which was given unto us' (Rom. v.5)." In Agape toward one's neighbor, therefore, "God is not the end, the ultimate object, but the starting point and permanent basis"—not the final cause of Agape but its efficient cause. Rather, in neighbor-love, "Agape-love is directed to the neighbor himself."[23]

Nygren has a polemical point here against Augustine, who can be interpreted with some plausibility as maintaining (in certain passages anyway) that in Christian love (or *caritas*) one should relate to one's neighbor, not as an ultimate object of love, but only as a means to be used to attain the ultimate end of enjoying God.[24] That Augustinian

21. Ibid., p. 210.
22. Ibid., pp. 211–212, 219.
23. Ibid., pp. 129, 215–216.
24. Augustine, *De doctrina Christiana*, I.xxii.20. See also Robert Merrihew Adams, *Finite and Infinite Goods* (New York: Oxford University Press, 1999), pp. 185–187.

view is not attractive. Shouldn't we love our neighbors for their own sake? Christians might well think that Christians themselves, and not just God, can and should be active subjects of such a love. With debatable consistency, Nygren too seems to suppose in many contexts that in some sense that is so, and that human beings sometimes love their neighbors in the sense of Agape.

Another striking aspect of Nygren's emphasis on God's grace is his insistence that Agape "must be spontaneous and unmotivated, uncalculating, unlimited, and unconditional."[25] Unlike Eros, which is essentially a response to perceived value, Agape is to be "unmotivated" in the sense that it finds no motive in the value of its object. It is grace not just in the sense that it is forgiving and looks past faults, and is not strictly proportioned to the value of its object, but in the sense that it is not a response to any value at all that it sees in the object. Agape is "*indifferent to value*," and "*any thought of valuation whatsoever* is out of place in connection with fellowship with God."[26] Indeed, it is Nygren's view that the object of Agape has no value prior to the Agape.

> God does not love that which is already in itself worthy of love, but on the contrary, that which in itself has no worth acquires worth just by becoming the object of God's love. . . . Agape does not recognize value, but creates it.[27]

This obviously suggests a divine love theory of the nature of value; but *Agape and Eros* manifests relatively little interest in metaethics, and no such theory is developed there.

One consequence that Nygren draws from the thesis that Agape must be "unmotivated" is that God can hardly be, in the most straight-

---

25. Nygren, *Agape and Eros*, p. 91.
26. Ibid., p. 77; italics in the original text.
27. Ibid., p. 78; cf. pp. 86–91.

forward sense, an object of our Agape. There is a "difficulty" in the conception of Agape toward God. "Agape is spontaneous, unmotivated love. But in relation to God, man's love can never be spontaneous and unmotivated." "Is not our love for God in fact 'motivated' in the very highest degree . . . by the Agape He has shown towards us?"[28]

Despite this difficulty, Nygren affirms that there is a sort of human Agape toward God. It is not wholly unmotivated, and if it is an expression of overflowing abundance, that can only be God's own abundance reflected back to God. But there is one main respect in which human Agape toward God is like God's love: it "is not an appetitive longing." Rather, in Agape "man's love for God signifies that man, moved by [God's] love, gratefully wills to belong wholly to God." This tells us rather little about what Agape's attitude toward God is. Elsewhere Nygren indicates that Agape's attitude toward God is one of *obedience*. He says that in Agape, love for God "devotes its whole attention to the carrying out of God's will. It is obedience to God, without any thought of reward."[29]

Contrasted with Agape are Platonic Eros toward the highest being (the Form of the Good) and Augustinian *caritas* toward God, which are forms of appetitive longing and expressions of human need. For Agape, God "is not the 'Highest Good', in the sense that He is more desirable than all other objects of desire, but He is simply not to be classed with any objects of desire whatsoever."[30] This is the point at which Nygren's critique of Eros and *caritas* is motivated by his commitment to a very strong form of the doctrine of salvation by grace alone. He thinks that in *seeking* God at all, Eros does not adequately recognize the primacy of grace. For it is part of Nygren's view of grace

28. Ibid., pp. 92, 213, 93.
29. Ibid., pp. 213, 94–95.
30. Ibid., p. 213.

that "*there is from man's side no way at all that leads to God*" but "God must Himself come to meet man."[31]

Should Rawls's attack on what he calls "naturalism" be seen, in Nygren's terms, as an argument for "Agape" as opposed to "Eros"? Rawls does not use the terms "Agape" and "Eros" in his own voice,[32] but the terminological point does not settle the question to what extent he was following Nygren. Specifically, we can ask whether Rawls uses the terms "desire" and "appetition," which he associates with the "natural" realm, to signify Eros, and whether the conception of "Christian love" that has an important place in the motivational ideal developed in his senior thesis (250–252) is a conception of Agape.

Nygren certainly associates desire and appetition with Eros.[33] And Rawls contrasts desire and Christian love in a way that clearly has something in common with Nygren's contrast of Eros and Agape as acquisitive and giving, respectively. Rawls says, "Desire leads us to acquire something. Christian love, on the other hand, seeks not its own; it manifests the spirit of giving" (250). Nonetheless I think it is misleading to read Rawls's contrast of the natural and the personal as a version of Nygren's contrast of Eros and Agape. The two contrasts differ both in structure and in content.

The structural differences are quite fundamental. Nygren's contrast is precisely between Eros and Agape. For Rawls, on the other hand, if Christian love is one pole of a binary polarity, the other pole is egotism, and the polarity is *within* the realm of personal relations. And the binary polarity in which desire and appetition are involved, in

---

31. Ibid., p. 80; italics in the original text.

32. They occur in his senior thesis only in citations of Nygren. Similarly, when Rawls uses the Latin term *caritas* in quoting or paraphrasing Augustine (174–175), there is no suggestion of Nygren's interpretation of Augustinian *caritas* as a synthesis of Eros and Agape.

33. Nygren, *Agape and Eros*, pp. 175, 180.

Rawls's view, puts not Christian love, but the interest in personal relations in general at the other pole.

An even more important structural difference concerns the strength of the opposition between desire and Eros and the opposite pole of each. For Nygren, Agape and Eros are "two entirely opposite motifs," "two general attitudes to life." He declares that "there cannot be any real synthesis between two forces so completely contrary to one another as Eros and Agape," although there have been repeated attempts in Christian history to join them together.[34] Rawls, on the other hand, despite his contrast between the natural and the personal, assumes that human lives that include personal relations will also include natural relations, with desires and appetitions related to them. This applies even to lives ruled by Christian love. Desires and appetitions that can be domesticated in this way within a life dominated by Christian love do not fit within Nygren's conception of Eros, which is defined primarily by the religious aspect in which it is incompatible with Agape. For Nygren, Eros is a "force . . . which, beginning with a sense of poverty and emptiness, seeks God in order to find in Him satisfaction for its own wants," as opposed to "the Agape which, being rich through God's grace, pours itself out in love."[35]

In content as well, Rawls's conception of appetition or desire is not a version of Nygren's conception of Eros. Rawls defines desire and appetition in terms of their object: they are not aimed at personal relationship as an end in itself. That is not a criterion of Eros for Nygren. For him, the difference between Eros and Agape "is not a question of the object of the love, but of its nature and ground."[36] Augustine's longing and quest for God has the character of Eros, in Nygren's view, even if it has fellowship with God among its ultimate ends, because

34. Ibid., pp. 227, 209, 231–232.
35. Ibid., p. 232.
36. Ibid., p. 142.

the fellowship is conceived as Augustine's own good and the quest is conceived (by Nygren at least) as "man's way to God."

Despite some points of agreement,[37] Rawls's conception of Christian love also differs fundamentally in content from Nygren's conception of Agape. For Rawls's conception is not constrained by Nygren's conception of divine grace. Rawls does emphasize the "givenness" of Christian love as "a fruit of faith which is given to us by the Word bursting in upon us" (251). He holds that the establishment of community is a gift of God, and impossible without God's grace (231). But Rawls does not see that as excluding our activity in establishing community. On the contrary, he says, "The elect are chosen to re-establish the community. To restore the community is their prime intention, or should be." He conceives of them as cooperating with God in this project: "By their efforts, together with the Holy Spirit, others can be brought into community" (247–248).

Likewise, Rawls does not imply that, strictly speaking, God is the only lover in Christian love. In his senior thesis, I believe, the anti-Pelagian emphasis on our need for grace is accommodated through a theology of conversion as wrought by God, rather than through a theory of a love of which we are merely conduits and not subjects. Rawls's alternative to ("natural") "appetition" is defined by its phenomenology and by the kind of relationship it seeks, not by who its subject is; he seems to think of us as potential subjects of it.

Nor does Rawls see our dependence on God's grace as a reason for disparaging motives and activities of *seeking* community with God. He speaks of "man's longing aloneness" in sin, and says, "Man seeks not to pry into [God's] privacy, or at least he should not; but he does seek to know *something* of His person." Rawls does not condemn this longing and seeking, for which indeed he mentions a good rea-

37. For instance, in emphasis on "the spirit of giving" (250).

son: "Man must have this knowledge of God before he can be restored. If the 'other' does not reveal itself, then the establishment of community must end in failure." He adds that "such knowledge of God can come only from God," but does not seem to draw any ethical conclusion from that except that "man must wait for God to speak to him" (224–225).

4. Values and Ends

In his senior thesis Rawls does not present a developed theory of value or of the good. He is more explicit in what he denies than in what he affirms about goodness as such. In what may be the clearest statement in the thesis on this subject, he says,

> The first concept to go, as we have already suggested, is the concept of the good as an object of desire. We maintain that objects of desire have nothing to do with salvation whatsoever except insofar as they are part of man's natural nature, which receives its due only after personality and community have been set in order. Community in the full sense, that is, the heavenly community, is the end in itself. It is the goal of creation, and while it may be true that man's natural being is fulfilled therein, such fulfillment is secondary to the community itself. (219–220)

On the negative side, Rawls denies that the good is to be identified with any object of desire. On the positive side, while the quoted passage is likely to leave readers with the impression that Rawls thinks the true good is community, that is not exactly what he says here. In a way that I think is typical for the text as a whole, he avoids the vocabulary of goodness and value in what he says positively about community. The preeminence he ascribes to community is expressed in terms of the way in which we should value it (as *end* in itself) rather than in terms of value that it has objectively (as *good* in itself). I will discuss first the way in which he relates objects of desire to the good, and then his treatment of community as an end in itself.

Rejecting "the concept of the good as an object of desire" is of a piece with Rawls's polemic against "naturalism." It is the starting point of banishing "all of the terms of the natural cosmos" from the discussion of salvation (220). The relativization to the topic of salvation is significant. At many places in the senior thesis Rawls says that "desires for food and drink, for beauty, and for truth and thus for the goods of nature as a whole . . . are good and their objects are good" (120). Indeed, it is a main thesis of his essay that "the natural cosmos is good and not bad" (179). Verbally, however, he is not altogether consistent on this point. He says of appetitions that "we can presume that they do not lead to good," and he uses "shudder quotes" when writing of "the 'good' which is the proper end of natural desire" (186–187, 120). But I think in these cases his point is to contrast appetitions with the seeking of community, which is what he values most. What Rawls most clearly rejects, I take it, is the idea (which he associates with Plato) of seeking our supreme end by way of "natural" rather than personal relationships (see also 160). As "part of man's natural nature," objects of desire are to receive their due, but "only after personality and community have been set in order." Rawls asserts a priority here—not exactly that the right is prior to the good, but that the ends of community are prior to the ends of "natural" desire.

He does not tell us *how* "man's natural being is fulfilled" in community, or *what* is the due that natural desires are to receive. So far as I can see, his view could be developed in either of two directions. He could suppose that what is due to natural desires is grounded in the ends of community, and that they are to be satisfied only insofar as that serves the ends of community. Or he could suppose that natural desires are worth satisfying for their own sake, but not at the expense of community, so that what is due to them is limited, but need not be grounded, by the ends of community. The tenor of Rawls's vindication of natural desire in Chapter Two suggests that he would, if asked, have endorsed the latter approach, which is clearly more generous to natural desire, as it does not require a positive community-based justification for each satisfaction of a natural desire.

On either approach it would be plausible to claim that there are at least *some* natural desires whose satisfaction, in some contexts, is supported, or even demanded, by the ends of community. In particular, it is plausible to think that good communal or interpersonal relations require us to try, altruistically, to satisfy some of each *other's* natural desires. It would be hasty, however, to jump to the conclusion that in this way altruism regarding the ends of other people's natural desires is unproblematic for the young Rawls. We can approach the problems altruism poses for him by reference to problems it poses for Leon and even for Nygren.

Nygren notes that for ancient Greek philosophical ethics, "the problem of the Good was . . . the problem of a 'Highest Good'—that is, of something which could in every respect satisfy the individual." It is the question, we might say, of what is supremely good *for* an individual. It is a central question of eudaemonism (in which the ethical criterion is the happiness of the agent) and utilitarianism (in which the ethical criterion is the greatest good of the greatest number of persons). That is the sense in which Nygren conceives of Eros as seeking the Highest Good. He denies that God is the Highest Good in that sense. Agape, he says, is less individualistic; it "is a social idea . . . and when the question of the Good is approached from the point of view of social relationships . . . it becomes dissociated from eudaemonism and utilitarianism and turns into the entirely independent question of 'the Good-in-itself.'"[38]

Viewed in such a social perspective, what is the Good-in-itself? In dissociating it from eudaemonism and utilitarianism, Nygren is evi-

38. Nygren, *Agape and Eros*, pp. 44–45; cf. p. 213.

dently implying that it is something whose goodness is not to be understood as goodness *for* particular persons, either individually or in aggregation. What else could the Good-in-itself be? Nygren's answer is, "The Good is *agape*."[39] I take him to mean that the decisive goodness of Agape is not a goodness *for* persons, but a non-person-relative intrinsic goodness of a feature of personal relations, a certain kind of love.

Agape, or Christian love, is generally supposed to be altruistic. Can it, or any form of altruism, really be wholly "dissociated from eudaemonism and utilitarianism" and uninterested in what is good *for* persons? Perhaps the likeliest alternative to caring about what is good for other persons, as a form of altruism, would be responsiveness to the preferences of other persons. Something of that sort is suggested by Philip Leon's account of the relation of the moral motive to appetitions.

Leon tries not to use "good" in his own voice (without quotation marks) to express the concept of goodness *for* a person. For him Goodness properly speaking (typically with a capital "G") "is that which we embody in individual right situations,"[40] which he conceives at least mainly as situations of personal relationship. But he does not locate it precisely in love. Leon thinks that "if [the reader] calls by the name of goodness that which is expressed in personal relationships, seeing how different in kind this goodness is from everything else, he will refuse that name to anything else." This consideration "may further persuade him that the whole domain of the so-called 'values' is a branch ... of Psychopathology."[41]

39. Ibid., p. 48.
40. Leon, *The Ethics of Power*, p. 297. He adds, "or in situations which embody Goodness"; the (otherwise unilluminating) circularity, he says, is intended "to show that no definition [of Goodness] is intended."
41. Leon, *The Ethics of Power*, p. 23.

In Leon's view "there is no class of really good appetitions or processes." He thinks appetitions for processes are presupposed by the moral motive, but they do not have the same kind of value as the moral motive. He holds that

> Morality does not presuppose 'goods'. . . . If anything is presupposed by morality, it is not good and bad processes, but processes which are liked and wanted and processes which are disliked and the objects of aversion.

In the view I take Leon to be proposing, the (largely social) requirements of "the right situation" do not call for us to regard the objects of appetition—our own or anyone else's—as really good, but only to be responsive in certain ways to each other's appetitions.[42]

Conceiving of altruism as responsiveness to other people's preferences rather than as caring for (what one takes to be) their good may have some appeal to thinkers worried about paternalism. But can it provide a wholly adequate account of altruism? Appropriately altruistic parents of young children, for instance, surely need to think in terms of what is good for their children, and not just in terms of their children's preferences. If the parents are philosophers, they may perhaps analyze the notion of what is good for a person in terms of the person's hypothetical preferences; but that does not touch the present argument. For hypothetical preferences are not actually preferences, and the parents in such a case are still relying on a conception of what is good for their children.

Because Rawls holds that the objects of many appetitions are good, his senior thesis, in any event, does not commit him to rejecting the conception of something being good for a person, or to denying that satisfying people's appetitions can be genuinely good for them. His position, however, might still severely limit how highly he can, con-

42. Ibid., pp. 285, 287–288; see also pp. 289–290.

sistently, value an altruistic concern for the satisfaction of another person's material needs. The end at which such a concern aims is not external to the single self of the other person for whom the altruist is concerned; it is, in Leon's terms, a "process" in that person. It seems to follow that such an altruistic motive must be placed in the "natural" part of Rawls's taxonomy of motives, in which all motives that do not aim at personal relationship as such are classified as natural.

It seems to follow also that an altruistic concern for satisfaction of the material needs of others as an end in itself must be valued by Rawls decidedly less highly than concern for the quality of personal relationships as an end in itself. Placing motives of satisfying others' material needs on a lower evaluative plane is certainly not unprecedented in Christian thought. But such an ordering of valuations seems at best very questionable in an account of Christian love, given the emphasis placed on the satisfaction of material needs in the New Testament.[43] I doubt that Rawls would have wanted to be saddled with this problem; and I have not noticed any indication in the senior thesis that he was aware of the problematic implications to which I have called attention.

Rawls has little to say there about altruism as such, and does not directly address the question of what place in his ethical taxonomy of motives should be assigned to altruistic interests in possible facts about other persons that would not be facts of personal relationship. But perhaps we can draw some inferences from things he says about other subjects. Concerning the motives belonging to the "natural" realm, Rawls says that all of them are acquisitive, egoistic, or self-centered. In "the natural cosmos . . . appetitional desires are the energies of all relations, and all love is acquisitive" (178). "Natural relations are

43. E.g., in Luke 10:25–37 and Matthew 25:31–46.

egoistic . . . Desires and appetitions are by nature egoistic, and therefore self-centered" (118).

So what would Rawls say about an altruistic interest in a process in another person, such as her recovery from illness, that does not essentially involve any personal relationship? Would Rawls deny that anyone has altruistic interests of that sort? Or would he agree with Leon in classifying them as egoistic or "alteregoistic" motives?[44] Or would he claim that such interests actually belong to the realm of personal relationships, simply by being interests in another person's well-being, even if one has no interest in interacting with the other person or being related to her otherwise than by wishing her well? All of these alternatives seem problematic, and none of them is addressed by Rawls.

As noted above, in his senior thesis Rawls tends to express his valuation of community in terms of the way in which we should value it (as *end* in itself) rather than in terms of value it has objectively (as *good* in itself). He associates the term "good" much more closely with his subordinate valuation of objects of "natural" appetition than with his supreme valuation of community. This is not to say that he never implies that community is good, and indeed supremely so. Rather, he manifests an ambivalence regarding the use of "good." This appears vividly in a single sentence in which Rawls both objects to the phrase "good life" and uses it to express his own valuing of personal relations above "any object." He says, "We do not believe that the so-called 'good life' (detestable phrase) consists in seeking any object, but that it is rather something totally different, a matter of personal relations" (161).

Rawls says that "community in the full sense, that is, the heavenly community, is the end in itself. It is the goal of creation." The implica-

44. Leon, *The Ethics of Power*, p. 23.

tion is clear that as "the goal of creation," community is the main and ultimate end that God sought in creating the world. There is also a very strong suggestion in this context that community is *our* highest end in that "salvation" or the fulfillment of our personal nature is to be found only in community (219). Rawls implies that community must be willed as an end in itself—that it cannot exist, properly speaking, except as it is willed as an end in itself by those who participate in it. "No community can be based on egoism" (187). A society based on social contract "is no community at all" if (as the young but not the later Rawls assumes) the social contract is "a scheme of mutual advantage which uses society as means only" (229).[45]

Rawls insists on valuing community as an end in itself. Nygren, on the other hand, seems to exclude analysis in terms of ends altogether where Agape is concerned. He declares that "no teleological explanation or motivation of [God's] love can be entertained." And he says of Luther, whom he considers a paradigmatic agape-ethicist, "The whole construction of his ethics is not teleological, but causal." These statements may be connected with Nygren's rejection of eudaemonism and utilitarianism. Nevertheless I believe they are misleading, because important distinctions are not made. The point Nygren seems to be after can be stated more precisely, and is relatively narrow. It is that Agape has in certain respects no *ulterior* end. In particular, "God does not love in order to obtain any advantage thereby, but quite simply because it is His nature to love." And in Agape toward one's neighbor, God's role is as cause of the Agape, not as a reward to which the neighbor is used as a means.[46] Neither of these points entails that the structure of Agape is not to be analyzed in terms of ends that are sought in

45. This view of social contract may have been influenced not only by Hobbes, but also by Leon's account of it (in *The Ethics of Power*, pp. 174–177) as a "mutual equilibration of egotisms."

46. Nygren, *Agape and Eros*, pp. 201, 737.

Agape. And in fact I think it is not easy to understand Agape in Nygren's account otherwise than as taking fellowship and the neighbor's good as ends in themselves.

Neither Nygren nor the young Rawls focuses on the sorts of alternatives to teleological motivation most likely to be discussed in moral philosophy today. Neither of them discusses either expressive action, or acting on a principle, as an alternative to trying to bring about an end extrinsic to the action. This is not to say that the senior thesis contains a teleological theory of right action; nowhere does it focus on defining the nature of right action as such. However, seeking to establish community is front and center in the ethics of the young Rawls without any expressed thought that there could be situations in which the end of this motive should be sacrificed to some less teleological consideration.

It is worth considering to what extent seeking community as an end in itself is a *selfless* motive in the view of the young Rawls. He had before him, in the work of Philip Leon, a clear formulation, if not an altogether clear discussion, of this issue. Leon holds that the moral motive is "objective" in the sense that it does not "refer essentially to the self." Its end is simply "that the right be done or that Goodness be embodied in a certain situation." The situation will normally be one involving some action of one's own.

We may have our doubts about this account of ethical objectivity. What about the desire that *I* embody rightness and goodness in my relations with others, as an end in itself and not for the sake of anything else? That desire refers essentially to the self, but looks like a very moral motive. Indeed, it looks very much like Leon's own conception of the moral motive when he says, "The genuinely moral man seeks to be at one with Goodness, to be inspired by Goodness, to embody Goodness."[47] For surely, insofar as you are seeking to embody

47. Leon, *The Ethics of Power*, p. 196.

Goodness, you have as an (essentially self-referential) end *your* embodying Goodness. The later moral philosophy of Rawls suggests a similarly self-referential motive: the interest in expressing one's own nature as a free and equal person.[48]

In his senior thesis Rawls is less articulate than Leon, but more cautious and arguably more consistent, in his treatment of self-referential motives in relation to his ethical ideal. He emphasizes that his ideal is not egoistic. "Christian love," he says, "seeks not its own . . . Its end is to give something to the other person as person" (250). Such a desire to give would not normally be counted as egoistic or self-seeking. Its end is not a process in oneself but a fact of personal relationship. But that fact of relationship, that stated end, is essentially self-referential. The end is not just that the other person receive a gift, but that the other person receive a gift from *me,* if I am the lover. That is implied if the end is *to* give something to the other person.

Moreover, Rawls says that Christian love, "although it is giving, does not overlook the personality of the giver. The self is not destroyed when it gives, but it is completed." To be sure, he goes on to say that in Christian love the self of the lover "is completed, however, not in an appetitional sense nor, of course, in an egotistical sense, i.e., by being glorified." But that just means that the self is not completed, "appetitionally," by satisfaction of a desire for "concrete impersonal processes," or "egotistically," by satisfaction of a lust for superiority over others. Rather, it is completed by participating in community in a way that essentially consists partly in loving. "The spirit completes itself in faith and love because it is communal by nature, and faith and love in all their intensity are proper to it" (250).

Nygren, I suppose, might still object to a love that in this way "does not overlook" the lover's own selfhood. He might think it comes much too close to an aspect of the self-love that he would exclude al-

48. Rawls, *A Theory of Justice* (1999), p. 417.

together from Agape, which has room only for love toward God and neighbor, and too close to the "sidelong glance" that he would exclude from Agape's neighbor-love.[49] But Nygren's ideal may be untenably austere on this point. If one's motivational ideal includes having it as an ultimate end to participate in a good community, doing one's part as a member of it—which is certainly a feature of Rawls's motivational ideal both in his senior thesis and in his theory of justice—then one idealizes having an end that is essentially self-referential (though not one that would normally be called "self-seeking").

One further issue about values calls for comment here. Both Nygren and the young Rawls refuse to speak of God as *beautiful*. Nygren situates his refusal in the contrast between Eros and Agape, with specific reference to the question "what it is that awakens love in man." With themes from Plato obviously in mind, he says that "Eros is of a markedly aesthetic character. It is the beauty of the Divine that attracts the eye of the soul and sets its love in motion." In Agape, on the other hand, "What awakens love in man is nothing else but the Agape shown to him by God." It is presumably a conception of beauty as inseparable from the competing value system of Eros that accounts for the otherwise surprising vehemence of Nygren's statement, "To speak of the 'beauty' of God in the context of Agape . . . sounds very like blasphemy."[50]

There may be an intentional echo of Nygren's vehement statement when Rawls says, "To speak of God as the most beautiful object, the most satisfying object, the most desired of all objects is to sin," and "if one cannot have faith in God just because He is what He is, but has to add that He is most satisfying in His beauty and such an *object* that we shall never crave anything else—then perhaps it is better not to be

49. Nygren, *Agape and Eros,* pp. 215–216.

50. Ibid., pp. 223–224.

a Christian at all." As suggested by Rawls's italicized use of the term "object," his claim is motivated, and has been thought through, on the basis of his contrast between the "natural" and the personal rather than Nygren's contrast between Eros and Agape. It is because it "is to turn a personal relation into a natural relation, and to do this misdeed in relation to God is surely sin," that to speak of God as the most beautiful object is to sin (182).

This reflects Rawls's classification of beauty as an object of appetition—"aesthetic appetition," which like all appetition belongs for Rawls to the "natural" realm (181). On that assumption, to speak of God as beautiful introduces the category of "religious appetition," and thus extends appetition beyond its rightful territory of the natural into that of the personal. Rawls's claim that it is sin to call God beautiful is explicitly part of his rejection of "religious appetition."

Issues arise here that Rawls does not address. Is it sin to speak (or think) of a human person as beautiful? Does that "turn a personal relation into a natural relation"? An affirmative answer to these questions looks pretty inhumane. As applied to sexual relations, it might have some resemblance to the particular form of inhumanity known as prudishness. The most plausible reading of the senior thesis, in my opinion, allows ascription of beauty to human persons to be innocent, as part of the normal mixture of the natural and the personal in our motivation. I suspect Rawls was thinking in terms merely of mixtures, and not of natural and personal motives as forming organic wholes with each other—though without providing (so far as I can see) any good reason for denying that such organic wholes occur. Be that as it may, it is only of God that Rawls actually says it is sinful, or contrary to community, to predicate beauty.

This suggests that the claim about God has another motive besides that of avoiding depersonalization. Perhaps the likeliest motive is simply the desire to avoid admitting any aesthetic value at the highest level of value. I think it is plausible to read the senior thesis as motivated by a belief that broadly moral relations among persons are, or can be, on a plane of value that transcends all other types of value, including the intellectual and the aesthetic. This belief might be compromised if the supreme being were acknowledged to have (also) aesthetic value. Why accept the belief, implying as it does that the value of the best personal relationships cannot have an aesthetic dimension? Two possible motives come to mind.

(1) It may be feared that admitting beauty of the beloved as a factor in love will compromise the unconditionality of love. This raises a serious problem. On the other hand, it may also be feared that refusing to admit beauty as a factor in love will compromise other important aspects of love.

(2) The other motive is that aesthetic values appeal to contemplation; and many strenuous moralists, as well as many interpreters of Christian ethics, are convinced that the more active moments of ethical and religious decision and enactment must be ranked above any more contemplative moment. This is not inevitable as interpretation of the Bible, however. Notable on the other side is a verse from the Psalms included in a passage that Rawls quotes from Augustine: "One thing have I desired of the Lord, that I will seek after; that I may dwell in the house of the Lord all the days of my life, that I may behold the beauty of the Lord" (175).[51] This passage ascribes beauty to God, as a theme of religious devotion, and expresses a clearly contemplative aspiration in doing so. Such themes have been important in several streams of biblically inspired piety. The opposite emphasis on religious and ethical decision and action, and a concomitant suspicion against the "contemplative life" and against mixing the aesthetic with

51. It is possible (though I am not sure how likely) that the biblical source did not register with Rawls. The reference (to Psalm 27:4) is supplied by the editors in the present edition of the senior thesis, but was not given by Rawls.

the religious, have arguably been more influential in Protestantism than in other forms of Christianity.

It may be significant in this connection that the writer Rawls cites as holding "much the same point of view" that he expresses in saying that it might be better not to be a Christian than to think one must say that God "is most satisfying in His beauty" is not Nygren but Kierkegaard (182). Kierkegaard does hold that it is important for Christianity, and for religion and ethics in general, not to grant aesthetic values a place at the highest level of value. And he connects this with the view that religious and ethical forms of life are centered in a stance of decision rather than contemplation.[52]

To what extent does Rawls's relegation of aesthetic values to a lower level remain in force in the rejection of "perfectionism" in his theory of justice? The first and most obvious thing to be said about that is that the perfectionism rejected by the older Rawls is a *political* doctrine which would treat excellence in aesthetic and other non-political dimensions as considerations appropriately grounding political decisions. In his final view, in *Political Liberalism* and later, Rawls is not necessarily objecting to individuals having beauty as one of the highest values in the "comprehensive view" that they personally embrace, so long as that valuation works, in their case, in such a way that they can join in an "overlapping consensus" supporting the liberal political principles of justice that Rawls advocates. Nevertheless, I do not believe that someone who did include beauty among her highest values would be likely to write exactly as Rawls wrote in *A Theory of Justice*.[53] We can say at any rate that in the senior thesis Rawls devel-

52. Rawls cites Søren Kierkegaard, *Concluding Unscientific Postscript,* trans. David F. Swenson and Walter Lowrie (Princeton: Princeton University Press, 1941), pp. 221–222. Statements of the relevant views are distributed widely in Kierkegaard's writings, including especially the *Postscript* and *Either/Or.*

53. See, e.g., *A Theory of Justice* (1999), pp. 387–388.

ops a religious outlook that, by virtue of the extreme priority it gives to broadly moral personal relations, is already a possible basis for participation in an overlapping consensus on political principles of justice.

5. Community

Acknowledging his debt to Emil Brunner's work, Rawls mentions, as something he particularly admires in it, "a clear and unflinching recognition that the universe is a *community* of Creator and created" (108; italics added). Brunner affirms the preeminence of community in terms that Rawls quotes and embraces with enthusiasm:

> As Brunner puts it: "The distinctively human element is not freedom, nor intellectual creative power, nor reason. These are rather the conditions of realization of man's real human existence, which consists in love. They do not contain their own meaning, but their meaning is love, true community."[54] Thus man is a being made to live in and to live for community. His gifts are means to this end. (192–193)

Rawls's use of the word "community" was likely inspired by (the English translation of) Brunner's *Man in Revolt*. The other sources that Rawls cites in the thesis make less prominent use of it. The English translation of Nygren's *Agape and Eros,* for example, usually prefers the term "fellowship."

Rawls says less by way of defining or explaining the notion of community than we might expect in an essay in which he declares that "the problem of ethics" is one of establishing community (128). He comments that "community" is "a difficult word to define" (111). I am not confident that Rawls was thinking of the distinction between *Gemeinschaft* (community) and *Gesellschaft* (society) in German social theory, although his conception of community agrees with standard

54. Brunner, *Man in Revolt,* p. 74.

conceptions of *Gemeinschaft* in signifying an association that is valued by its members for its own sake and not merely for its service to self-interest (189, 229). In stark contrast to Rawls's later work, the senior thesis says virtually nothing about *institutions* that might structure community. We might see a foreshadowing of a main theme of his later political philosophy in a comment on the traditional Christian doctrine of the *equality* of the three persons of the divine Trinity: he says they are "each equal with the other because that perfect community is bound by that perfect love and faith, and love seeks equality with the person to whom its givenness is directed" (207).[55]

Perhaps the best indication of what sort of personal relationship, or system of personal relationships, Rawls has in mind in speaking of community is to be found in his account of Christian love (250–252). Love is "giving," not self-seeking (see also 186). "There is . . . affection in love." More than that, "love is an intense and full personal contact," which involves "the very center of the spirit" rather than "the border of the person." It is directed toward the other person, but completes the personality or self of the lover. It is not egotistic, and thus is not interested in obtaining any sort of superiority in relation to other persons.

Other characteristics of community as Rawls understands it are that "community involves responsibility and obligations," and trust rather than fear and suspicion (249, 229). He holds that community cannot be based on merit, and indeed that an interest in merit is a barrier to community (229–230, 241)—a point that I will discuss more fully in section 7. He emphasizes that community is characterized by "openness," and by communication or mutual revelation of feelings and thoughts (250, 153–155). His connection of commu-

---

55. That love seeks equality with the beloved is a central idea of the second chapter of Kierkegaard's *Philosophical Fragments*, which Rawls cites at this point.

nity with communication is shared with Brunner, whom he cites as his source for the thought that "speech is something for community" (155). Brunner speaks of speech as "reason-in-community."[56]

In excluding egotism and emphasizing communication, Rawls's conception of community also has something in common with the conception of the good or right relational situation, which holds a corresponding place in Leon's scheme of things. Leon says,

> The right situation is . . . made up of personal relationships . . . such that in them these persons seek and maintain neither mutual separation nor mutual identification, no form of conquest, but at-oneness in distinction, cooperation through complementation, harmony through diversity, communication without fusion or confusion.

And the last words of his book describe "the development of free personalities living and growing and having their being in that free, full and intimate communication with each other in which is embodied Goodness."[57]

A significant aspect of Leon's statements just quoted is their emphasis on the "at-oneness in distinction" of "free personalities." A similar emphasis is present in Rawls's senior thesis, and it is extremely important for a sound understanding of that document in relation to the popular contrast between individualism and communitarianism. The word "individualism" is used a number of times in the thesis, always as something that Rawls is against (e.g., 227, 246). It is explicitly connected with sin (230), and contrasted with "communal thinking" (108). The word "communitarianism" does not occur in the thesis.

Clearly there is nothing that Rawls commends more highly in the thesis than community. And it is an explicit and emphatic doctrine of the thesis that "unless we have community we do not have personal-

---

56. Brunner, *Man in Revolt*, pp. 176–177.
57. Leon, *The Ethics of Power*, pp. 282, 309.

ity. Individuals become persons insofar as they live in community" (112). This is something affirmed by many who regard themselves as communitarians, and it is often regarded as a communitarian doctrine. Rawls does not really argue for it, nor does he cite a source for it. It could have been inspired by Kierkegaard's claim that "the measure for the self is always that in the face of which it is a self."[58] But here again I think the likeliest source is Brunner, who says, "I am not man at all apart from others. I am not 'I' apart from the 'Thou,'" and "man can only be fully 'himself' when he lives in love."[59] This flows from Brunner's interpretation of the idea of the human person as an image of God, which Rawls adopts. In contrast with the majority of traditional accounts of this idea, which identify the image of God in us with our rationality, Brunner identifies it with our capacity, and divinely ordained destiny, for personal relationship—responsible, broadly moral relationship above all with God, but also with each other.[60]

However, Rawls also affirms that "all persons are individuals, that is, separate and distinct units," and "unless we have personality, we do not have community" (111–112). Like Leon, he explicitly refuses to regard the values of community and personality as opposed to each other. He says,

> Likewise mistaken are the fears of those who, in wanting to preserve the independence of the person apart from the community, repudiate the person's necessary dependence on community. They fail to see that a person is not a person apart from community and also that true com-

58. Søren Kierkegaard, *The Sickness unto Death,* trans. Walter Lowrie (published with Kierkegaard's *Fear and Trembling*) (Princeton: Princeton University Press, 1954), p. 210. *The Sickness unto Death* is explicitly cited in the senior thesis: at 244 for an idea that is clearly Kierkegaard's, and at 208 for a thought that features "aloneness" where Kierkegaard evidently had despair in mind.

59. Brunner, *Man in Revolt,* pp. 140, 291.

60. Ibid., pp. 91–113. Rawls's appropriation of Brunner's view is evident at 192–193, 206; see also 202, 205.

munity does not absorb the individual but rather makes his personality possible. True community, meaning one integrated in faith under God, does not dissolve the person, but sustains him. (127)

The senior thesis does not speak of a good of the community as a whole to which individual interests must be sacrificed—nor even of principles of justice or right for a community as constraining conceptions of individuals' good, as in Rawls's later theory of justice. To be sure, if such thoughts of sacrifice or constraint did not seem necessary to the younger Rawls, that could be due chiefly to the dominance of aspirations for community in his conception of appropriate aspirations for individual lives. More deeply significant, therefore, in relation to present-day debates about individualism and communitarianism may be the absence from the senior thesis of any thought that ideals of individual autonomy should be regarded with suspicion, out of deference to the *authority* of a community's institutions or traditions.

These points reflect a tendency in Rawls's senior thesis to describe community in terms of person-to-person relations rather than in more holistic terms. A similar tendency is present in Brunner, whose discussion of "the individual and the community" surely influenced Rawls. They both could be described as having, in a sense, an "individualistic" conception of community. Brunner, moreover, is emphatic in affirming a positive rather than a negative relation between individual autonomy and community. "True independence [can] be developed," he says, only in the right sort of community, which for him as for the young Rawls is one that lives in contact with God. And "love is free self-positing in perceiving the claim of God which meets us in the other." The target of Brunner's fiercest polemic in his discussion of community is "collectivism," which he describes as a misunderstanding of "the destiny for community," a "perversion" which subordinates "personal being" to what should have been merely means to personal life. Such "means" include "the associations of civilization"; the culture and institutions which should have served personal life; the State; and even, or especially, "the collective power of the Church."[61] Writing in German in 1937, Brunner undoubtedly had Nazism in mind in this polemic (but not only Nazism). I see no reason in Rawls's senior thesis to doubt that he was thoroughly in sympathy with Brunner's attack on collectivism (though his own criticisms of Nazism there are rooted in the rejection of egotism, and thus more in line with Leon's arguments than with Brunner's).

It seems fair to say, on the whole, that in his senior thesis Rawls values both individuality and community very highly, and the same is true of his mature writings, as is argued in the Introduction to the present volume. In the thesis, and especially in the later theory of justice, themes of individuality and community are interwoven in complex and subtle ways. If we are going to speak of Rawls as an "individualist" or a "communitarian" at all, I think it would be most accurate to use those terms in a sense in which he is both an individualist and a communitarian. That applies in similar, though not identical, ways to both his senior thesis and his later theories of justice and political liberalism.

6. Sin and Egotism

Rawls defines sin as "the repudiation and negation of community." It is plausible to suppose that in this he is following Brunner, who says,

> The sin of Adam is the destruction of communion with God . . . ; it is that state of 'being against God' which also means 'being against one another.' . . . As we know ourselves in Christ . . . as the community of the elect, so we perceive in Him also sin as the opposition to the electing Word and the dissolution of this community intended and prepared in the fact of election.[62]

61. Brunner, *Man in Revolt*, pp. 292–295.
62. Ibid., p. 141.

Brunner's formulations in this passage are more theological than the definition I have quoted from Rawls, but Rawls supports his definition with theological ideas similar to Brunner's. Given that "'sin' is a word which we use solely in relation to God," Rawls asks, "Why use the word 'sin'?" He devotes several paragraphs to answering this question. "The repudiation of another, the negation of community," he argues, "is therefore repudiation of God as well. Implied in the abuse of our neighbor, is sin against God," because of "the nexus-like character of personal relations." He connects God's participation in the nexus with the thought that "we are all related to God, by virtue of being persons in His image." Further theological arguments for Rawls's definition of sin are indicated in his statements that "egotism is sin because it is the negation and destruction of that spiritual community for which man was made," and "thus, repudiation of community is the repudiation of man's end and of his Creator" (204–205; see also 193).

In addition to his definition of sin, supported in the manner indicated above, Rawls's account of sin has two main parts. One is a vivid portrayal of "aloneness" as "the result of sin" for the sinner, in the third and final section of Chapter Four. The other, larger part is an argument for the view that moral evil or sin has its root mainly, or even solely in the spiritual part of a person—not in the "natural" part and its "appetitions" but in interests in personal relations, and specifically in egotism or pride. It is a rambling argument, extended through the first three sections of Chapter Two and the first two sections of Chapter Four. It is largely devoted to subsidiary arguments for three theses regarded as supporting the view.

In the first subsidiary argument Rawls addresses the view that physical appetites as such are morally bad, or something to be escaped. Rawls gives himself an easy victory over that view, which he presumably did not take seriously as a live option. He does this in the first two sections of Chapter Two by marshaling evidence from the early "fathers" of the church for the thesis that Christianity historically supports the view that the human body and its physical appetites are good rather than bad. There is nothing new in Rawls's historical account in these sections, and he follows an interpretive line that was extremely influential in mid-twentieth-century Christian theology. Certainly the Christian theologies most widely regarded as orthodox have maintained that the human body is in principle a good creation of God, and that its normal and natural processes are in principle good too. This historical argument, at best, supports rejection only of quite extreme views. Even among orthodox church "fathers" one often meets quite negative or ambivalent attitudes toward physical appetites, as Rawls acknowledges to some extent. And most scholars writing today would be less ready than scholarship was half a century ago to let orthodoxy dominate the narrative.[63]

The alternative to his own view that Rawls, rightly, takes more seriously is a view typified by Aristotle. It sees physical appetites as necessary and appropriate for human life, if wisely governed by reason and ethical understanding, but also as taking, sometimes, the form of passions that threaten to overturn or prevent such wise self-government. In accordance with this view, the idea of a struggle of moral reason to dominate the passions and physical appetites has persistently played a major part in many streams of moral and spiritual thought. Rawls's other two subsidiary arguments are directed against this view, and they do not rest on an appeal to ecclesiastical authority. They are both concerned with the question, "Does the spirit pervert the flesh, or does the flesh pervert the spirit?" (148). Or to use Leon's terminology, which Rawls employs in parts of his discussion of sin, does egoistic

63. Peter Brown, *The Body and Society: Men, Women and Sexual Renunciation in Early Christianity* (New York: Columbia University Press, 1988), is a splendid example of the more recent historical approach to this topic.

sin arise from more fundamental egotistic sin, or does egotistic sin arise from more fundamental egoistic sin? That is, does an excessive, selfish, or otherwise perverse interest in "processes" in individuals arise from a perverse (superiority-seeking) interest in personal relationships, or does the latter sort of sinful interest arise from the former sort?

Rawls quotes Leon as holding that "there is nothing in appetition itself to bring about egotism in any of its expressions," and Rawls heartily agrees (151; 183).[64] His argument that egotistic sin cannot be grounded in merely egoistic sin, found chiefly toward the end of the first section of Chapter Four, consists mainly of phenomenological argument for the distinctness of interests in personal relations (including those of superiority) from "appetitional" interests in individuals' life processes. If we accept its premises, such an argument might well persuade us that appetition cannot ground an interest in social superiority purely or mainly for its own sake, which is what both Leon and Rawls mean by "egotism." Rawls does not seriously address the hypothesis that apparently "egotistic" grasping for superiority in wealth or power, for example, might actually have purely or mainly instrumental motivation, being inspired by "egoistic" anxiety about the satisfaction of one's own life process needs. Such a hypothesis should have been recognized as a serious competitor, however, in the theological context in which Rawls was writing in 1942. It is suggested, for example, by Reinhold Niebuhr's account of sin in the first volume of *The Nature and Destiny of Man*. Niebuhr's was certainly the theological treatment of sin that was most discussed in America then, and Rawls explicitly drew on it.

Of the three subsidiary arguments, the most important to Rawls, I think, was the argument for a grounding of egoistic sin in egotistic

---

64. Citing Leon, *The Ethics of Power*, p. 158.

sin, which is found mainly in the third section of Chapter Two, and is reinforced in Chapter Four. The argument in Chapter Two proceeds by offering rather speculative psychological explanations of some imaginary or generic cases of sexual sins and gluttony and drunkenness, largely drawn from Niebuhr's attempts to explain apparently "sensual" sin as rooted in a deeper spiritual sin. Rawls explains sensual sins as manifestations of underlying pride or egotism. As he admits, these arguments are "superficial." Their largely anecdotal character (not to mention the largely fictional character of the anecdotes) renders them plainly insufficient to justify his sweeping conclusion that "sensuality, whenever it becomes sin, will be found to be completely interfused with those spiritual perversions and aspirations from which no man is free" (149–150). Nor does his similar use, in Chapter Four, of a fictional example of the greed of an egotistical capitalist provide support of a stronger sort for such a conclusion about the motivation of greed (194–195). We may well agree that many cases of greed, drunkenness, and sexual aggressiveness or insatiability have deeper roots in desires for social superiority, without being persuaded that all cases of those vices have a correct explanation of that sort. And Rawls provides no compelling argument for even the more cautious conclusion that although "it is conceivable that appetitions may lead to sin, . . . (a) such is not often the case, and (b) in any event the appetition itself is not evil, but rather the situation to which it leads" (152).

Misgivings about the thesis of the derivative character of egoistic sin may also be suggested by Rawls's argument for the distinctness of appetition from interests in personal relationships. In discussing the "pure" appetition of a cold and weary man for rest and warmth, he imagines him asking someone else to warm a cup of coffee for him, and comments that "other people can only enter into his consciousness as means to the achievement of the desired end. The other persons do not enter as persons at all, but purely as means" (187). A Kantian might well think that a state of consciousness in which one regards other persons as means only and not as persons is already a sinful state, which could easily lead to immoral disregard of their interests and well-being, without any egotistic motive of competition.

Another problem, involving consistency, in Rawls's marginalization of egoism cuts close to the center of his account of the spiritual life. As we have seen, in the first section of Chapter Four Rawls rejects what he calls "the religious appetition" for God as a source of personal satisfaction. He classifies it as sin precisely because he sees it as an appetition and *not* a seeking for personal relationship, and therefore as depersonalizing one's relation to God. He does not suggest that this sin is rooted in an egotistic interest in social superiority. I imagine that Rawls would have agreed that such an explanation would implausibly trivialize the Augustinian type of piety that he has in view in his critique of religious appetition. His target here seems to be in his terms a fundamentally egoistic sin, and not an unimportant one.

Nonetheless, I believe that the desire to see both moral good and moral evil as rooted primarily in interests in social relations is deeply connected with central motives of Rawls's senior thesis, and indeed of his later work. This point can be developed in comparison with Niebuhr's account of sin. Niebuhr begins a chapter on the roots of sin by stating that "the uniqueness of the Biblical approach to the human problem lies in its subordination of the problem of finiteness to the problem of sin."[65] Rawls would not have been entirely wrong in seeing in this statement (which he had surely read) a commitment, similar to his own, to the priority of the ethical as an area of human con-

---

65. Reinhold Niebuhr, *The Nature and Destiny of Man,* vol. 1 (New York: Charles Scribner's Sons, 1941), p. 178.

cern. There are important differences, however, in their views of both the nature and the priority of the problem of sin. In a nutshell, Niebuhr's conception of the nature of sin is more metaphysical than Rawls's, and not as thoroughly social; and the priority Niebuhr ascribes to the problem of sin is a priority on the moral and spiritual agenda and not a priority in explanation. He in fact holds that the problem of finiteness occasions and motivates sin at the deepest level.

The most fundamental sin, in Niebuhr's view, is refusal to accept our own finiteness. This is the "pride" that he has in mind when he says it is the predominant "biblical and Christian" view "that pride is more basic than sensuality and that the latter is, in some way, derived from the former."[66] This pride can take the form of trying to override one's social limits in competition with others; but it can equally take the form of an indiscriminate struggle for resources to prolong one's life, or of escaping from knowledge of one's finite self. It is thus not an essentially social pride, except insofar as it is rebellion in relation to God; and even that rebellion, as such, is not necessarily part of the proud person's intention, since the refusal to accept our own finiteness is a motive as accessible to atheists as to theists.

Rawls actually quotes Niebuhr as arguing, "Does the drunkard or the glutton merely press self-love to the limit and lose all control over himself by his effort to gratify a particular desire so unreservedly that its gratification comes in conflict with other desires? Or is lack of moderation an effort to escape from the self?"[67] But when Rawls tries to incorporate Niebuhr's argument into his own by paraphrase ("put in our terms," as he says), it becomes, "Does [sensuality] involve merely natural relations or does it include personal relations, and if

66. Ibid., p. 186.
67. Ibid., p. 233.

both are present, which is dominant?" (149). Escape from self has disappeared from the argument, and has been replaced by an interest in personal relations which is not part of the explanation quoted from Niebuhr.

The differences between Niebuhr and Rawls in the conception of sin are, I think, profound. Rawls offers one sharp criticism of Niebuhr, noting that Niebuhr

> wants to argue that man, being both bound and free, both limited and unlimited, is in a state of anxiety. Although anxiety is not sin, it is the precondition of sin. Man sins when by pride he tries to deny his contingency and when by sensuality he tries to escape from his own freedom. (191)[68]

Rawls disagrees in two ways with this account of the root of sin (in which Niebuhr was evidently inspired by Kierkegaard's book, *The Concept of Dread*).

The disagreement more emphasized in this context may involve more misunderstanding than real disagreement. Rawls regards Niebuhr's account as an instance of the "Manichean" effort to blame our sin on something external to ourselves. Instead, Rawls says, "We have to admit that the spirit simply corrupts itself. Personality depraves itself for no reason that can be found external to it." But Niebuhr largely agrees that the human spirit corrupts itself. "Sin posits itself," he says; and "the situation of finiteness and freedom would not lead to sin if sin were not already introduced into the situation. . . . For this reason even the knowledge of [sin's] inevitability does not extinguish the sense of responsibility."[69] And on the whole, Rawls seems largely to agree with Niebuhr about the inevitability of sin. He refers to "the apparent inevitable tendency" of the spirit to deprave itself, and com-

---

68. Citing ibid., pp. 182–186.
69. Ibid., pp. 181, 254.

ments that "the beginning of sin must be conceived as taking place in this unfathomable 'causeless' way." That is substantially Niebuhr's view (191).

It is also part of Rawls's objection to Niebuhr, however, that far from being part of the explanation of sin, "anxiety is the result of sin. It is the state of the sinner in the cosmos he creates for himself, namely, the cosmos of aloneness." This is a deep disagreement. For Rawls, hell is aloneness—so to speak. He does not speak of hell in his own voice, but quotes lines from T. S. Eliot that speak of "active shapes of hell" as less fearsome than "emptiness, absence, separation from God" (191, 208). This is a passionate personal conviction for Rawls, as his portrayal of aloneness makes clear. I think it is fair to say that the senior thesis expresses a view in which our nature is most fully expressed in preferences regarding personal relations, and he finds it difficult to believe that such preferences would be grounded in even deeper, less social, more metaphysical or physical concerns regarding our finitude or, more concretely, regarding death and material insufficiency.

That remains true to a large extent of Rawls's mature work as well. Certainly *A Theory of Justice* manifests a serious respect for reasonable economic sufficiency as a necessary condition of a well-ordered society. But Rawls still expects those who enjoy a good and just social and political system to satisfice easily regarding non-social goods. This is clearly expressed at the end of his career, in *The Law of Peoples*, in his argument that liberal peoples will be "satisfied peoples," and, being freed from temptations of social superiority-seeking by the just internal structure of their societies, they will "have nothing to go to war about."[70]

70. John Rawls, *The Law of Peoples* (Cambridge, Mass.: Harvard University Press, 1999), p. 47.

This argument is connected with one of the most striking and important differences between Rawls's view of sin and Niebuhr's. Niebuhr's views on the relation of sensuality to pride are not particularly distinctive, and his account of the root of sin, or inescapable temptation, in anxiety is largely borrowed from Kierkegaard. What is most characteristic about Niebuhr in this area, and most strongly connected with the "Christian realism" that he championed in his role as one of the most influential political thinkers in mid-twentieth-century America, is his belief in the *persistence* of sin. "There is," he declares, "no historical development which gradually eliminates those sinful corruptions of brotherhood which stand in contradiction to the law of love."[71]

Both at an individual and at a sociopolitical level Niebuhr sees real possibilities of important victories over sin, but no possibility of eliminating sin as a terrible problem. At an individual level, he says that "it is logical to assume that when man has become aware of the character of his self-love and of its incompatibility with the divine will, this very awareness would break its power." The account of conversion in Rawls's senior thesis can easily be read as an account of just such a breaking of the power of sin. Niebuhr thinks that "this logic is at least partially validated by experience. Repentance does initiate a new life." But he does not believe that any conversion observable in history comes even close to eliminating sin from a person's life. "The sad experiences of Christian history show how human pride and spiritual arrogance rise to new heights precisely at the point where the claims of sanctity are made without due qualification."[72]

At the collective level Niebuhr says, on the one hand, that there is "no social or political problem in which men do not face new possi-

71. Reinhold Niebuhr, *The Nature and Destiny of Man,* vol. 2 (New York: Charles Scribner's Sons, 1943), p. 96.

72. Ibid., pp. 121–122.

bilities of the good and the obligation to realize them." He insists there are approximations to justice that are achievable and worth working for. Niebuhr would surely have criticized Rawls's senior thesis as expecting too much from individual conversion and too little from reformation of institutions. On the other hand, he says, "No human community is . . . a simple construction of conscience or reason. All communities . . . are governed by power." At the heart of democracy he sees conflict, limited so as not to result in anarchy or violence. He says, "It is the highest achievement of democratic societies that they embody the principle of resistance to government within the principle of government itself."[73]

The difference between Niebuhr's hopes for a democratic political order and those of the older Rawls is undeniable, even if it is to some extent a difference of tone and emphasis. It is associated with a difference in their choice of political problems to write about. In the first chapter of *A Theory of Justice*, explaining his decision to focus on ideal theory and on cases of "full compliance" with principles of justice, Rawls acknowledges that "the problems of partial compliance theory are the pressing and urgent matters. These are the things that we are faced with in everyday life." He argues for "beginning with ideal theory" as offering the best prospects for a "systematic grasp of these more pressing problems."[74] Niebuhr's voluminous writings on politics, on the other hand, focus largely on non-ideal situations. This may reflect to some extent his greater personal engagement with

73. Ibid., pp. 207, 257, 268. The second volume of Niebuhr's work was first published in January 1943, the month after Rawls submitted his senior thesis; but Niebuhr's views about the permanence of sin in politics were already well known, in an even more pessimistic form, from his earlier book, *Moral Man and Immoral Society* (New York: Charles Scribner's Sons, 1932). See Fox, *Reinhold Niebuhr*, pp. 212–214.

74. Rawls, *A Theory of Justice*, p. 8.

practical (and partisan) politics. But Niebuhr's more pessimistic view of the prospects for ideally just political systems doubtless led him to see the problems of moral wisdom in dealing with non-ideal situations as even more urgent, and more difficult, than they seemed to Rawls.[75]

These differences are deeply connected with the disagreement between Niebuhr and the younger Rawls regarding the root of sin. The problem of finiteness, in which Niebuhr sees the deepest temptation to sin, is not going away. It is not a problem that we could *solve*, individually or collectively. Nor does Niebuhr think that God is going to take the problem away at any time in human history. Our moral and spiritual task, in Niebuhr's view, is not to solve this problem but to learn to live with it. He does not think we should learn to be *satisfied* with the best attainable spiritual and political conditions. On the contrary, he believes we should constantly subject such conditions to criticism by reference to a standard of transcendent goodness (that is, a standard of sacrificial love). But he also regards the belief that we might actually realize the ideal as a dangerous delusion.

The problem of egotism, in which Rawls saw the root of sin, seems more amenable at least than the problem of finiteness to individual and social moral improvement. And Rawls might well think this an advantage in providing a basis for the hopefulness that he and Niebuhr agree is necessary for moral and political effort. I think the basis of hopefulness is indeed one of the most difficult points in Niebuhr's thought. To the extent that Niebuhr thinks that anxiety about our finitude can be purged of "the tendency toward sinful self-assertion," it is through "faith in the ultimate security of God's love." How does God's love address the source of the anxiety? Niebuhr speaks, for instance, of a hope that "eternity will fulfill and not annul the richness

---

75. See, e.g., Niebuhr, *The Nature and Destiny of Man,* vol. 2, p. 88.

and variety which the temporal process has elaborated." But he speaks vaguely about such things, and is less ready than Rawls was in his senior thesis to affirm in literal terms the traditional Christian hopes of a future life beyond the vicissitudes of history.[76] On the other hand, Niebuhr would surely say that his account of the root of sin is more realistic than Rawls's. In particular, he might well think it an advantage of his account, an aspect of its realism, that it does not assign a uniquely fundamental motivational role to interests in personal relations, and therefore gives him no reason to deny that we remain capable of selfishness in regard to economic goods quite independently of competitive interests in social relations.

7. Conversion and the Rejection of Merit

The section on conversion (Chapter Five, section III) is perhaps the most original and interesting in the whole senior thesis. Rawls himself affirms emphatically the centrality of conversion for Christian thought. He says, "It is undoubtedly true that a full understanding of conversion is absolutely essential for the understanding of Christianity. . . . conversion is crucial because its character constitutes the womb of Christian theology. It is in this experience that Revelation, Sin, and Faith achieve their full meaning and contrast." He sees in it "the true source of the doctrine[s] of election" and creation and, more generally, of "the true conception of God" (233, 242).

The emphasis on conversion is characteristic of some traditions in Protestantism. And Rawls's account of "the Word of God break[ing] into the closedness of sin" in the event of conversion is classically Protestant (233). Strikingly personal, however, and I believe quite original, is Rawls's account of the phenomenology of conversion, in terms of the "flatness" of "lying in exposure before the Word of God"

---

76. Ibid., vol. 1, p. 183; vol. 2, p. 295. See also Fox, *Reinhold Niebuhr*, p. 215.

(233–237). The experience is outwardly undramatic, inwardly transforming. Rawls goes so far as to say, "Sin cannot help but be destroyed
before the grace of the Word. . . . The in-coming of the Word has so
exposed the sins of the self that they have no longer a hiding place"
(239).

This seems to affirm an extirpation of sin more radical than Niebuhr would have asserted without emphatic qualifications. Brunner
too holds that conversion from sin is never completed in this life:
"The eggshells of the old nature still cling to [the person who has re-
sponded to God in faith] as something which has been overcome, but
still also as something which has to be overcome again and again."[77]
Rawls himself would perhaps have wished, on further reflection, to
qualify his claims of efficacy for conversion, but his discussion in the
senior thesis evinces little sense of a need to do so. A note of caution
appears when he says that as a result of "the experience of [God's]
Word . . . we act, *or try to,* according to the analogy of His grace" (249;
italics added). But he states flatly, in the same context, that the converted sinner "now leads his life in right relations to others. . . . Therefore there grow from the conversion experience those actions which
restore and reconstruct community. Thus obligations are now fulfilled" (248).

The account of conversion is a central node in an argument and
theoretical structure that integrates much of the contents of the thesis. The following points (at least) are linked here.

(1) The fundamental sin, which closes us off from community, is
egotism (that is, the sin of pride, more or less—or perhaps, more fundamentally, lust for social position).

(2) Although the conversion which is required for salvation is
depressing in some ways, it is not pain that is crucial in it, but the

77. Brunner, *Man in Revolt,* p. 488.

crumbling of egotism "into the flatness of exposure" (238), without histrionics.

(3) In this (and even before this, in the hearing of God's Word) the conversion is an encounter with the generosity, the gently judging love and mercy of God. "It is mercy and not wrath which is the most powerful condemnation of all" (239). It is the perception of the contrast between God's love and the sinner's own egotism that precipitates the dissolution or crumbling of the egotism. The idea that it is only in the revelation of God's mercy that we can truly recognize our sin was certainly current in Protestant theology in the 1930s,[78] but Rawls develops it with uncommon richness and vigor in the thesis (237–242).

(4) Rawls's account of conversion is deeply connected with the denial that God is angry or punitive. This connection is reflected in the emotional flatness he ascribes to conversion, and in the claim that it is God's *mercy* that undoes our sin. "Fear," says Rawls, citing William Temple, "is the most self-centering of all the emotions." Because it gives rise to fear, the belief (false, according to Rawls) that God is angry is a barrier to faith, and leads to a further barrier that Rawls calls "the bargain basis" of interpersonal relationships. Bargaining, he says, is "a method used by the sinner to bind the 'other' and to protect his own self," and it "springs from fear." This is true, as Rawls points out, of the social contract as Hobbes conceived of it; but it cannot result in genuine community, which must be based on mutual trust rather than distrust. Similarly in religion, distrust of God motivates bargaining with God and is the source of "any 'merit' scheme of salvation" (227–230).

(5) The senior thesis proposes two reasons for rejecting *merit* as a

78. This idea is expressed succinctly, for instance, in Emil Brunner's christological book, *The Mediator: A Study of the Central Doctrine of the Christian Faith,* trans. Olive Wyon (New York: Macmillan, 1934), p. 602.

basis for salvation, or indeed as an object of any legitimate interest whatever. Both reasons are connected with the conversion experience. One is that with the crumbling of egotism, "The human person recognizes that every thing he has received is a gift and that he has nothing that had not been given to him." This is partly a matter of what parents, friends, and "community" have given him; but there are also "the land" and "nature," and "he can now see that the totality of what he has possessed and enjoyed has been the gift of God" (238–240).

(6) The other reason for rejecting merit is that "achieving good deeds as merits serves only the demon of spiritual pride," and that therefore "merit is beside the point [indeed counter-productive] in establishing community" (241, 230). Merit is viewed here as a sort of social superiority. And if interest in social superiority of any sort is egotism, and conversion is in large and essential part a turning away from egotism, then conversion involves a turning away from interest in merit.

Rawls identifies "a lack of faith and trust," issuing in a desire "to flaunt some merit before the decisions of the divine election," as "the real core of Pelagian falsity" (229). This is not proposed, I take it, as exegesis of Pelagius, but as Rawls's own view of what is most deeply wrong with views that have been called Pelagian. It is an authentic expression of the Pauline theme of salvation by grace alone through faith which was central to the theologies of Augustine and Luther, and it is developed by Rawls in what seems to me an original and interesting way. That "God . . . does not want merit that He can reward" (241) is not stated in the letters of Paul in the New Testament, but it articulates an idea that can plausibly be seen as motivating such passages as Romans 10:3-4.

In his critique of the interest in merit Rawls has more in common with Leon, among his contemporary sources, than with the more traditionally theological writers Brunner and Niebuhr. That the interest in merit is an expression of egotism is an idea extensively developed by Leon. In fact, Leon's discussion provides an explanation of a curious extension of the idea that emerges in Rawls's thesis only in an occasional turn of phrase. Rawls says, "Egotism seeks to set the 'thou' below itself, to turn the 'thou' into an admirer or into an object of admiration" (194; see also 203). It is easy to see how turning the "thou" into an admirer would be setting the "thou" below oneself, but by the same token we might think that turning the "thou" into an object of admiration would be setting the "thou" *above* oneself—setting the "thou" on a pedestal, as we say. Rawls offers no explanation on this point, but Leon has a lot to say about it. He explains admiration of another as a manifestation of a covert egotism exalting itself by "identification" with the admired other. He argues further that admiration is incompatible with community because it turns away from the individuality of the other person to "generic attributes" which are abstractions from the individual.[79] He says that

> there can be no intimacy with abstractions (qualities, attributes), which are the objects of valuation. Nor is there intimacy with persons whom we esteem, respect, honour, praise, admire, or otherwise laud (that is, we laud their attributes or "characters").[80]

Leon carries this idea to a point that is contrary to the traditions and practices of virtually all the theistic religions: he objects to admiring and praising God. He asks, "Does the moral or objective life exclude, then, worshipping, awe, reverence, veneration, all of which have been called laudatory attitudes?" He answers,

> It only does not exclude that at-oneness with, and inspiration from, God experienced as Goodness and Love, which . . . is certainly not de-

79. Leon, *The Ethics of Power,* pp. 196–201; see also pp. 98–99.
80. Ibid., p. 201.

scribable nor described by the terms 'awe,' 'worship,' 'reverence,' 'veneration,' 'the sense of the numinous,' as these are ordinarily used.

In a note, Leon adds that he "is prepared to be judged and sent to the stake" for "the assertion that all religion which centres around the notions of power, absoluteness, and supremacy is sheer egotism."[81]

I do not believe the young Rawls had any intention of following Leon in this rejection of worship. Considered in isolation, Rawls's statement, "God's call is not a call to praise, but a call to repentance," might perhaps be read in such a sense. In its context, however, its sense is pretty clearly that we are not to *be* praised, but to repent. "To make God's motive His own honor is to make Him into an egotist," Rawls says; and he objects to "imagin[ing] God as a glorified egotist." But though God is not "seeking His own glory," still "His community will manifest His glory." And in the final paragraph of the senior thesis, the joyous consummation of community is envisaged as one in which "all the creatures of God will kneel at His feet" (242, 246, 227, 252).

As pointed out in the Introduction to the present volume, the rejection of merit is a point of "particularly striking continuity between the thesis and Rawls's later views." It is one of the distinctive, and controversial, features of Rawls's theory of justice that it does not treat either reward of merit or punishment of demerit as a fundamental requirement of justice. This feature of the theory is supported by arguments that the sources of moral merit depend on advantages that were not earned and that no one individual deserved any more than anyone else. These arguments have much in common with the argument, in the senior thesis, that every advantage any one of us may have enjoyed "has been the gift of God." The less essentially theological argument of the senior thesis, that the interest in merit is inimical to community, as an egotistic interest in social superiority, is not fea-

81. Ibid., pp. 196–197.

tured in *A Theory of Justice*, perhaps because it is less directly and obviously connected with ideas of fairness and deserving.

In *A Theory of Justice*, to be sure, the argument against desert is not presented in theological terms, but in terms of a natural lottery, the idea of being fortunate or favored by nature.[82] Rawls certainly had reason enough in his conception of the nature and aims of political theory to avoid arguing in theological terms in his theory of justice. But he may also have been motivated by a personal unwillingness to "interpret history as expressing God's will," as he put it decades later in "On My Religion" (263).

I doubt, however, that seeing everything as a gift of God is simply superfluous as a support for the rejection of meritarian perfectionism. It is not obvious that the merely negative consideration that one's acquisition of any perfection is never wholly one's own doing gets a strong grip on perfectionist thinking. For the perfectionist claims that Rawls most wishes to oppose are typically seen by perfectionists as grounded in the actual or possible *possession* of perfections, rather than in any *earning* of a reward by the mode of acquisition of the perfections. Seeing everything as a gift of God provides a positive motive of gratitude for giving back to God by giving to the community that God is establishing.

8. God and Revelation

The way in which Rawls speaks of God in his senior thesis gives no reason to doubt the accuracy of his recollection, in "On My Religion," that he was "a believing orthodox Episcopalian Christian" at the time he wrote the thesis (261). No doctrine of God is systematically developed in the thesis; but many fragments of a conception of God emerge in passing comments, and they are mostly quite orthodox

---

82. Rawls, *A Theory of Justice*, §§17 and 48, and p. 64.

from a traditional point of view. The doctrine of Creation is mentioned as having its source, as noted above, in the experience of conversion. It is explained, very briefly, as meaning "primarily . . . first, that man is dependent on God, and second, that everything is a gift of God" (242). Such creating surely requires an extremely powerful God, and Rawls in fact affirms divine omnipotence, in the biblical formulation "all things are possible with God" (252).[83] The orthodox affirmation that "God is . . . Three Persons in One, each equal with the other" is made in the course of discussing human community (206; see also 193). The linking claim that "God is communal," however, fits some traditions of Christian orthodoxy better than others.

A modernizing aspect of the conception of God that emerges in the senior thesis is the rejection of the doctrine of divine immutability, which, as Rawls suggests, has roots that are more philosophical than biblical (246). This is not a surprising position to take. The changelessness of God, though almost universally affirmed in medieval and early modern theology, was widely (but by no means universally) denied in twentieth-century theology. Rawls does not articulate any positive theory of God's relation to time and change.

More interesting, perhaps, is the question of the *neo*-orthodoxy of Rawls's conception of God. He shows little of Barth's zealous emphasis on the transcendence and "otherness" of God. On at least two distinctive points, however—the doctrine of election and the conception of God's self-revelation—Rawls's account of God shows the influence of neo-orthodox theologians—in particular, of Brunner.

(1) One of the aspects of a Protestant conception of God that Rawls discusses most extensively in his thesis is the doctrine of *election*— that is, the belief that God elects or chooses those who are the objects of God's redemptive activity. Rawls states that he accepts "the New

83. Mark 10:27; compare Luke 1:37; Genesis 18:14.

Testament concept of election . . . in its full sense." But he wants to "avoid . . . harsh predestinarian conclusions," which he associates with Augustine and Aquinas, but which certainly can be associated also with Luther and Calvin. This aspiration, to retain a doctrine of divine election but without a harsh doctrine of predestination, can be found in modern theology at least as early as the archetypal liberal theologian Schleiermacher, and hence is not distinctively neo-orthodox; but it was certainly shared by Barth and Brunner. The five-hundred-page chapter in which Barth tries to accomplish this ambition is one of the most excitingly innovative parts of his *Church Dogmatics.* But it is Brunner's two-page treatment that Rawls would have read, and Rawls has more to say about election than he would have found there.[84]

Rawls's first suggestion for avoiding the harsh conclusions is that the conception of God as changeless should be abandoned. Presumably his thought, in connecting this proposal to issues of predestination, is that if God's plans can change over the course of time, then God's election of persons can reflect changing circumstances and contingent choices of those persons. His main suggestion, however, is that a theology of election should reject "radical individualism" and the misunderstanding of election as intended "to save an isolated person here and there." Rawls's preferred alternative is that God's electing has a communal rather than an individualistic purpose; it is intended "to restore and to gather together a community of His created ones." "The elect are chosen to re-establish the community." Their own conversion is the first step in the re-establishment of community, which continues through their telling others the "good news." God's electing the apostle Paul, for example, means that "he is chosen

---

84. See Brunner, *Man in Revolt,* pp. 76–78; Karl Barth, *Church Dogmatics,* vol. 2, part 2, trans. G. W. Bromiley et al. (Edinburgh: T. & T. Clark, 1957), pp. 3–506; first published in German in 1942.

to preach the Word; God will use him as a means for further election" (244–247).

How does this constitute an alternative to harsh predestinarian doctrines? Rawls does not address that question as clearly as one might wish, but I believe that in his account it is the *purpose* of God's electing that is communal rather than individualistic. He does not deny that persons are called individually, and at different times, into the community by conversion. His view differs from a predestinarian view of election, I take it, in that he sees God's election of a person not as choosing that person, rather than others, for eventual salvation, but rather as choosing that person for a role in the establishment of the community, for membership and service in it at a particular time.

It is hard to believe that these strategies are really sufficient for Rawls to avoid the harsh implications of more traditional doctrines of election. Given his argument that we are not in a position to claim merit or credit for any moral attributes we may have, it seems that the harshness, and indeed the unfairness, will remain in his theology unless he denies the doctrine of hell, which would exclude some individuals forever from membership in God's community. It is not the divine determinism, but the belief in hell or damnation, which is the main source of moral offensiveness in the doctrine of election, as was already clearly recognized by Schleiermacher.[85] Barth and Brunner did not reject the doctrine of hell as unequivocally as Schleiermacher, though I think it is fair to say that they invite their readers to *hope* for

---

85. Schleiermacher, *The Christian Faith,* pp. 536–560 (§§117–120) and pp. 720–722; and especially *Über die Lehre von der Erwählung,* in Schleiermacher, *Kritische Gesamtausgabe,* series I, vol. 10 (Berlin: Walter de Gruyter, 1990). Much of what Rawls affirms positively about election can already be found in Schleiermacher.

universal salvation.[86] Others were going farther in the 1930s. In a commentary cited (though not on this point) in Rawls's thesis, C. H. Dodd advocates an unequivocally universalist reading of the last part of chapter 11 of St. Paul's Epistle to the Romans.[87] Rawls is perhaps not equivocal, but not fully explicit on the point either, in his senior thesis; but some statements in the thesis seem to indicate a belief that all people will eventually be saved. He says, for instance, that those who have already been elected and restored "are to gather together with [God's] aid *all* those who still remain behind, and are to help bring the *totality* of the creation before Him." In the end, "The *whole* creation will be bound together and *all* the creatures of God will kneel at His feet. This community joining *all* together under God is the goal towards which God moves His creation" (252; italics added).

(2) In the views that Rawls expresses in his senior thesis about how God can be known we find an emphasis on revelation, conceived as God's personal self-disclosure in communicative action, and a corresponding disparagement of "natural theology." These are typical neo-orthodox themes, though they appear, for the most part, in much less polemical contexts in Rawls's thesis than in the work of the leading neo-orthodox theologians. Rawls's conception of revelation manifests the personalism that animates the main arguments of his thesis, and in which he is particularly close to Brunner.

"It is doubtful," Rawls says, "whether natural theology can tell us

86. Barth, *Church Dogmatics,* vol. 2, part 2, e.g., pp. 477, 496–497, 506. Brunner is vague on the crucial point in *Man in Revolt,* pp. 470–477. He is not vague at all, but crisply and frankly inconsistent, in *The Christian Doctrine of the Church, Faith, and the Consummation* (the third volume of his *Dogmatics*), trans. David Cairns (Philadelphia: Westminster Press, 1962), pp. 415–424, which was written long after Rawls finished his senior thesis.

87. C. H. Dodd, *The Epistle of Paul to the Romans* (London: Hodder and Stoughton, 1932), ad loc.

very much" (111). He may be making some allowance for skepticism about philosophical arguments for theism here and when he says such things as

> Reason cannot tell us whether God is Creator, Eternal, all-powerful and so forth. But He himself can tell us. . . . The nature of God, insofar as it is intelligible to us, is not discovered by playing with metaphysical categories, but is rather presented to us unmistakably in the experience of His Word. (242–243)

It seems fair to say that in youth, as later in life, Rawls did not wish to rest his most cherished convictions on metaphysical arguments.

Most often in his senior thesis, however, the disparagement of natural theology, and the insistence on revelation, are grounded in the personal character of the knowledge of God to which he aspires. "Personal relations proceed on the basis of mutual revelation. . . . Personal relations require this self-revelatory action, else no personal contact can be established" (117–118). This applies to God too. "Natural theology cannot tell us of God's person. His personality must be revealed by Him" (124). Rawls explains this point very vividly:

> Imagine the person who seeks to re-establish community and who receives no response from the "other." Suppose that throughout all our efforts the "other" remains silent and makes no answer, then what can we do? If the other person makes no disclosure on his own part, then our efforts are certain to fail. . . . Natural theology is helpless before the personality of God. Why? Because all knowledge of other persons is knowledge given to us by them. Personal knowledge is revealed knowledge. (224)

Rawls declares that in the experience of conversion "the Word of God breaks into the closedness of sin and bends back its walls." This expresses a dynamic view of God's Word. That word is not just a written text; it is also something preached by human beings who have already heard it. But more than that, the Word of God is a divine action revealing God to us, which can even constitute God's being knowably present to us at a particular time. As Rawls says in this context, "Revelation is God's action; it is His coming to us and speaking to us; it is His presence bursting into the aloneness of sin." Similarly, "it is the Word of God Himself speaking to us which destroys sin and which converts the inner spirit and immediately sets it open to and into community" (233, 248).

These statements express a characteristically neo-orthodox conception of revelation and God's Word. It offered the neo-orthodox theologians ways of avoiding "fundamentalist" biblical literalism, although Rawls does not appeal to it for that purpose. He seems to have met most of the main points of this view in Brunner, including the points that the Word of God is preached as well as written, that "God Himself actually speaks to *us*," and that "Knowledge of a person is possible only through revelation, and he reveals himself through his word."[88] Rawls's formulations also have something in common with Barth's, although it seems unlikely that he had read Barth.[89]

In Barth and Brunner the doctrine of revelation has an extremely christocentric form. They both emphasize that Jesus Christ, in person, is the primary form of the Word of God. Rawls does affirm God's incarnation in Jesus as an important part of God's self-revelation, but he does not insist on its primacy. He can easily be read as assigning a fully coordinate role to God's presence with us as Holy Spirit. Because of the personal nature of revelation, Rawls says, "God Himself had to come in His own person." But he goes on to explain, "First He comes

88. Brunner, *Man in Revolt,* p. 67; *The Theology of Crisis,* p. 32. The latter passage is cited by Rawls (233).

89. See the now classic treatment in Karl Barth, *Church Dogmatics,* vol. 1, part 1, trans. G. W. Bromiley, 2nd ed. (Edinburgh: T. & T. Clark, 1975), §§4 and 5; first published in German in 1932, and in English in 1936.

in His own person as Christ Jesus, converting many to faith. Then by His own presence as the Holy Spirit after the resurrection of His Son He elects apostles to spread the 'good news'" (124–125). Similarly, Rawls says that "the Gospels represent the Word; Christ is the Revelation of the Word, and the Cross is the symbol of the Word"—but he places the "climax" of the converting activity of the Word in the New Testament in the Acts of the Apostles, with no suggestion that Christ is the agent there (233–234). This is in keeping with the general lack of emphasis on christology in the senior thesis, and it is perhaps the least neo-orthodox feature of Rawls's treatment of revelation there.

One of the most intriguing things that Rawls says in the senior thesis about God is best read, I believe, as an attempt to link his polemic against "naturalism" with his conception of revelation. He claims that "the extended natural cosmos excludes . . . God, although it may use His name" (120). If the "extended natural cosmos" is the universe of all the things with which we are related, or try to be related, impersonally, the claim should mean that if we try to be related to something impersonally (for instance, by way of appetition for it) that thing must not be God, even if we call it God.

This is puzzling. It says more (and in a way, perhaps, less) than the claim that it is wrong, a sin, to try to be related impersonally to God. If someone treats you as if you were not a person, although you are in fact a (human) person, that does not keep you from being the one who is treated in that way. If it did, the treatment would not be so offensive to you. Similarly, when Rawls says that "one of the forms of sin . . . is to turn a personal relation into a natural relation, and *to do this misdeed in relation to God* is surely sin" (182; italics added), he seems to imply that it can after all be God whom one treats impersonally. It is not hard to see why Rawls would think it is a sin to treat God as a non-person, but why would he think it is simply impossible to do so?

There is an obvious analogy between Rawls's claim that "the extended natural cosmos" excludes God and Martin Buber's characterization of God as "the eternal Thou . . . the Thou that by its nature cannot become It"—a claim from which it seems to follow that God does not exist in the world of It.[90] Buber's claim is grounded in a theory of I-Thou and I-It relations that includes a richly and subtly developed epistemological and semantical framework. One key point for understanding his claim, I believe, is that he thinks that we cannot have experience *(Erfahrung)* of God, in what I take to be a Kantian sense. In the world of *Erfahrung,* so to speak, there is no God. A second key point is that Buber believes that we can nonetheless *encounter* God, in an I-Thou mode; such an encounter gives us a sort of cognitive access to God, and is in a broader sense an experience (an *Erlebnis* but not an *Erfahrung,* in Buber's usual terminology). Rawls had probably not read Buber, but Brunner certainly had; and though they do not seem to presuppose a Kantian framework in their discussions of revelation, they do both affirm something very close to the second Buberian point.

I take that as a clue to the motivation of Rawls's puzzling claim. Its intended point, I suggest, is epistemological rather than metaphysical. Rawls is motivated here by a view about revelation that he shares with Brunner. Rawls is prepared to grant that traditional arguments of natural theology "can tell us perhaps that [God] is intelligent, that He is powerful and that He is eternal." But if we have only such impersonal arguments, "God still remains the great unknown," because it is a divine *person* that Rawls really wants to know, and "natural theology is helpless before the personality of God." That is because "personal knowledge . . . comes about through communication in com-

90. Martin Buber, *I and Thou,* trans. Ronald Gregor Smith, 2nd ed. (New York: Charles Scribner's Sons, 1958), p. 75.

munity" (224). I take it that Rawls infers that God cannot be known to us as a person unless we are in community with God; and that in that sense we cannot find God as a person in the "extended natural cosmos."

Similar conclusions are suggested by things that Brunner says. He declares that "the content of the Christian conception of God . . . cannot be conceived as a rational content; it can only be believed as a revelation"; and similarly that "we cannot conceive the Living God; we can only perceive Him in His Word." He contrasts "the rational God . . . whom I construct for myself" with "the revealed God who speaks to me . . . this One who is the 'Thou' 'over against me.'" Further, he maintains that "only in my faith does God Himself speak to me," and "faith is real communion with the Creator"—that is, personal relationship with God.[91]

Even with this rationale, I think the claim that the extended natural cosmos *excludes* God should be regarded as a misstep on the part of Rawls. It is not absurd to suggest that cognitive access to *some* aspects of another person could be available only in a certain kind of personal relationship. For instance, it would not be absurd for Rawls to claim that some insights about God have their source in the sort of conversion experience that he describes, and cannot be fully appreciated by anyone who has not had such an experience. It seems much harder, however, to defend the supposition that a person of some kind could be recognized *at all* only in a certain kind of personal relationship.

Aspects of Rawls's own account of personal self-revelation do not support a strong exclusion of God from the realm of possible objects of appetition. As part of his argument, in Chapter Two, that it is a good thing rather than a bad thing that we have bodies, Rawls puts forward

91. Brunner, *Man in Revolt*, pp. 242–243, 103, 67, 494.

the thought that "we have bodies ... as signs which make community possible." He explains that "personal relations of necessity [proceed] on the basis of mutual revelation," that a person "must reveal his feelings to us by means of sense-data," and that we use our bodies to produce the sense data by which we communicate (153). This is a sketch of a plausible account of how we manage to communicate with each other so that community is possible. But the indicated process of communication relies on recognition of sense data as caused by voluntary agents intending to communicate by causing them; and that recognition is a sort of knowledge of other persons that seems quite independent of whether our relation with them is a natural one or a broadly moral, personal one. On the whole I think that Rawls's account of personal relations, including relations with God, would be more coherent if he simply held that God is not an *appropriate* object of appetition, and did not add anything implying that God is not even a *possible* object of appetition.

This simplification would affect very few passages in the senior thesis, and would not affect its main aims and arguments, as I understand them. Buber would not (and doubtless should not) so lightly give up his claim that God cannot become an It, though it too seems problematic. That claim stands at the center of a whole theology for him. But the analogous claim did not have that role for Rawls; nor was he invested in a rich epistemological and semantical theory for personal relationships. His main investment in what is said about God in his senior thesis was in *ethical* aspects of the subject, which I believe would not be touched by the simplification I have suggested.

A concluding question about Rawls's conception of God in the senior thesis is to what extent it is repudiated in his later essay, "On My Religion." No theistic belief is unambiguously affirmed there, but neither are all forms of belief in God ruled out as live alternatives. Rawls seems still very interested in "religious faith," broadly understood, but he pretty clearly no longer considers himself a Christian. That position presumably entails abandonment of christological doctrines and the doctrine of the Trinity. This short autobiographical paper manifests no positive abiding interest in the concept of revelation, though it clearly does not dismiss the idea of taking the existence of God on faith. The most telling silence in "On My Religion" may be that Rawls has nothing to say about the reality of a personal encounter with God in the conversion experience, which has such central importance in the senior thesis. Among the aspects of the concept of God that are not specifically Christian, the supremacy of God's will in history is perhaps the main one that is clearly implied in the senior thesis and rejected in "On My Religion." There is also a pretty strong hint that the older Rawls, unlike the undergraduate Rawls, shared Philip Leon's disapproval of glorifying God (264).

It is striking that several doctrines associated with Christianity that are repudiated in the later essay are already rejected or avoided in the senior thesis. This is clearly true about harsh doctrines of predestination; and, on what I think is the most plausible reading of the senior thesis, it is true also about the doctrine of hell. The older Rawls denounced these as beliefs that "depict God as a monster moved solely by God's own power and glory" (264). But whereas in his senior thesis he had treated similar objections to such beliefs as considerations to be taken into account in formulating Christian doctrines, in "On My Religion" Rawls treats them as objections to "main doctrines of Christianity" as such. Similarly, in "On My Religion" he says, "Christianity is a solitary religion: each is saved or damned individually, and we naturally focus on our own salvation to the point where nothing else might seem to matter" (265), whereas the undergraduate Rawls had envisaged a Christianity of which that would decidedly not be true. In these ways the later autobiographical piece seems to represent a standpoint more external to Christianity, and a disengagement from a process of theological reinterpretation which (whether acknowledged or not) is a permanent enterprise of Christianity as a living religion.

I do not see in "On My Religion" a similar disengagement or externality in relation to generic theism as distinct from Christianity. The discussion of the similarity of God's will and reason to ours, and their relation to the truth of moral claims, in the last section of that essay is at least as thorough and careful as any discussion of God's nature in the senior thesis. Rawls does not appear to be engaged there in what he elsewhere calls "conjecture," arguing from premises that other people accept but he explicitly does not, in order to persuade them that they can rationally accept practical conclusions that he supports.[92] Rather, he seems clearly to be working out what he himself, if a theist, would say about God's practical rationality. His statement, "Yet God's reason, I believe, is the same as ours in that it recognizes the same inferences as valid and the same facts as true that we recognize as valid and true," could easily be read as implying that he still considers himself a theist. This statement should perhaps be seen as more ambiguous as to commitment, in the context of the essay as a whole, but it surely is not a product of disengagement from constructive theistic thinking.

92. Rawls, *The Law of Peoples*, pp. 155–156.

A BRIEF INQUIRY INTO THE MEANING OF SIN AND FAITH

(1942)

A Note on the Text

The two existing copies of the thesis are almost identical. The one deposited in the Princeton University library, a carbon copy, has a small number of corrections made by hand, some of which have been typed into the Harvard library copy. Corrections made by hand in the Harvard copy, the one Rawls kept, seem to have been added by the two Princeton faculty readers, along with their marginal comments.

The thesis has been lightly edited. The numbering of the sections, divisions within sections, and subsections has been rationalized, and a few paragraph breaks have been added. I have corrected obvious typos and solecisms, and in a few cases made minor changes in an awkward passage so that it would read more smoothly. But essentially I have left Rawls's text as it was. Most of the editing is in the quotations and references. The footnotes have been made accurate and complete, and some have been added. The bibliography has been expanded. I have checked all quotations against the originals, consulting the translations Rawls used, where I could identify them. (For example, he used the Healy translation of *The City of God,* but quoted other works of Augustine from the *Post-Nicene Fathers.*)

The one exception is the Bible. Even with the help of others, and with a search of several biblical translation databases, I have been unable to find the translation from which Rawls's biblical quotations come. So I have left them as they are, noting only one evident misquotation in a footnote.

I am most grateful to Patricia O'Brien for transcribing the thesis and to Robert Adams for his advice and suggestions.

Thomas Nagel

A Brief Inquiry into the Meaning of Sin and Faith:

An Interpretation Based on the Concept of Community

By
John Bordley Rawls

A Senior Thesis Submitted to the
Department of Philosophy
of
Princeton University
December, 1942

Preface

To avoid confusion I want to preface this thesis with a few remarks. First I want to say that I have not attempted to solve any particular problem of theology. I have touched upon a number of questions, but I have not been primarily concerned with any of them. What I have tried to do can best be explained by listing the two aims which have always been uppermost:

(1) To enter a strong protest against a certain scheme of thought which I have called naturalism. By naturalism I mean something far broader than is usually meant by the term. Naturalism is the universe in which all relations are natural and in which spiritual life is reduced to the level of desire and appetition. I believe that naturalism leads inevitably to individualism, that it cannot explain community and personality, and that it loses the inner core of the universe. Since this manner of thought has been prevalent in the West since Augustine, we are proposing more or less of a "revolution" by repudiating this traditional line of thought. I do not believe that the Greek tradition mixes very well with Christianity, and the sooner we stop kow-towing to Plato and Aristotle the better. An ounce of the Bible is worth a pound (possibly a ton) of Aristotle.

(2) The second aim is to attack a specific Christian problem (like that of sin and faith) using the concepts which are derived from Biblical thought. I have suggested that the reconstruction of theology must take place by using such concepts as that of community and personality. The naturalistic concepts have crept in to mess up our thought. Therefore, the second aim of this thesis is to consider a specific Christian problem and try to answer it in terms of the correct categories. In this way we not only see the tremendous divergence from the answer given by naturalistic thinkers, but we also are exposed to the categories "in action."

The above aims cover a wide range of territory, and I am fully aware that my treatment of the problem is not adequate. Nevertheless I do believe that enough has been said to present the reader with my objection to naturalism and with the way I believe the reconstruction of theology should take place. I believe myself that the flavor of the times seems to point to a revival of "communal" thinking after centuries of individualism. Amongst theologians I think Brunner is the person whom I have learned the most from, and I think that his work best illustrates what I mean by a theology based on the intimate and personal quality of the universe, together with a clear and unflinching recognition that the universe is a community of Creator and created.

If the reader will bear the above remarks in mind, the thread of the argument will be a lot clearer. Chapter One gives a general prospectus; Chapters Two and Three are largely concerned with naturalism; Chapters Four and Five form the constructive part of the argument and consist in an analysis of sin and faith in terms of community.

John Rawls

Contents

A General Prospectus

Section I

1. It seems that every theology and every philosophy proceeds to investigate experience with certain fundamental presuppositions. If the presuppositions appear reasonable, then the basis of the philosophy or theology is sound, but if the presuppositions are invalid, then the view presented would appear to fall to the ground. Therefore, we propose to outline and investigate our fundamental presuppositions, and thereby to suggest what is to follow. This introduction is intended as a background for everything that follows, and it likewise sums up briefly most everything that we have to say. Although our argument may seem to be drawn out at certain times, the main theme is extremely simple, and can be grasped at a glance. We intend to state nothing new, startling or original. What follows is a rehash of what everybody knows. But because everybody knows it, we are liable to forget it. By analyzing experience with the simple presuppositions we intend to use, some results are achieved which are not obvious at first sight. Our view has implications for political theory, ethics, and theology, although we can do little more than to suggest these implications.

2. There are four fundamental presuppositions around which the entire discussion will revolve.

(i) It is assumed at the outset that there is a being whom Christians call God and who has revealed Himself in Christ Jesus. As to what sort of being God is—that is, whether He possesses all the metaphysical attributes assigned Him—we do not presume to know. It is doubtful whether natural theology can tell us very much. The Bible has told us all we need to know about Him, and everyone who tries to learn more is doomed to failure. We assume, then, that God is, and that He is the sort of God that the Bible says He is, and that He revealed His nature in Christ.

(ii) Implicit in the one major assumption above are the two following ones. First of all there is in the world something which we call personality. By personality we do not mean "individual." There are individual dogs and trees, but not necessarily dogs and trees which are persons. Personality is something over and above individuals as such. All persons are individuals, that is, separate and distinct units, but all individuals are not persons. Personality is equivalent, perhaps, to what we mean by "spirit." When we speak of spiritual life, it seems that we mean personal life. Personality and spirit, which we shall use more or less interchangeably, are difficult terms to define. There is little definite objective meaning which we can assign to them, and yet we all seem to know what they mean. Our second assumption consists, then, in the belief that there is something which we call personality existing in the world, and that persons as such exist. We believe that personality is something unique and that it is not reducible to the possession of a particular body or to the sum of mental states.

(iii) The third assumption is that there is something in the world which we designate by the term "community." It, likewise, is a difficult word to define. We certainly do not mean by community an aggregate of individuals. We are not in the habit of calling forests a community of trees. Community, therefore, would appear to involve the concept of personality. Unless we have personality, we do not have community. Further, unless we have community we do not have personality. Individuals become persons insofar as they live in community. Therefore, our third presupposition is the belief that communities are irreducible and unique in the sense that personality is unique.

(iv) The fourth presupposition consists in the belief that the realm or the character of the personal and the communal is qualitatively distinct from the realm of nature. By nature we mean what is usually meant by that term, i.e., the expanse of space filled by bodies, all that we see, feel, touch and so forth. As a result of this distinction between the natural and the personal, there are two types of relations, natural and personal. It will be one of our main tasks to elaborate and clarify this distinction.

The above four presuppositions form the categories of all our thought. We are to discuss our problems in terms of God, personality, community, and nature. As we proceed we shall see how certain other philosophers and theologians employ different concepts, and that therefore we cannot accept their analysis. Further, a simple development of the above presuppositions will yield our conception of the universe, i.e., that the universe in its spiritual aspect is a community of persons manifesting the glory of God and being related to Him. God created the world, as far as we can tell, for the establishing of such a community, and the end towards which creation moves is just such a community. Man, being a person, belongs to this community, and it is membership in this community which is the distinctive thing about man and which sets him apart from the creatures of nature. By being a person, man lives in relationship with God, the angels, with the devils and his fellow men, and he cannot destroy this relationship or this attachment to community. Thus the universe is at its root a spiritual or personal one. It was created by God, who is as He has revealed Himself, and among the creation are created persons. The world in its essence, is a community, a community of creator and created, and has as its source, God.

3. In passing we should make a few remarks about these assumptions.

(i) They are not postulates in the sense in which the term is used in logic, and therefore we are not engaged in a deductive system. These statements are assumed from the outset because we have not time to show their validity. They have empirical meaning and are derived from experience. For example, the existence of personality and community, and the difference between personal and natural relations, are a matter of examining experience. The belief in God's existence is, of course, not strictly empirical. There are reasons to believe that He exists and that such beliefs are not sheer fancy. We have made the above remarks because the tendency of the times is to imagine all speculation as either nonsense or as a deductive system. We do not consider that what we say is nonsense, nor is it deduction from arbitrary postulates.

(ii) These principles are the basis of our other views, and our other opinions are closely related to them. For example, sin will be defined and explained as the destruction and repudiation of community; faith as the inner state of a person who is properly integrated and related to community; grace as the activity on God's part which seeks to restore the person to community; the *Imago Dei* as that which in man makes him capable of entering into community by virtue of likeness to God, who is in Himself community, being the Triune God.

(iii) To understand the chief ethical and religious problems which face us, we have to understand these principles, since it is our belief that the ethical problem is a social or communal problem. Ethics should be an inquiry into the nature of community and personality.

Man's chief moral problem is how to live with himself and with other men. The religious problem is likewise communal. It considers how man is to relate himself to God. The ethical and religious situations are similar because they both involve the establishment of community. There can be no separation between religion and ethics since the problems they deal with are in the same nexus of relations, namely those personal relations which involve all persons existing in the universe, whether in heaven, in hell, or on earth. The outlook which these principles lead us to accept will be contrasted with another point of view which we shall call "natural ethics," which is the ethics of Plato and Aristotle, and to which we oppose the Christian or "communal" ethics. Proper ethics is not the relating of a person to some objective "good" for which he should strive, but is the relating of person to person and finally to God.

Section II

1. Our fourth principle stated that there was a difference between the realm of personality and community as opposed to that of nature. In this section we want to clarify this distinction by giving a number of contrasting characteristics of each type of relation.

In experience as we know it there are actually three types of relations: (a) personal and communal, (b) natural, and (c) causal. The first type is between two persons, the second between a person and some object insofar as personality is involved in the relation, and the third is the relation between two objects. The relation between the "I" and the "thou" is therefore personal, that between the "I" as desiring and the thing desired such as food and drink is natural, while the relation between any two things is causal, such as the relation between the food and drink and the table upon which it rests. These distinctions seem clear and should cause little difficulty.

Since our subject concerns chiefly the problems of personality and community, we will not deal with causal relations, or attempt to describe them. Natural relations, however, will concern us as much as personal relations for two reasons:

(i) Many philosophers and theologians have confused them with personal relations, and therefore we are forced to criticize such thinkers. We have to point out that ethics is not primarily concerned with natural relations. Those who have failed to distinguish between natural and personal relations include such figures as Plato, Aristotle, Augustine, and Aquinas. They have all failed to understand the communal problem and consider ethics a matter of relating persons to proper objects, such as the Form of the Good, Truth, or God, who is conceived by Augustine and Aquinas as the most desirable object.

(ii) It is necessary to distinguish the two sorts of relations in order to show that nature itself is not evil, but good, and that sin does not result from desires or appetitions but from the perverseness of the spirit. In short, in order to understand sin, faith, and grace we must make this fundamental distinction.

2. We now come to list the contrasting characteristics of personal and natural relations.

(i) A personal relation is characterized by a "thou" over on the "other" side. A natural relation has as its "beyond" a "that" or an "it", i.e., some object. The fact that a "thou" stands over against us and not an object changes the entire atmosphere of the relation. There is no man who acts the same way to objects as he does to persons. In personal relations we are conscious that we are related to "others" who resemble ourselves.

(ii) Thus personal relations are active on both sides. The "I" and the "thou" meet in some kind of rapport or "dis-rapport." In natural relations the object is always irrelevant to us as persons; the other usually is an object, unconscious, unknowing and always impersonal.

The object is always a brute fact, as something "there" to be desired or grasped or else ignored and avoided.

(iii) Personal relations form a nexus, i.e., they are all intimately bound up with one another. A reverberation in one of them creates a disturbance in all the others, and vice versa. Further, the nexus is a personal nexus, i.e., the disturbances which result involve personality. Philosophers have long spoken of the causal nexus of the universe and how all events are causally related. In the same sense we mean that personal events are personally related. The nexus-like character of personal relations is illustrated time and time again. By abusing a man's children we abuse him; by running off with some other person's beloved we find ourselves in considerable difficulty. Ultimately all personal relations are so connected for the reason that we all exist before God, and by being related to Him we are all related to each other although we may never have met one another. That personal relations form such a nexus leads us to the conclusion that religion and ethics cannot be separated. While personal relations form a personal nexus, natural relations do not involve us in this way. We can dislike bananas without incurring the wrath of apples. But we cannot like Englishmen without being frowned on by the Irish, and so forth.

(iv) Personal relations are characterized by a "thou" on the other side, as we have already stated, and it is this "thou" which constitutes the judge in personal relations, i.e., we know that we are existing before someone and that this someone is judging us. It is also the "thou" which gives, shares, and loves. This latter fact we all know. But we do not realize so clearly that it is the "thou" that judges that at the same time gives. The importance of judgment in personal relations, and its connection with the Divine self-giving, will be clear when we come to discuss the doctrine of Grace and Election. It need hardly be added that the "other" in a natural relation does not judge or give itself. It is just "there."

(v) In personal relations the "I" seeks to establish a definite personal relation with the "thou". The relations fall into two broad classes: (a) relations of fellowship and givenness, i.e., relations of true community; (b) relations in which the other is made an admirer or an audience, as in the case of sinful and anti-communal relations infected by pride. There is a third type of relation in which the "thou" is used as a thing. Such a relation is one type of sin, but it is an impersonalized personal relation and not in itself personal. Personal relations manifest a certain amount of "juggling for position," and in the case of egotism the proud man will often throw away his life to win admirers. The most demonic sin is always setting up a relation with other people which is intensely personal. There could be no pride in a world of objects. On the other hand, the appetition which seeks its object does not set up any relation between it and its object. The whole phenomenon of desire, though it seems to include personality to a degree, moves along the level of biological causation, and the end desired is an impersonal state which uses the object as means only.

(vi) As a consequence of the above, personal relations are unique in the case of each person in relation to another, whereas natural relations are readily exchangeable. If there are several apples on the table, one apple is as good as another provided they all will satisfy the taste. In personal relations not only ought we to regard each relation as unique, but we often, even in the case of sinful actions, realize the uniqueness of personal relations. The egotist wants to make a particular person his admirer; he wants to be admired not by any person but by a particular one. We are jealous and envious of certain persons and not of others, and for special reasons. All personal relations have their character of being unique in each case, and not exchangeable.

(vii) Personal relations proceed on the basis of mutual revelation. One person establishes contact with another person not directly, because the nature of the case makes that impossible, but by means of signs, such as words, facial expressions, gestures and so forth. Personal relations require this self-revelatory action, or else no personal contact can be established. The implication of this characteristic is important in discussion of the Incarnation. Natural relations, on the other hand, are self-revelatory. An apple immediately reveals itself as round, hard, sweet and so forth. To find out what a person is thinking requires subtle and often insidious methods of maneuvering.

(viii) The dynamic "energy" which flows in the respective types of relations is of two sorts: (a) in natural relations the "energy" is desire, appetition, bodily want, desire for beauty and so forth; and (b) in personal relations the "energy" is hate, jealousy, pride, envy and sometimes givingness, fellowship and so forth. Hence it appears that natural relations are egoistic (desires for concrete objects or for objective relations) while personal relations are motivated by egotism or by fellowship and love. Desires and appetitions are by nature egoistic, and therefore self-centered. The machinations of pride and jealousy are egotistic, meaning that they are endeavors not found in nature, but only in the spiritual and communal sphere. They are not purely self-centered since they take the other person into consideration. Pride, as we have already remarked, is pride before other people. Pride presupposes community, as does jealousy, hate, envy and so forth. Appetitions do not presuppose community. They are purely natural in that they seek objects as such.

3. The above list of characteristics is incomplete. We have just touched the surface of the difference between the two, which is the difference between nature and spirit. The dualism which runs through our experience is between these two types of relations, representing qualitatively distinct realms of experience and of the universe as a whole. It seems far more adequate to explain the dualism in this fashion than to explain it in terms of mind and body, spirit and matter, rational

and irrational, and so forth. It is our hope that the dualism which we all feel in experience is explained by the two types of relations analyzed above. Personal relations open us to the realm of spirit; natural relations to the realm of nature; and because man participates in both realms, he is the peculiar creature that he is.

Section III

1. In this section we want to suggest briefly the meaning of the "extended natural cosmos." This phenomenon will be treated more fully in Chapter Three, but it is advisable to introduce the notion here. By the natural cosmos we mean any universe in which all of the relations are conceived of in natural terms. Such a view we shall call naturalism. We intend to use the word in a different sense than it is usually used. When we think of naturalism we are inclined to imagine a view resembling materialism and kindred philosophies. For us, however, naturalism is the type of thought which speaks of all relations in natural terms. It makes no difference what types of objects are included in such a universe. Natural systems which include such objects as God or the One, we might term theistic naturalism; systems including ideals as objects we may call humanistic naturalism; and other more positivistic views may be called materialistic naturalism. These terms, however, are provisional. Our main point is the following: naturalism as we understand it is not materialism, but is any view which constructs the cosmos in naturalistic terms. For us the philosophies of Plato and Aristotle, together with the theologies of Augustine and Aquinas, are naturalistic. This statement may be a shock to some. In Chapter Three we shall try to support our somewhat radical statement.

2. The terminology of the natural cosmos has already been suggested. Its favorite words are "desire", "object", "good", "end", "appetite",

"proper-act" (Aristotle and Aquinas particularly), "enjoy" (Augustine) and so forth. Natural ethics consists of a discussion of the proper objects of desire, of the training of character to indulge in right activity after right development of the correct habits, of the way to seek the "good" which is the proper end of natural desire. In short, natural ethics, whether in Plato or Augustine, and in Aristotle or Aquinas, is concerned with the problem of turning desire *(caritas)* to its proper object and end. Earthly objects are improper objects for man; man should seek otherworldly objects. Man should strive to be satisfied by God rather than by food and drink.[1] In this fashion the whole universe is naturalized.

3. The result of a complete naturalization of the cosmos is to lose community, personality, and of course the real nature of God. God is not just a satisfying object of supreme desirability. Nor can personality and community be explained in naturalistic terms. As a result the extended natural cosmos excludes personality, community, and God, although it may use His name. All naturalistic thinkers have completely missed the spiritual and personal element which forms the deep inner core of the universe. It will be part of our task to criticize this extended natural cosmos and to analyze sin and faith not in natural terms, but in relation to God, personality, and community.

4. While repudiating the extended natural cosmos we do not repudiate nature as such. Man does possess appetitions by nature and desires for food and drink, for beauty, and for truth and thus for the goods of nature as a whole. These desires are good and their objects are good. The created world of nature is good because God made it.

1. For Plato see *Symposium* and *Phaedrus* especially. For Aristotle see *Nicomachean Ethics*, bk. 10; *Metaphysics*, bk. 12. For Augustine see bk. XV of *City of God, Morals of the Catholic Church*, etc. For Aquinas see *Summa Contra Gentiles*, bk. III.

We therefore call nature good and praise the bounty of nature, which is God's gift to man.[2] The error lies, not in accepting nature, but in extending natural relations to include all of those in the cosmos. We are mistaken if we think of God as another object of desire. We thereby make Him a part of nature. This extension of the natural cosmos is sin because it results in transforming personal relations into natural relations, which process is one form of sin, as we shall see later. Our problem, then, is to limit the sphere of nature to its proper limits, and to make room for the heart of the universe, namely, community and personality. This spiritual realm, always dependent on and connected with God, must never be confused with nature. These remarks should suffice to illustrate what we mean by the extended natural cosmos, and what errors it results in.

Section IV

1. In this section we want to put forth briefly our own view of community, personality, sin, and faith, and suggest certain problems related to them.

First of all, what is man? We believe that man is a communal being and thereby possesses personality. The distinctive thing about man is not his reason, not his appreciation of beauty, not his various powers; no, man's distinctiveness from other worldly creatures is that he was made for community and that he is a personality necessarily related to community. Man's likeness to God consists in this ability to enter into community, since God Himself is community, being the Triune God. Because man is a communal being, he belongs to the spiritual order of the universe. Man is thereby related to God, to the angels, to his fellow men, and also to the devil and his angels.

Since each man bears the image of God, he is a responsible being,

---

2. In Chapter Two we shall vindicate the natural world, and argue for its goodness.

and a personality with obligations. The image enables man to answer to God's call, to respond to His love, to have faith in God and, God willing, to live with Him. The image of God provides the basis for man's moral being. There is no morality in isolation, except for natural morality, i.e., the morality which concerns the proper objects of appetitions. Christian morality is morality in community, whether it be the earthly community or the heavenly community. Man is a moral being because he is a communal being.

Man is a communal being by nature. This fact means that man can never escape community, and therefore that he is always responsible and always under obligations. Many theories of salvation consist in destroying this communal nature of man. Rousseau bids us to return to the woods, the Epicureans ask us to retire from society, while the Yoga philosophy urges us to proceed to a state of peaceful "nothing." Man's true salvation consists not in escaping community but in being properly integrated to community. Salvation restores and completes man's nature; it is not a process destroying that nature.

The above three paragraphs give the following conclusions: (a) man is communal and personal in nature by virtue of the Image of God; (b) in this communality of man is rooted his moral being; and (c) man can never escape from his nature. God always claims him, and therefore, salvation must consist in the fulfillment of man's nature by re-integrating him into community.

2. What is sin? We believe that sin is the destruction, annihilation, and repudiation of community. Any action which destroys community is a sinful action. Therefore the denial of obligations, the refusal to answer to givingness (love), and the rupturing of any personal relations are the acts of the sinner.

There are two main types of sin: (a) egotism, which is that perverse self-love of the spirit for itself, which craves honor, distinction, glory, and praise. The egotist will go to all sorts of extremes, overt and subtle, to win his goal. His actions are by nature destructive of community; (b) egoism, which is not in itself evil insofar as it is limited to natural appetitions, but which supported by egotism, turns personal and communal relations into natural relations. The egoist treats other people as so many objects to be used as instruments for his own appetitional satisfaction, and thereby he destroys community. There is a third kind of sin which has never been prevalent in Western culture, but which has often dominated the East, namely the sin of despair, which seeks to escape from community into nothingness. It is a sin which is caused by the result of sin, meaning that it is a further sin committed once egotistic and egoistic sin has disrupted community. Because the sin of despair has not been prevalent in the West we shall not deal with it in this thesis. The time may not be far off, however, when the West will add to its sins the last sin of despair.[3]

The result and consequence of sin is "aloneness". Since man is by nature communal, and since sin destroys community, the result of sin is to make man alone, to cut him off and to leave him in isolation. This spiritual cut-offness, this desolating "closedness" is the inevitable end and result of sin.

The above three paragraphs assert the following conclusions: (a) sin is the destruction of community; (b) there are three types of sin: egotistic, egoistic, and the sin of despair; and (c) the result of sin is "aloneness."

3. What is faith? Faith is the spiritual disposition of the whole of a personality which is fully integrated into community and thereby rooted in the source which sustains it. Faith is the perfect relation of person to person. It is the relation out of which grow the bonds which

3. The signs can be seen in Schopenhauer, Nietzsche, and Spengler.

tie community together. To have faith means to be grounded in that community which supports personality and which is the fountainhead of spiritual gifts.

Faith is often confused with belief. We have faith in persons, therefore faith is a personal and communal relation. Belief is a cognitive attitude which holds certain propositions as being true or false. Properly speaking, we do not have faith that God exists; rather we believe that He exists. Once believing that He exists and in the Revelation through His Son, we have faith in Him. Therefore the body of Christian dogma should not, strictly speaking, be called "The Faith," but should be called according to what it is, namely, belief. Dogma is a group of statements and propositions to be interpreted as the Church sees fit. Faith is a relation of one person to another and to community. To have faith in God means to be related to Him by faith. It does not mean merely to believe that He exists. Therefore, as sin is the destruction of community, so faith is the construction and building of community. A sinner is isolated from God; a man of faith is in community with God. As sin is closedness, shut-offness, and aloneness, so faith is openness, restoredness, and togetherness.

Since personal relations proceed on the basis of mutual revelation, and since man had turned away from God, it follows that God Himself had to come in His own person to restore man to faith, both to Himself and to his fellow man. Man by his intelligence might have learned that God is, but then he would merely have belief. He would only accept the proposition that He existed. To restore man's faith, God had to come, He had to reveal His own self, and He had to call man. Natural theology cannot tell us of God's person. His personality must be revealed by Him. It is the presence of God Himself which penetrates into and shatters man's aloneness, thereby restoring him and calling him back to community.

Restoration to community is called conversion. Conversion is the direct or indirect result of God's election. The apostle Paul was elected by God and accepted into the community. But Paul, knowing that his election was not for his own sake, sought to spread the "good news" to the whole of those lost from community. Paul, sustained by God and strengthened by Him, worked to restore many of the heathen into the community. The apostle, being directly and marvelously elected, knew the call of God first-hand. The rest of us, who have not received such favor in His sight, must listen to Paul and receive the "good news" from him. Those of us who are not elected receive the Gospel through his preaching. The "good news" which Paul tells us is of the coming of God Himself, who must come in His Presence to restore us. God works in the way in which the Gospel or the Word is spread. First He comes in His own person as Christ Jesus, converting many to faith. Then by His own presence as the Holy Spirit after the resurrection of His Son, He elects apostles to spread the "good news." Being ever present with His apostles and to their listeners, He restores us all to community. This descent of God into our aloneness and isolation is another gift of His bounteous love. He comes to us not on account of merit on our own part. We have no claim upon Him. That He restores us to the community from which we have been isolated is an act of mercy which must be accepted in gratitude and trust. Once restored, we look up to Him in faith.

The above four paragraphs assert the following conclusions: (a) to have faith means to be restored to the community; (b) we must distinguish between faith and belief; (c) God Himself must descend to our aloneness to restore us; and (d) restoration is called conversion and is the result of God's election and a gift of His love. Also implied is (e) that God's election means not that a certain person is chosen to the necessary exclusion of others, but that He uses His elect by working with them to win the lost back to His community. In this way He used Israel and His apostles.

Section V

1. In this last section we should suggest a few implications of the view put forth above. First of all we reject mysticism because it seeks a union which excludes all particularity, and wants to overcome all distinctions. Since the universe is in its essence communal and personal, mysticism cannot be accepted. The Christian dogma of the resurrection of the body shows considerable profundity on this point. The doctrine means that we shall be resurrected in our full personality and particularity, and that salvation is the full restoration of the whole person, not the wiping away of particularity. Salvation integrates personality into community; it does not destroy personality to dissolve it into some mysterious and meaningless "One."

2. Concerning political theory, our view suggests that any contract theory of society is false. Therefore theories along the order of Hobbes and Locke must be rejected. The person does not bring anything to society for the simple reason that he is nothing until he is in community. Once the human person is in society, he can give something to it; but he cannot bring anything to it. Once integrated into community we become persons, and then we can contribute to the life of the community. When a newborn child enters a family, he brings nothing to that family. His presence may offer occasions of satisfaction for his parents and older brothers and sisters, but he of his own will contributes nothing. He is utterly dependent on others. In this way all of us begin our life. It is not until after a long period of dependence that we can contribute to society. Even then we never become independent, nor should we want to. But we do become independent

in the provisional sense that we can live positively in community, fulfilling our obligations and creating possibilities of mutual co-exis-
tence.

It is also false to hold that dependence of the person upon the community implies his subjection to some "general will" or to some
"group soul" of the community. The existence of such a general will is
a fiction. A community is always a group of persons integrated together by faith, and there is no mysterious principle which subsumes
all persons into one person. Likewise mistaken are the fears of those
who, in wanting to preserve the independence of the person apart
from the community, repudiate the person's necessary dependence on
community. They fail to see that a person is not a person apart from
community and also that true community does not absorb the individual but rather makes his personality possible. True community,
meaning one integrated in faith under God, does not dissolve the
person, but sustains him. Likewise, true community contains the only
possibility of personality. What does destroy the human person in
community is not society itself but the *sin* which infects all earthly
society. It is the sin of one group which seeks to dominate another
group that gives rise to the fear of communal dependence; but in
community as such, and in the heavenly community, we have no
such fear.

Therefore the reconciliation between the person and community,
between the individual and society, can be understood by analyzing
the concepts themselves. They are mutually interdependent. One cannot exist without the other. The dichotomy between the individual
and society which recent Western thought has puzzled over is really
no dichotomy at all. Where the difficulty arises is how personality and
community can be achieved in face of the pervasive sin which exists
in the world. Therefore, the chief problem of politics is to work out

some scheme of social arrangements which can so harness human sin as to make the natural correlates of community and personality possible.

If our culture is to solve the problem of individual and society, the answer suggested above seems to be the right one. We must realize that an individual is not merely an individual, but a person, and that a society is not a group of individuals but a community. Once we realize this fact, any solution which advocates a balance between independence and absorption is seen to be false. It is false because there is no such thing as independent personality free of community, and further, community as such does not absorb personality but creates and sustains it. The problem is, as already stated, one of controlling and ridding the world of sin. Our solution to this problem is not a matter of finding the mean between two extremes. We should always be suspicious of such facile answers. Our solution is to examine and find out what community and personality really are, and to see that the tensions in society are not between personality and community, but between various types of sin which seek to destroy community.

3. The problem of ethics, like the problem of politics, is how to establish community in the face of sin in the world. The ethical problem is therefore communal and personal. Any ethical theory which tries to find the "good" in some objective value, i.e., in some object, is what we call a natural ethic. But since man is by nature personal and communal, ethics must deal with his communality; and because man belongs to the heavenly community, ethics must not separate itself from theology.

With these remarks we can pass on to the next chapter.

chapter two

Vindication of the Natural Cosmos

Section I

1. The world is evil; it is the source of all corruption and sin. The visible universe is a region controlled by fate; in it the spiritual souls are held captive by the planetary aeons. Time continues in unending cycles; worlds and events repeat themselves and man is bound here to suffer in this wicked cosmos.

Such has been the verdict of many, particularly of the Gnostic sects which existed in the first four centuries of our Christian era. It is a view which human weakness is often tempted to accept. For man, no matter how hard his heart may become, at least knows that evil and sin do exist in the world; and to answer the question as to why such evil exists, man often replies that the world by nature is evil. There results from this view the notion that all corporeal things are evil; that nature is but a lowly beauty, if a beauty at all; and that man's body, being part of him subject to natural laws, is that which makes man the sinner that he is. Man's sin, then, is that he was born a creature, that he possesses a body, and that he lives in this sensible world.

The other half of this world view states that there is another world: a world of spirit, of freedom, of spiritual beauty and rationality; a world wholly invisible, transcendent, beyond, but nevertheless existing. It is to this glorious realm that man belongs. Here on earth he lives in an alien world, a world into which he has been thrust by some wicked transaction between the aeons; or a world into which he has fallen as a consequence of some prenatal imperfection. It must be man's aim to redeem himself from his sinful existence in this corporeal reality, and to return to his home. Or if man cannot save himself, he must turn to some redeemer, some savior who has provided knowledge and secret passwords for the return-trip past the wicked demons, and there be united once again to the heavenly realm where man's immortal soul is to rest in peace.

The world cosmology outlined above was widely held throughout the Hellenistic world when Christianity began to spread from the city of Jerusalem. The view admits of all sorts of variations, some of which we propose to briefly investigate. At bottom, however, they are one in that they find the sensible world the root of evil and man's creatureliness the cause of man's depravity. Sin is attributed to some sort of defection in the nature of the sinner before the "fall" occurred. And this is true whether the view is presented in a Platonic dialogue, or in the vast humanitarian theology of Origen, or in the crude and syncretic fancies of Gnostics like Basilides and Saturninus.

2. The first heresy which Christianity encountered was Docetism. It is the view which teaches that Christ had no real body or human nature, and that His human existence was merely an appearance. For the Greeks of the time it was perhaps permissible to say that a savior from the other realm had entered the world to redeem men, but to go on to say that he assumed a real human nature was folly. It was to them impossible that a divine savior would immerse himself in the defective and sinful material of the sensible world. Hence there was an immediate tendency to say that Christ only "appeared" to have as-

sumed a full human nature; or else it was stated that the man Jesus had become the instrument of the Saving Spirit, the spirit itself remaining untouched by matter and in no way subject to the material flesh.

The latter speculation is suggested by the following lines from the Gospel of Peter, a document early suspected and later condemned by the Church: "And one of them said, give him to drink gall with vinegar. And they mixed and gave him to drink, and fulfilled all things, and accomplished their sins against their own head. And many went about with lamps, supposing it was night and fell down. And the Lord cried out, saying, My Power, My Power, thou hast forsaken me."[1]

Irenaeus related that according to the opinion of Basilides, "he [Christ] did not himself suffer death, but Simon, a certain man of Cyrene, being compelled, bore the cross in his stead . . . For since he [Christ] was an incorporeal power . . . he transfigured himself as he pleased, and thus ascended to him who had sent him, deriding them [i.e., his persecutors] inasmuch as he could not be laid hold of, and was invisible to all."[2] It is by such speculations that the Hellenistic cults tried to avoid the Christian dogma of the Incarnation. This doctrinal tendency was no mere isolated phenomenon; it continued well down into Augustine's time, because we know that he found it necessary to defend the orthodox dogma against the Manicheans. In the long dispute which Augustine held with Faustus, the famous Manichean called the virgin birth a sorcery, to which charge Augustine answered: "We deny that there is anything disgraceful in the bodies of the saints,"[3] which is a way of saying, as he does immediately follow-

1. Verses 16–19. *Ante-Nicene Fathers* (hereafter *A.N.F.*) vol. X, p. 21. (See also introduction to the Gospel in *A.N.F.* vol. X.)

2. Irenaeus, *Against Heresies*, bk. I, ch. 24:4, *A.N.F.* vol. I, p. 349.

3. *Reply to Faustus the Manichean*, bk. XXIX, *Post-Nicene Fathers*, Series I (hereafter *P.N.F.*) vol. IV, p. 327.

ing, that "the licentious and intemperate use of those members is disgraceful, but not the members themselves."[4] As a Christian doctor, Augustine defends the flesh from the charge of being evil; for it was the hatred of matter, known at the time as encratism, which fostered the docetistic tendency.[5]

3. The deprecation of this world manifested itself in various tendencies in the first few centuries. Perhaps the most prominent of these was Gnosticism, which was widely scattered throughout the empire. No two Gnostics agree completely with one another, but they have enough views in common to enable us to discuss them as a group. On the whole they believed that the sensible material world had been created by a low demiurge or by emanation. Matter and spirit were in complete opposition; and matter was categorically evil. Salvation was from this intrinsically evil world of matter, and also from the fate under which all who lived in this world were held by the planetary aeons.[6] The means of salvation were given by a savior, in this case Christ, who being one of the aeons, descended to give man knowledge of how to escape from the world. Not all men were to be saved, but only those who contained a divine spark, implanted in some men by the true God, not by the wicked demiurge who created the world and who was identified with the God of the Old Testament.[7] Gnosticism, like most of the ancient mystery cults, was thereby aristocratic, and it is perhaps this element which manifests most clearly its despisal of the world. Irenaeus tells us how the Gnostics of the Valentin-

4. Ibid.

5. See article on Docetism by Adrian Fortescue in James Hastings, ed., *Encyclopaedia of Religion and Ethics*.

6. See article by E. F. Scott on Gnosticism in Hastings, *Encyclopaedia of Religion and Ethics*.

7. See McGiffert, *A History of Christian Thought*, vol. I, ch. 4.

ian sect conceived of three kinds of men: spiritual, material, and animal.[8] The material class of men goes to certain corruption; they are children of wicked matter. The animal man, if he makes a choice for the better (whatever this may mean), finds repose in an intermediate place between this earth and the true heaven; but the spiritual men, after "being disciplined and nourished here," will someday attain perfection and "shall be given as brides to the angels of the Savior." Hence there are those who are good by nature, and they will be saved as members belonging to the other realm; but those evil by nature are doomed to corruption.

Irenaeus likewise tells us that the Gnostics took two very opposed views towards the flesh. In each case, however, the flesh was the object of abuse. They either condemned marriage as "nothing else than a corruption and fornication," or took the view that extreme licentiousness and promiscuity were permissible since they helped destroy the despised body and also because "God does not greatly regard such matters."[9]

4. Origen, the greatest of the Alexandrian theologians, is likewise extremely unorthodox in his view of the creation of the visible world. For him the creation consisted of two parts: (a) the spiritual creation, which is eternal; and (b) the temporal or material world, which will only endure for a definite length of time. In the spiritual creation all men and angels were created as fully rational spirits, who were free because they were rational, and who were to enjoy God. The material creation came into existence when the free rational spirits fell away from God by defection. Origen states his view in the following way: "on account of their excessive mental defects [those souls] stood in

8. Irenaeus, *Against Heresies,* bk. I, ch.7:5, *A.N.F.* vol. I, p. 326.
9. Ibid., ch. 28:2, p. 353.

need of bodies of a grosser and more solid nature; and for the sake of those for whom this arrangement was necessary, this visible world was also called into being."[10] The world is a place where these defective souls who "deserved to enter into bodies"[11] are to be trained and disciplined. "This subjection," as Origen puts it, "will be accomplished in certain ways, and after certain training and at certain times" not by force but by "word, reason and doctrine; by a call to a better course of things, by the best systems of training,"[12] and thereby to bring the souls back to God, following the instructions of Christ who came "that He might teach obedience to those who could not otherwise than by obedience obtain salvation."[13]

It is true that Origen lacks any violent deprecation of the material creation; being a Christian theologian, he must limit his utterances. He remains partly orthodox by saying that the rational souls brought the punishment upon themselves of their own free will. The Greek element in Origen is, however, unmistakable. The implication of the phrase "deserve to enter into bodies" is clear; it can only mean that to possess a material body is somehow an evil from which the soul in its full created essence should be free. The created world is God's way of making use of a bad situation; the state which called the world into existence is a previous state of sin, on the part of souls who were punished by being cast into a material nature. The world, then, is something lower. In short, it is a mere expedient, a school-house for naughty souls. Hence Origen can intimate that the wisdom of the flesh is hostile to the wisdom of God; and that those souls are weak who are "carried away by their desire for visible things."[14]

10. *De Principiis*, bk. III, ch. 5:4, *A.N.F.* vol. IV, p. 342.
11. Ibid., ch. 5:5, p. 343.
12. Ibid., ch. 5:8, p. 344.
13. Ibid., ch. 5:6, p. 343.
14. Ibid., ch. 5:5, p. 343.

5. The deprecation and despisal of the flesh, no doubt, have a long history in Greek thought. Certain Greek myths of the fifth century B.C. present us with a dualism between spirit and matter, the divine and the earthly. The central myth of the Orphic cult[15] was the story of Zagreus. The whole myth is too long for exposition, but the significant point for us, as it is for Nygren, is that it purports to explain man's "double nature." Man, being formed from the ashes of the Titans who opposed Zeus, is thereby connected with evil, but since in the Titans there remains the nature of the god they devoured, man has in him a divine spark. Man thus is a participator in two worlds, the earthly and the divine, the evil and the good. As Nygren goes on to say, "It is this Divine part of man which needs to be liberated from its incongruous association with the earthly and sensual element; it needs to break its bonds, to purify itself from its earthly defilement, and pass out from the environment of physical nature into the Divine life to which it is by nature akin. To this end Orphism provides a way of salvation by purification and by ecstasy, that at last the soul may be united again with the Divine and taken up into it."[16]

In the Platonism of the early dialogues[17] this oriental mysticism which had made its way into Greece becomes marvelously combined

---

15. Nygren, *Agape and Eros*, vol. I, p. 121, gives the narrative of the myth. [This is a reference to the 1932 edition. It corresponds to p. 163 of the one-volume 1953 edition.]

16. Ibid., p. 122. [See p. 164 of the one-volume edition, where the passage reads: "It is this Divine element in man that must be liberated from its unwarrantable bondage to the earthly and sensual element; the Divine reason or Divine soul needs above all things to break its bonds, to purify itself from the defilement of the senses, and to pass out from this unnatural environment into the Divine life to which it is by nature akin. The way of salvation for the Divine soul is therefore in Orphism the way of purification and ecstasy, and the goal is the final reunion of the soul with the Divine and its absorption into it."]

17. As before the *Parmenides*.

with Plato's rationalism by means of the doctrine of the forms. Plato's elaborate metaphysics often hides from us the fact that his philosophy contains a similar view towards the soul as found in the myth above, only carefully refined and rationalized. It is this fundamental concept which as time goes on will become more and more pessimistic until it degenerates into the fantastic systems of the Gnostics, with their violent hatred of the world of sense.

A few quotations from Plato will illustrate more precisely how Platonism philosophically laid down the position that was to become extended into Gnosticism under the pressure of disintegration and a new influx of orientalism. From the *Republic:* "To understand her real nature, we must look at her [the soul], not as we see her now, marred by association with the body and other evils, but when she has regained that pure condition which the eye of reason can discern; you will then find her to be a far lovelier thing and will distinguish more clearly justice and injustice and all the qualities we have discussed ... we must rather fix our eyes ... on her love of wisdom and note how she seeks to apprehend and hold converse with the divine, immortal, and everlasting world to which she is akin, and what she would become if her affections were entirely set on following the impulse that would lift her out of the sea in which she is now sunken, and disencumber her of all that wild profusion of rock and shell, whose earthy substance has encrusted her, because she seeks what men call happiness by making earth her food."[18]

Or take certain passages from the second speech of Socrates in the *Phaedrus:* "Let the soul be likened to the conjoint nature of a team of winged horses and charioteer. Now with the gods the horses and the charioteers are noble, all of them, both in themselves and by descent, whereas with other races there is a mixture. With us, first note, the driver has to guide a pair of horses, and, secondly, one of them is

18. *Republic,* 611c–612a.

beautiful and good, the other the reverse in character and stock. [Hence the soul's fall is the result of a defect in its nature.] . . . But the soul that has lost its wings is borne along until it fastens upon something solid, and there finds a dwelling place, taking on an earthly body."[19] Hence the soul's material body is the result of its previous fall; cf. Origen. ". . . when we had no mark upon us of this tomb we call the body, our prison which we bear about, shackled to it like a shell fish to its shell."[20] Demos has summed up the situation in the following manner: for Plato, man has something sublime which is his reason; but man is also earthly, being a creature. Thus "his earthly aspect gives rise to the diversity and confusion in human nature; and the clue to his unity and simplicity is to be found in his immortal nature."[21]

These quotations will illustrate my point clearly enough when I say that the fancies of Gnosticism were in a sense implicit in the dialogues of the enthusiastic young Plato. The mature Plato is a philosopher of different inflections, but the earlier dialogues, once written, formed a philosophical literature of incalculable influence.

Section II

1. What does Christianity have to say on this point? Is the flesh evil, or is it good? The Christian answer to this question is so simple that it is often overlooked. We are told frequently by certain modern writers that Christianity has a "morbid" attitude towards sex and so forth. As we shall see, it was Christianity that first launched the attack on the Greek point of view, and finally emerged victorious. Because for Christianity the answer has been contained in the simple dictum in Genesis: "And so it was God saw all that He had made, and very good it was."[22]

19. *Phaedrus,* 246a–c.
20. Ibid., 250c.
21. Demos, *The Philosophy of Plato,* p. 304.
22. Genesis 1:31.

The material world is good; it is good because God made it. All through Christian ages, theologians have returned to this dictum to refute heretics; and more than once this statement in Genesis has kept certain theologians from becoming heretics themselves. Wherever the Greek influence becomes manifest, the world-denying tendency appears. It is fair to say, however, that the main stream of Christian thought has always kept its bearings on this point.

2. St. Paul, who is supposed by some to be an example of Christian asceticism, states clearly in First Corinthians that the body is not to be condemned. "The body is not meant for immorality but for the Lord, and the Lord is for the body; and the God who raised the Lord will also raise us by His power. Do you not know that your bodies are members of Christ?"[23] "Do you not know that your body is the temple of the Holy Spirit within you—the Spirit you have received from God? You are not your own, you were bought with a price, then glorify God with your body."[24] The body, then, is fully part of our nature and is designed, like everything else, to fit us for community with God, and abuse of the body makes such community impossible. It must further be noted that the strictness with which Paul views marriage in the seventh chapter of Corinthians is strongly colored by two facts: (a) the admitted immorality of the Corinthian Church, and (b) Paul's expectations of the Lord's speedy return. In light of these considerations, Paul adopts a "courageous realism." Further, Paul is expressing his own preferences. The one dogmatic command is the words of Christ demanding permanence of the marriage bond.[25]

In the fifteenth chapter of First Corinthians, St. Paul speaks of the resurrection of the body, which is thoroughly Christian. Greek

23. 1 Corinthians 6:13–15.

24. 1 Corinthians 6:19–20.

25. See article by W. F. Howard in *Abingdon Bible Commentary* on 1 Corinthians.

thought wanted to escape from the body, and for them resurrection of the body meant the denial of their religious intentions. For the Hebrew, however, the Greek notion of immortality was nothing but a shadowy survival. He wanted the restoration of the whole person, with the body included. He knew nothing of the soul as something immersed in and imprisoned in a body. Paul's thought is Biblical on this point. It is true that Paul speaks of a spiritual body in the resurrection; but a body is still resurrected. The body which is raised by God is to be of the second man, for "we are to bear the likeness of the heavenly man";[26] "What is sown is mortal, what rises is immortal; sown inglorious, rises in glory; sown in weakness, rises in power; sown an animate body, it rises a spiritual body,"[27] and so forth. We are, then, most certainly to be resurrected in the body; but with a body adapted to its new heavenly realm, for "there are heavenly bodies and also earthly bodies,"[28] each sort of body being adjusted according to its station. Our heavenly body will be one fitted to the needs of heaven; it will be a proper instrument of self-expression and communication in the spiritual condition of the new life.[29] The body, then, is not to be despised but praised. It is the temple of the Holy Spirit, and a most gracious gift of the Lord God who made it.

3. Irenaeus has spoken aptly concerning the view which despises the flesh. He writes concerning the Encratites (including Marcion, Tatian, and others) that they "preached against marriage, thus setting aside the original creation of God, and indirectly blaming Him who made the male and female for the propagation of the human race. Some of those reckoned among them have also introduced abstinence from animal food, thus proving themselves ungrateful to God, who formed

26. 1 Corinthians 15:49.
27. 1 Corinthians 15:42–44.
28. 1 Corinthians 15:40.
29. Howard, in *Abingdon Bible Commentary.*

all things."[30] Those who disparage God's creation are "ungrateful." The world is God's gift; to turn away from the gift is to offend God. Hence, if nothing else, to enjoy the world is a matter of obligation. But we must enjoy it rightly; we must never misuse the gift any more than be unthankful for it.

4. Tertullian, despite his Montanism, earnestly vindicates marriage against those who would blaspheme it. Marriage is not a "polluted thing"; consequently "it is not an institution of this nature that is to be blamed, but the extravagant use of it; according to the judgment of the founder Himself who not only said 'Be fruitful and multiply' [Gen. 1:28] but also, 'Thou shalt not commit adultery' and 'thou shalt not covet thy neighbor's wife' [Ex. 20:14–17]."[31] The following passage is one of the most eloquent defenses of the body to be found among the Fathers: "Why then, O soul, should you envy the flesh? There is none, after the Lord, whom you should love so dearly; none more like a brother to you, which is even born along with yourself in God. You ought rather to have been by your prayers obtaining resurrection for her: her sins, whatever they were, were owing to you. However, it is no wonder if you hate her; for you have repudiated her Creator."[32] The spirit and the body are to be ever united as bride and bridegroom; and the flesh most certainly will be raised in its integrity.

5. St. Augustine is perhaps the most "other-worldly" of all the great Fathers. In him, if anywhere, we should expect to find renunciation of the flesh. He came to Christianity from the background of neo-Platonism, and remained a neo-Platonist throughout his life. (This point, however, is debatable.) He was always inflamed with a typical

30. Irenaeus, *Against Heresies*, bk. I, ch. 27:1, *A.N.F.* vol. I, p. 353.
31. Tertullian, *Against Marcion*, bk. I, ch. 29, *A.N.F.* vol. III, p. 294.
32. Tertullian, *On Resurrection of the Flesh*, ch. 63, *A.N.F.* vol. III, p. 594.

Platonic longing for things unseen—for beauty, truth, goodness and so on. Examining two of his treatises on marriage, one finds him approaching the danger point, but never crossing it. He knows full well that the order of nature is good. In *De Bono Conjugali*, written against Jovinian, Augustine writes that married people owe one another faith in intercourse for the begetting of children, for such a fellowship was the first in their mortal state. They also owe each other a mutual service of sustaining one another.[33] Marriage is, therefore, a natural bond.[34] For the begetting of children is the natural function of marriage, and is not a fault; it is the satisfying of lust which is the fault. Immediately following Augustine comes perilously close to denying marriage its proper place, but is forced to give it its due. "Continence," he writes, "from all intercourse is indeed better even than intercourse of marriage itself, which takes place for the sake of begetting. But because that Continence is of larger desert, but to pay the due of marriage is no crime . . ."[35] hence "marriage and continence are two goods, whereof the second is better";[36] but note that marriage, Augustine insists, is a good. Marriage is one of those goods which is given as a means to something, in this case to friendship by propagation. Using marriage for its end, one uses it well; using it for its own sake, one sins. But to need the end not at all is better.[37] Nevertheless, insofar as marriage is not corrupted by the lust of concupiscence and is "natural," it is a good.

In another work on marriage Augustine seeks to distinguish between marriage as a natural good and what has corrupted it, namely lust. The latter, he argues, does not form part of the natural state of

33. *De Bono Conjugali*, ch. 6, *P.N.F.* vol. III, p. 401.
34. Ibid., ch. 1, p. 399.
35. Ibid., ch. 6, p. 402.
36. Ibid., ch. 8, p. 403.
37. Ibid., ch. 9, p. 403.

marriage, but is the consequence of sin, and in the descendants of the first man, it manifests itself as concupiscence. When man sinned, he began to feel another law in his members; for if man refused to obey God, why should man's body obey his own will? Concupiscence is the refusal of the body to obey the will; it gives rise to the sense of shame and is the punishment of sin, not the natural state of the body as created.[38] Augustine states his view as follows: "Carnal concupiscence ... must not be ascribed to marriage; it is only to be tolerated in marriage. It is not a good which comes out of the essence of marriage, but an evil which is the accident of original sin."[39] Augustine has come close to denying marriage, but he has not forsaken it. The view seems harsh to us, but in the time of Augustine such an attitude was reasonably "moderate." Elsewhere Augustine stoutly defends the body against Origen[40] and Plato.[41] So we may conclude that although Augustine still remained imbued with neo-Platonism, he realized that the neo-Platonic attitude toward the body was untenable, when he discovered that the Catholic faith in the Word made flesh was more than "teaching by example." When he arrived at the heart of the doctrine of the Incarnation, he accepted the body as a good.[42]

6. The Christian view, then, is anything but ascetic. When Christian theologians turn away from the world we can be sure that it is because of some alien influence. Hebraic thought throughout holds the family in high reverence. One has only to point to the sorrow of childless marriages told in the Bible to illustrate what should be the true Christian attitude. For example, the stories of Hannah, Rebecca, and Elizabeth, mother of John, are representative of the Hebraic view point.

38. *De Nuptiis et Concupiscentiis, P.N.F.* vol. V.
39. Ibid., bk. I, ch. 19, p. 271.
40. *City of God,* bk. XI, ch. 23, *P.N.F.* vol. II, pp. 217–218.
41. Ibid., bk. XII, ch. 26, *P.N.F.* vol. II, p. 243.
42. See Burnaby, *Amor Dei,* p. 69.

The world is a gift; a bounteous creation of God. If we say there are three main concepts which have to be integrated in religious thought, namely, God, nature, and man, then the Christian would say that nature is a gift from God to man. Man's existence as part of nature is a gift, nature is a gift; all the food he eats, all the clothes he wears, all the happiness he wins depend on God's willingness to give, and God is willing to give, despite our sinful rebellions, because He is God.

Section III

1. We have now to consider the view that the flesh, or the appetites or the sensible world in general, is the cause of evil; these may not be called evil in themselves but at least they are the cause of wickedness and sin. The wicked man is considered as one who is overcome by passion, unable to control his appetites and swept away by the love of visible things. Here again, we are confronted with the Greek, and the view we oppose can be illustrated from Aristotle and Plato.

(i) In Book 7 of the *Nicomachean Ethics,* Aristotle considers the problem of a man acting contrary to his proper knowledge. He remarks concerning Socrates' belief that there is no such thing as incontinence, i.e., that no one acts against what he judges best, but that notion, says Aristotle, "plainly contradicts the observed facts."[43] The Socratic distinction between opinion and knowledge is brushed aside. The chief answer which Aristotle gives to the problem is contained in his discussion of the practical syllogism. He points out first that in the practical syllogism there are two sorts of premise, one predicable of the object, the other predicable of the agent. For example, "apples are poisonous for all men" and "I am a man." The incontinent man drawn by the apple either would not have knowledge or would not be exercising it.[44] When one has knowledge but fails to use it one is like a

---

43. *Nicomachean Ethics,* 1145b28.
44. Ibid., 1147a7.

man asleep, mad, or drunk, for "this is just the condition of men under the influence of passions; for outbursts of anger and sexual appetites and some other such passions, it is evident actually alter our bodily condition, and in some men even produce fits of madness. It is plain, then, that incontinent people must be said to be in a similar condition to men asleep, mad or drunk."[45] Hence, when appetite is present in us, we are led to the object contrary to our right opinion and so behave incontinently. If we are habituated in this procedure we pass through the unstable stage of incontinence and develop a wicked nature, meaning one which has been so habituated that its bad character is incurable. The self-indulgent man is the man of vice. He pursues to excess improper pleasures by free choice; whereas the incontinent man is one who is temporarily beside himself. He does not act by choice, but is overwhelmed by desire. Incontinence and continence are intermediate stages between virtue and vice; they have not yet been sufficiently habituated to choose their course of action, but must battle against desire.[46]

(ii) Earlier in Greek philosophy Plato had expressed much the same view. Plato's description of the tyrannical man will serve to illustrate the point.[47] Imagine the son of the democratic man, says Plato, whose father has grown old, and he (the son) has been exposed to the same libertine influences. Then "when those terrible wizards who would conjure up an absolute ruler in the young man's soul begin to doubt the power of their spells, in the last resort they contrive to engender in him a master passion, to champion the mob of idle appetites which are for dividing among themselves all available plunder—a passion that can only be compared to a winged horse. Like a swarm buzzing around this creature, the other desires come laden

45. Ibid., 1147a14–18.
46. Ibid., see 1150a–1152a.
47. *Republic*, 562–576.

with incense and perfumes, garlands and wine, feeding its growth to the full on the pleasures of the dissolute life, until they have implanted the sting of a longing that cannot be satisfied. Then at last this passion, as leader of the soul takes madness for the captain of its guard and breaks out in frenzy; if it can lay hold upon any thoughts or desires that are of good report and still capable of shame, it kills them or drives them forth, until it has purged the soul of all sobriety and called in the partisans of madness to fill the vacant place."[48] The birth of the tyrant is thus pictured in terms of passion. Take, for example, the phrases "master passion," "mob of idle appetites," "desires come laden with incense and perfume," "garlands and wine," and so forth. The sphere of ethics, in Plato as in Aristotle, is often spoken of purely in terms of reason vs. desire. They both may have said a great deal that is profound about the harmony of the soul in the good life and so on; but that which corrupts the good life is desire, passion, and the appetites.

(iii) In a sense, both Plato and Aristotle reiterate the poetry of Aeschylus in the *Suppliants*. The chorus says:

> Let death come upon me before to the ravisher's bed I am thrust;
> What champion, what saviour but death can I find, or what refuge
>   from lust?[49]

Later lust is pictured as preying on beauty:

> Lovely is beauty's ripening harvest-field,
> But ill to guard; and men and hearts, I wot,
> And birds and creeping things make prey of it.[50]

Passion, then, is the root of sin; and for reason to control passion is one of the marks of the virtuous man.

48. Ibid., 572–573.
49. *Suppliants,* lines 806–807.
50. Ibid., lines 1000–1003.

2. How are we to answer this charge? First of all, we must distinguish between three questions: (a) If the appetites do cause sin, how serious is the sin so caused? (b) Is there any factor distinct from appetite which may cause sin? (c) Assuming the second question to be answered positively, which of the two factors, appetite or our at present unknown "X", is responsible for the most demonic sin and which most concerns us? The first and second questions will be implicit in the third.

3. (i) We must first attempt to show that there is a factor in experience totally distinct from appetition, either for drink, for beauty, or for truth. The failure to distinguish this factor results in a complete misunderstanding of the whole complex of moral relations. The great mistake has been to classify desire for food and drink together with envy, hatred, etc., as representative of the so-called passions. For example, the following is from Aristotle: "by passions I mean appetite, anger, fear, confidence etc. . . . and in general the feelings accompanied by pleasure or pain."[51]

Again, Schopenhauer falls into the same blunder. In the second book of his best-known work he expressed the view that in all grades of nature one finds the constant conflict of individuals and species which is the necessary expression of the will to live within itself. In the fourth book he considers the problem on a higher level, namely in man himself. Here the same phenomenon is found, only exhibited with greater distinctness. Man as a knowing individual has the knowledge within him that he contains the whole will to live or the inner being of the world itself. As a result of this fact, every man, though he is in a sense nothing in a boundless world, "yet makes him (it) self the centre of the world, has regard for his own well-being before every-

---

51. *Nicomachean Ethics*, 1105b22.

thing else; indeed . . . (he) is ready to annihilate the world in order to maintain his own self, this drop in the ocean a little longer. This disposition is *egoism,* which is essential to everything in Nature."[52]

The error to be found here is simply the failure to realize qualitative distinction between the will to live on the animal level, and the will to live as it is involved in human egotism on the higher level. For Schopenhauer, the higher is simply a more developed state of the lower; the suffering found on the human level is still the result of the contradiction of the will to live within itself. He has failed to realize that egotism is something different—a craving for honor and glory, for which it will gladly lay down its life (i.e., destroy and repudiate the "mere" will to live).[53] The distinction which Schopenhauer has failed to grasp is the qualitative difference between natural and personal relations, between appetition on one hand and pride and love on the other.

(ii) St. Augustine perceived the distinction so clearly that the force of his argument in the *City of God* depends upon a keen analysis of the difference. Augustine, referring to Paul,[54] lists as works of the "flesh" (i.e., the earthly, sinful man) adultery, fornication, idolatry, hatred, envy, drunkenness and so on; but, he says, "we find not only such as appertain to bodily and luxurious delight, as fornications, uncleanness, luxury, and drunkenness, but such also as discover the viciousness of the mind, truly (distinct) from fleshly pleasures. For who does not think that idolatry, witchcraft, enmity, contention, emulation, wrath, envy, sedition, and heresy, are rather mental vices than corporal?"[55] Here Augustine makes the distinction we are looking for.

---

52. *The World as Will and Idea,* bk. IV, sec. 61. (vol. I, p. 428 in the Haldane and Kemp translation).

53. See Subsection (iv) on Leon below.

54. Galatians 5:18–21.

55. *City of God,* bk. XIV, ch. 2, *P.N.F.* vol. II, p. 263.

There is something in human nature, he asserts, totally different from the flesh. Call it spirit, if you will; but whatever it is, by spirit we mean that capacity to enter into community, that ability to respond to love, to repudiate love and thereby to sin.

St. Augustine earlier uses an argument which illustrates the difference between spiritual sin and the flesh. He is discussing Origen's view of the body as a punishment for sin; and he states that this assertion is most assuredly false, since the "devils (the worse prevaricators) should rather have been thrust into the basest, that is, earthly bodies, than the worst men. But that we might know that the spirits' merits are not repaid by the bodies' qualities, the worst devil has an airy body."[56] The merit of this argument is not whether we believe in devils or not (although the writer happens to), but it illustrates that we conceive of the devil, the worst of all sinners, as a spiritual being. He is not a being "weighed down" by a body; he does not struggle with appetites; he has no need for the so-called goods of worldly fortune. No, he is a being powerful and mighty, of great intellectual acumen and, no doubt, of considerable aesthetic appreciation; but he is proud, vainglorious, full of spite and envy, hate and jealousy. He is the complete repudiation of love, living isolated in his barren egotistic "aloneness." He is a creature possessing all the Greek virtues, but nevertheless, the most wicked of all souls created by God. He lives eternally cut off from God, in that most terrible abyss of spiritual separation.

(iii) We can get at the heart of the matter by asking, "Does the spirit pervert the flesh, or does the flesh pervert the spirit?" Concerning this problem we shall follow the suggestions made by Niebuhr, since he has treated the question with considerable skill. Niebuhr has put the point thus: "Does the drunkard or the glutton merely press self-love to the limit and lose all control over himself by his effort to

56. Ibid., bk. XI, ch. 23, *P.N.F.* vol. II, p. 218.

gratify a particular desire so unreservedly that its gratification comes in conflict with other desires? Or is lack of moderation an effort to escape from the self?"[57] In other words, is sensuality, in those extreme forms in which it becomes sin, a result of desire or of some spiritual puffed-upness or pride; is sensuality a case of mere appetition, or is it a case of spiritual perversion? Or, put in our terms, does it involve merely natural relations or does it include personal relations, and if both are present, which is dominant?

Which view we accept is naturally the result of our analysis of experience. It seems, however, that sensuality always contains the personal element; and that demonic sensuality is invariably a case of spiritual sin which is using sensual means for its satisfaction. Hence, Niebuhr is right when he says that "the sexual, as every other physical, impulse in man is subject to and compounded with the freedom of man's spirit. It is not something which a man could conceivably leave embedded in some natural harmony of animal impulses. Its force reaches up into the highest pinnacles of human spirituality; and the insecurity of man in the heights of his freedom reaches down to the sex impulse as an instrument of compensation and as an avenue of escape."[58]

We can test the validity of the conclusion by asking in what manner drunkards behave. As far as I know, they fall into two large categories: either they are extremely jovial, friendly and more sociable than usual, or else they are considerably more reserved, often approaching the point of plain surliness. Admitting all sorts of subtle varieties, we can say that the first kind is not seeking the mere enjoyment of drink but rather some sort of community or fellowship. Our ordinary life is in a sense cold and separated; drunkenness gives an

57. *The Nature and Destiny of Man*, vol. I, p. 233.
58. Ibid., p. 236.

excuse to overcome this defect. The second sort of drunkard usually has something on his mind, a quick remembrance of his trouble immediately throwing him into an unusually bad humor. He often tries to find someone to fight in order to demonstrate his mastery; or perhaps he indulges in an extended speech of vituperation which eases his inner tension. In sexual sensuality we can find the same perversities as Niebuhr has suggested. Men get egotistic satisfaction by retelling their supposed love-life, each conquered woman being presented to the listener along the same order as a medal won in war or in a track meet.

The analysis above is admittedly superficial. The matter is really so complex that a complete analysis would reveal innumerable subtleties and variations. But at least I believe the main outlines of our view are correct. Sensuality, whenever it becomes sin, will be found to be completely interfused with those spiritual perversions and aspirations from which no man is free. In sensuality we seek satisfaction of pride, escape from the closedness of the self, forgetfulness,[59] community and fellowship. Were sensuality merely appetition, our troubles would be comparatively simple.

(iv) Philip Leon in an admirable study of human egotism[60] has carefully drawn the distinction between what he calls "egoism" and "egotism." By the former he means much the same as we mean by a natural relation. Egoism for him means a biological striving for a concrete process, for a definite object or state of affairs. By egotism he means something totally different, such as the craving for position, desire for fame and supremacy, and so on. The egotist seeks processes not in themselves, as in the case of pure appetition, but he seeks them as symbols for his superiority and for the sake of his superiority.[61]

59. Ibid., pp. 236–240.
60. *The Ethics of Power.*
61. Ibid., p. 87.

Thus, Leon's definition of egotism is what we mean by pride in personal relations; and he has properly seen that egotism is not only indifferent to appetition but is often totally opposed to it. "Finally," he writes, "the despotism of ambition over appetition . . . is most extreme and most apparent when, from pride, vanity, stubbornness, resentment or hatred, or in general from desire to assert, or at least, to save, his supremacy or self-esteem, the egotist risks, or throws away, his own life."[62]

Leon asserts that appetitions do not cause egotism. The latter is of a wholly different nature, or as he puts it, "There is nothing in appetition itself to bring about egotism in any of its expressions."[63] But, he continues, appetition can qualify and sometimes determine the particular channel of egotistic expression, as it is sometimes the vehicle of such expression. Leon believes this egotism is not only the cause of sin, but is in itself sin. As he puts it: "The root of evil, to put it roughly, is madness . . . the theory is this: At one pole there is sanctity or sanity or the genuinely moral life; at the other, insanity, the triumphant extreme of egotism—of pride, conceit, ambition, the lust for power. Between the two lie many different limbos of methodical madnesses or insane sanities which are all the civilization and the savageries that have ever been."[64]

4. We are now in a position to answer the three questions which were posed earlier.[65] To the second question we reply that the factor responsible for sin, as distinct from appetition, and which is in itself sin, is that spiritual perversion which corrupts personal relations.[66]

---

62. Ibid., p. 89.
63. Ibid., p. 158.
64. Ibid., pp. 18–19.
65. See division 2 of this section.
66. For a complete analysis of sin, we must wait until Chapter Four.

To the third question we say that it is this spiritual perversion which makes sin demonic and possessive of its destructive power. To the first question we can now reply that it is conceivable that appetitions may lead to sin, but with the following reservations: (a) such is not often the case, and (b) in any event the appetition itself is not evil, but rather the situation to which it leads. In reply to the Greek accusation with which we began, we can now say with Berdyaev: "The spirit which belonged to the highest degree of existence was the first to separate itself from God by his own free act, and his self assertion and spiritual pride exercised a corrupting influence upon the whole ordered hierarchy of being. It was in the highest ranges of the spiritual and not in the shallows of the material world that evil first showed itself."[67] The Greek analysis in terms of reason and desire is totally inadequate to understand this truth. Given such presuppositions, it is no surprise that the Greeks never arrived at an adequate or convincing concept of sin.

Section IV

1. So far we have been chiefly critical of the Greek view of the body, although we did try to anticipate our own theory of sin by making the distinction between what Leon calls "egoism" and "egotism." In this section we shall put forth briefly a more positive theory of what we consider the body to be, and we shall find out that our conception is remote from the Greek attitude which we have just considered.

2. It has already been mentioned in our section on Paul that the body is to be considered as a temple of the Holy Spirit and as a gift of God. Nature as a whole must be so considered. This much has previously been stated. Now we want to examine another concept of the body,

---

67. *Freedom and Spirit*, pp. 161–162.

the body as a "sign in community" and not as the peculiar limitation of a creature.

(i) We stated in our introductory chapter that personal relations of necessity proceeded on the basis of mutual revelation. Natural objects immediately reveal their nature as being colored in such a way, as such and such a shape, and so forth. But personal relations are different; what the person feels cannot be seen as a sense-datum, but that person must reveal his feelings to us by means of sense-data, using those which have been determined by convention as representing the feeling and state of mind in question. Now it is our belief that the body is included as among the signs necessary for communication. We have bodies, then, as signs which make community possible. My body is a sign of me, yours of you. Whenever the sense-data of your body appear in my consciousness, then I know that you are in the vicinity and that I can establish contact with you by speech or gesture or any other means at my disposal. The body is thus an indispensable means of communication. It enables us to know when a certain person is in a position standing in immediate communicable contact. When a person dies and we lay his body beneath the ground, we have chosen another way of saying that we shall not meet him again in our present lives and that for some time to come he is beyond reach of any communication. Communication without some sort of sign, i.e., without some sort of body, is to me unintelligible. A community of disembodied spirits would be particularly upsetting. One would never know where the other person was, what he looked like, what he thought, whether he was angry or happy and so forth. In other words, it would not be a community at all. Thus, the Bible is right when it insists that we will be resurrected in some sort of body, whatever sort it may be, which will be adapted to the spiritual realm of heaven and which will be sufficient for communication and self-expression; and since the form of our present body is no disgrace, we may expect that the heavenly body will not be greatly altered in visible appearances.

(ii) The tremendous importance of signs in community is often overlooked. In personal life we cannot set up any sort of community at all until we know the other person's name and he knows ours. Hence, when two people meet for the first time the first transaction which takes place is a mutual disclosure of their names, or signs. Where natural religion fails is just at this point. What is God's name? Obviously, man cannot find out because names are self-revealed. Man can call God the One, or the All, or the Principle and such-like empty phrases, but that is as far as he can get. Revelation tells us that God's name is Christ, so when we pray we do not mumble empty metaphysical phrases, but we address God as Christ, the Son of God, who is our mediator.

This longing to know God's name is expressed early in the Bible. Moses, after God has appeared to him in the burning bush, cried out: "When they ask me 'What is his name?' what am I to say?" God said to Moses: "I am who I am ... tell the Israelites that I am [who I am] sent you ... This is my name for all time, this is my title for all ages."[68] This cry for a name is justified, for how could we establish community otherwise?

(iii) A further analysis of signs would reveal all sorts of variations. Take, for example, facial expressions. They represent the most subtle system of signs imaginable. The ability of the face to express the most delicate feeling is incredible. It is, thus, extremely important that we should have faces. A person without a face, or a person whose expression never changed, would be cut off from community because community depends on the mutual revelation of feelings, thoughts, and so forth, which are passed along by visible signs. Gestures also manifest the same complexity. An analysis of speech would yield, of course,

---

68. Exodus 3:13–15. [The bracketed words are not in the biblical text, but are supplied (without brackets) by Rawls.]

the same view. Men do not speak for the sake of isolated thoughts; but speech is something for community.[69] A lie is so damnable because it abuses the use of signs.[70]

(iv) The body is, then, an indispensable precondition of community. It is a sign by means of which community is established, and it possesses much the same function as names, words, facial expressions, gestures and so forth. In this sense of body, i.e., as a sign, and not body as a token of creature, I believe that God Himself most assuredly has a sign.

3. Another point which we want to consider is that the body, being a mark of creatureliness, is a restraint upon sin. It is the presence of the body which prevents human sin from being purely satanic. Mixed in man's revolt is always some weakness, some infirmity, some doubt, some of the pathetic "lostness" peculiar to a creature. Only the devil, mighty and powerful, can be purely satanic. The devil is surely a creature, but the limits upon him are less than those upon us; and hence his egotism can carry itself to the fullest extreme known. Man is, so to speak, just a "little sinner." There is always something pathetic and naïve about his rebellion. The parable of the Prodigal Son[71] will illustrate our point. The younger son, we are told, went off from home and squandered his fortune in "loose living." But soon a famine spread through the land, and he was "fain to fill his belly with the pods the swine were eating"; realizing that the hired men in his father's estate had more to eat than he, he returned home willing to give up his claim of son, hoping his father would make him one of the hired men and feed him. He knows he has sinned against his father,

69. See Emil Brunner, *Man in Revolt*, pp. 176–177.

70. Augustine has an interesting comment on this point: *Enchiridion,* ch. 22, *P.N.F.* vol. III, p. 245.

71. Luke 15:11–32.

but the necessity of his creatureliness forces him to return and be humbled. Now our argument becomes clear. If he had not been a creature subject to starvation and famine, would he have returned? Or to put it another way, suppose he possessed the might of the devil, free from such extreme creaturely subjection, would he have repented? It is certainly at least doubtful that he would. Thus the body, far from being the occasion to sin, is in countless cases that element in us which batters down our conceit, makes us realize our sin, and brings us to repentance. Thus, the natural cosmos is vindicated.

chapter three

The Extended Natural Cosmos

Section I

1. In this chapter we want to inquire into the meaning of the natural cosmos, and thereby to understand how the whole universe, including God, can be naturalized. We will attempt to achieve our end by examining the thought of Plato and Augustine. We begin with the hypothetical hypothesis of the *Protagoras* that virtue is knowledge, and then pass on to the *Republic* and finally to Augustine. In this way we shall uncover the assumptions and principles of the natural cosmos, and how they can be falsely extended to include the entire universe.

2. Plato in the *Protagoras* puts forth a view which states that knowledge is what enables us to achieve virtue, and that ignorance is the cause of error. It is stated in the dialogue that the view is only hypothetical, as Taylor has pointed out. The equation of pleasure with "good" enters the discussion only on problematic grounds, the dialogue ending with the admission that the problem of what goodness is has only been raised. Also the tenor of the discussion suggests that Plato is arguing that even if one accepts a hedonistic ethics, knowl-

edge is still virtue.[1] For these reasons we must not accept the view in the *Protagoras* as Plato's real view, and further, we know that Plato's own ethics differ considerably from the philosophy here presented. But since we are not interested in whether Plato was presenting his mature opinions, we can use the dialogue to illustrate our point. It really makes no difference whether it was Plato who wrote the dialogue, or whether the conclusions are accepted only hypothetically.

3. Socrates begins the argument by asking Protagoras if virtue can be taught, and Protagoras assents, believing that it can. A number of questions are raised, which need not bother us, until Protagoras hesitates in identifying valor or courage with knowledge. He is willing to admit that the other virtues are a matter of knowledge, but is inclined to believe that those without knowledge can yet be courageous and vice versa. Socrates is anxious to equate all virtue or goodness with knowledge, and by accepting the hypothesis that pleasure equals good and pain is equivalent to evil, he proceeds to convince Protagoras that the courageous man does possess and act in accordance with a proper knowledge whereas the coward does not.

The part of the discussion that is crucial for us comes near the end of the dialogue.[2] Socrates begins by asking Protagoras if he accepts the popular opinion concerning knowledge, namely that it can be dragged about by the influence of the passions, or whether he considers that "knowledge is something noble and able to govern man, and that whoever learns what is good and what is bad will never be swayed by anything to act otherwise than as knowledge bids, and that intelligence is a sufficient succour for mankind."[3] Protagoras, being a professional teacher, naturally agrees with Socrates. But the "many"

1. A. E. Taylor, *Plato, the Man and His Work*, pp. 258–61.
2. *Protagoras*, 352–358.
3. Ibid., 352c.

do not hold knowledge to be such a noble thing, but argue on the contrary that men are often overcome by passions which influence them on the spur of the moment to act against their better knowledge. Hence Socrates must try to discover what the "many" mean by "being overcome by passion."

To answer the problem Socrates assumes the identification of the pleasant with the good and of the unpleasant or painful with the bad. The effects of action may, however, not be immediate. That is, we call such things as gluttony and sexual license evil, not because at the time they are not pleasant, but because they result in painful consequences. Likewise physical training, military training and so forth, though not pleasant immediately, lead to greater happiness in the end. If such is the case, we must judge actions not only in accordance with their immediate pleasure or pain but with careful consideration as to their future consequences. Hence, we use the art of measuring pleasures and pains in the same way as we use measuring in any other activity. The measuring in matters of virtue is of course a matter of knowledge derived from experience. Thus, it is possible for Socrates to conclude that "the salvation of our life depends on making a right choice of pleasure and pain—of the more and the fewer, the greater and the smaller, and the nearer and the remoter"[4]—all of which is possible by a sort of mental "hedonic calculus."

Further, all men will choose the most pleasant action once the hedonic calculus has been performed because "no one willingly goes after evil or what he thinks to be evil; it is not in human nature, apparently, to do so—to wish to go after what one thinks to be evil in preference to the good; and when compelled to choose one of two evils, nobody will choose the greater when he may the lesser."[5] Now

4. Ibid., 357ab.
5. Ibid., 358cd.

if such is the case, then most assuredly knowledge is virtue. Since all men seek the good, all men will certainly choose the good if they know it; hence virtue must be a matter of knowledge and of the methods of calculating pleasures and pains. Not to be virtuous must mean to be ignorant of the proper manipulation of pleasures and pains. Using these conclusions, Socrates succeeds in convincing Protagoras that courage is, like the other virtues, a question of knowledge.

4. What is the importance of the above discussion for us? If we uncover two of the underlying presuppositions, the goal of our efforts will become clear. We maintain that Plato, in the above argument, has assumed two things: (a) that the good is an object, that is, that it exists as the "other" in what we have termed a natural relation; (b) that all men do in fact seek this good, since it is apparently not in human nature not to do so. If these two presuppositions are correct, if the good exists in natural relations and all men seek it, then I think Plato is absolutely right in arguing that knowledge is virtue. It is almost undeniable that if such were the case, knowledge would be the pathway to virtue.

Moreover, the strength of the argument does not depend on equating the good with the pleasure. The good might well be equated with pain, and yet if all men did in fact seek good, knowledge would be the means of acquiring pains instead of pleasures. This alternative is not considered because it is not empirically true that men seek pain. But what I am anxious to point out is that it makes no difference what the object of virtue may consist in for it to be true that, if men do in fact seek that object, then virtue is knowledge. The object of virtue may be God, or it may be the crudest pleasures. As long as virtue is seeking a certain object, and as long as men are said to seek it as part of their nature, then I believe Plato is right in calling knowledge virtue.

I believe that Plato is right, granting his presuppositions, because

examination of our actions bears him out. If, for example, I am seeking for blackberries, and most earnestly desire them, certainly my actions will depend on knowledge of where they are to be found. Further, a man may seek a more ethereal object such as the alone which
Plotinus speaks about, and if he does earnestly long for it, then instruction will certainly determine his future actions and his endeavor
to seek it. If we seek for the object which the neo-Thomists say we do,
namely God, and if all our actions are signs of our seeking Him,[6] then
knowledge would lead us to Him. The neo-Thomists are saved from
this most extreme Pelagianism by various dogmas of predestination
and whatnot, but chiefly by the assertion that God, being a supernat-
ural object, cannot be gained by any natural actions. Hence, we have
their doctrine of grace, which is the divine mechanizer and habit-for-
mer which prepares man for the appreciation of the "Master Value."

What then are we to say? Are we to agree with Plato? Most certainly
not. We must say a vigorous "no" to all the foregoing considerations.
And how do we propose to answer him? Very simply. We shall deny
both presuppositions. (a) We do not believe that the so-called "good
life" (detestable phrase) consists in seeking any object, but that it is
rather something totally different, a matter of personal relations; and
(b) we deny that men seek the "good" so named. Our own view, then,
consists in the denial of both these presuppositions, the consequences
of which denial shall occupy us in the last two chapters.

It is now time, however, to pass on to the view which denies only
one of them, namely, the view of Plato (in the *Republic*), Aristotle,
Augustine, and Aquinas. We want to demonstrate that these men
consider it true that the good is some object, but point out the obvious fact that men do not in fact seek it, or are unable to. Plato and
Aristotle resort to education and habituation on the natural plane as

6. Gilson, *The Spirit of Medieval Philosophy*, pp. 271–274.

a remedy; Augustine and Aquinas, having a more pessimistic view of human nature and considerably higher aspirations, feel it incumbent to invoke divine habituation and instruction. On the whole, however, their difference from Aristotle and Plato is merely a matter of degree. Their thought moves in fundamentally Greek categories, so they too must be discarded. Augustine and Aquinas deny only the second presupposition, namely, they hold that men do not seek the good (and that they cannot because of the Fall and various other reasons); thus they fail to deny the first presupposition. For them God is merely a bigger and better object for our enjoyment, an object which shall so satisfy our various appetitions that we shall cry "Abba father," and rest contentedly.

Section II

1. Plato saw clearly that the second hypothetical presupposition, which he assumes for the sake of argument in the *Protagoras,* is false. Men do not seek the good. The numerous wars among the Greek city states during Plato's time convinced him that perhaps the larger part of men's efforts is getting money. The horrors of the Peloponnesian War had demonstrated that men are not by nature good, or at least that their nature as exhibited is not good, and that a program to remedy the situation must be put forth. In the *Republic* Plato puts forth an elaborate scheme for setting up the ideal state, and from this scheme we can infer what he would have said to the question "How can the now misguided and corrupted human nature be saved?" Plato would have said that we must train and educate men from childhood, and that their training and education must proceed along the lines dictated by true philosophy.

2. We must now inquire briefly into Plato's theory of education and training, and uncover, if possible, its basic principle. Plato follows in

outline the education which was given Athenian boys at the time. Hence his program for education falls into two main parts, gymnastic for training of the body and music for the education of the soul. "Music" is used in a much wider sense than today, since it included art, letters, philosophy, and anything which we might term cultural or liberal. Likewise, it included theology and other matters pertaining to religion. It is Plato's intention to control carefully the training of the young so as to mold them properly, and for this reason he censors the poets for their sayings about the gods, because young men will be tempted to use such impious representations as excuses for their bad conduct.[7] Plato thus justifies a strict censorship of education which seems a bit harsh to us.

Not only is the intellectual instruction carefully regulated, but likewise music (in our sense) and gymnastic, and also the various sorts of prose style. For example, concerning the proper melody and song, Plato urges that the Lydian or sorrowful mode must be banished along with the Ionian or drunken mode, since they will be of no use in training warriors and will encourage drunkenness, effeminacy, and inactivity.[8] The Dorian and Phrygian harmonies are to be kept because they are fitting to represent the brave man, and will strengthen courage and temperance for war and invoke prudence in times of peace. The simple harmonies, then, will be used in education. Also, the musical instruments are to be strictly regulated. Only the lyre and the harp are to be allowed, while the flute is to be excluded. The shepherd, if he wishes, may have his pipe.[9] These two aspects, music (in the broad sense) and gymnastic, must be joined in the fairest proportions to give the best harmony to the soul. Plato puts it as follows: "There are, then, these two elements in the soul, the spirited and phil-

7. *Republic,* 391.
8. Ibid., 398e.
9. Ibid, 399d.

osophic; and it is for their sake . . . that heaven has given to mankind those two branches of education. The purpose is to bring the two elements into tune with one another by adjusting the tension of each to the right pitch."[10] Plato urges this careful balance, because a man who surrenders himself to music alone becomes softened and the "iron" in him melts away.[11] On the other hand, if a man is not trained in music, but in mere bodily exercise, he becomes a brute and seeks to gain all his ends by savage violence.[12] In Plato's view, then, the object of education in this preliminary stage, and likewise in more developed states, appears to be to create a spirit of harmony, for such a harmony in the soul will cause it to love the loveliest, which is beauty and order. Such a soul will thus be temperate, prudent, and well-balanced. It will be not inflamed by excess passion, nor will it be dull and brutish.

The higher education of the guardians proceeds along the same lines. Once they have been identified as those who have natural capabilities for such training, they are instructed in the highest of all learning, philosophy. The end of their education is to enable them to behold the form of the good; and by a gradual process of intellectual ascent,[13] along the path of abstract mathematics and dialectic, they are able to achieve their goal. Then, and only then, is the training of the guardians complete. Others not capable of such high exploits are assigned their proper place; for human nature is such that it can perform only one duty well.[14] Thus, each person has his proper station in the state, for which he must be trained. The training of each fits him for his proper station, from the tradesman to the philosopher king.

10. Ibid., 411e.
11. Ibid., 411ab.
12. Ibid., 411de.
13. The outline of higher education is given in *Republic,* 521–541.
14. Ibid., 394e.

Each is set in order and in harmony with himself and others by virtue of this perfect education.

3. What are the presuppositions of the above view? Why does Plato believe that his theory will work? Plato does not believe, as he suggests he might in the *Protagoras,* that men naturally seek the good and in fact do so. Rather, his elaborate educational scheme is a means of bringing this state of affairs about. What, we may ask, are the presuppositions of his solution? They may be roughly considered as two: (a) The soul is easily determined by its surroundings, especially in youth. Or we may say that the soul is an imitator of what it knows. (b) If the soul is shown its good, if amidst the "flux" of being it perceives the good, then it will follow that good, seek it, and try to actualize it in the world.

(a) Plato states the first presupposition explicitly several times. In discussing the undesirability of risqué stories about the gods, he writes: "A child cannot distinguish the allegorical sense from the literal, and the ideas he takes in at that age are likely to become indelibly fixed; hence the great importance of seeing that the first stories he hears shall be designed to produce the best possible effect on his character."[15] Plato further speaks of how, if the amusements become lawless, then the youths themselves become likewise.[16] Later when Plato is trying to explain the corruption of those with a talented and philosophic nature, he gives a number of reasons such as the evil influence of the Sophists, friends using them for selfish purposes, the confusion of popular opinion; but the chief reason is that they fail to meet the proper climate and environment proportionate to their vigor, and so receive more injury than weaker natures by following the lower goods

15. Ibid., 378de.
16. Ibid., 425a.

of the crowds. Being preeminently good, they become all the worse when exposed to improper surroundings.

Plato writes: "We know it to be true of any seed or growing thing, whether plant or animal, that if it fails to find its proper nourishment or climate or soil, then the more vigorous it is, the more it will lack the qualities it should possess. Evil is a worse enemy to the good than to the indifferent; so it is natural that bad conditions of nurture should be peculiarly uncongenial to the finest nature and that it should come off worse under them than natures of an insignificant order."[17] Nurture and climate, then, as Plato tells us, are crucial for the development of the human person. Indeed, this law applies as well to all animals and plants. Nettleship appears to have summed up the conclusion well in the following lines: "Nature and nurture are the two things which go to make up human character. Neither will do without the other; you can not create the required nature, but you can by nurture do everything short of that; and without the proper nurture the best nature is as likely to turn out ill as to turn out well."[18] Thus we can conclude that "the method Plato advocates depends upon the theory that the human soul is essentially an imitative thing, that is, that it naturally assimilates itself to its surroundings."[19]

(b) The above presupposition is not the only one, however, since Plato assumes that the soul, once perceiving the good, will seek it. Plato assumes that the soul, at least that of the guardians, has somehow a natural aspiration for the good, a certain "reminiscence" of the good,[20] and that if the soul can once again be made to see the good, then it will seek it as a lost one seeks its home. Hence education does not merely create a proper environment which will make a person

17. Ibid., 491d.
18. Nettleship, *Lectures on the Republic of Plato*, p. 77.
19. Ibid., p. 78.
20. See the *Phaedo*.

congenial and social. It also presents the soul with the objects which it seeks when it is functioning properly. Education must draw the soul to its proper object; it must harmonize the soul by presenting its proper object to it; "so the philosopher, in constant companionship with the divine order of the world, will reproduce that order in his soul, and, so far as man may, become godlike."[21] Thus, as Nettleship remarks, "the ultimate purpose of both kinds of education is to present to the soul the good under certain forms."[22] Barker puts the same point in another way. In answer to the question as to what sort of environment is needed, he writes that Plato's view is that "mind develops through contact with the products of mind."[23] The soul develops according as it is exposed to the good, which is ultimately closely connected with the essence of soul itself. Education is turning the natural aspiration of the soul for the light to the light, and to accomplish this transformation "the teacher sets the light to catch the eye."[24]

The process of education, then, is a very delicate one. Its purpose is somehow to turn the soul from lower objects to higher ones by presenting the higher objects to it. Since the soul naturally seeks the higher objects, it will certainly follow a course to gain them, once it has seen them. That the soul will seek the good, provided it once knows it, Plato has no doubt. In the *Republic*[25] he reminds Glaucon that the philosophers will be forced to return to manage the affairs of men, although this return will of course be repugnant to them once they have beheld the form of the good. The second presupposition of Plato is now clear. It is that the soul, having deep down in its nature a natural appetition for the highest good, no matter how much this

21. *Republic*, 500c.
22. Nettleship, *Lectures*, p. 81.
23. Barker, *The Political Thought of Plato and Aristotle*, p. 125.
24. Ibid., p. 123.
25. 517cd.

fundamental aspiration may appear to be covered, will, if it is shown this good, seek and long for it. The highest good, or the form of the good, is the best and most glorious object for the soul to seek. The soul, then, can, by gradual "exposures" to the good, be led to this most perfect of all objects.

We are once again back at the same position maintained in the *Protagoras,* with one important difference. The end of virtue or goodness is still to seek some object, but instead of unrealistically asserting that men do seek it, Plato has realized that a long process of education must intervene to enable men to seek it. Plato has simply become more pessimistic about the matter of attaining virtue. Being good is no simple thing, but requires a good nature to begin with and proper nurture. We are, however, still moving in the same categories, namely, that the good is an object to be sought, and that men (or men of appropriate natures) have a natural aspiration to seek this good.

It is for this reason that the process of salvation consists in illumination and habituation, to give the soul a "taste" of the good and thereby to lead it upward. By accepting a more realistic view of man's present state, and by clearly seeing the difficulties involved in turning men to the good, Plato has inserted a determinant between the present state of badness and the future state of goodness. This determinant so inserted we may call a "will" (using it in the sense of the principle of determination within the personality) which must be conditioned by education, which must be so exposed to its natural object of choice and to its natural object of longing that it will be drawn upwards by its own spontaneous determination. This concept of will is never explicit in Plato. As a determinant between the present and future state, it is never openly spoken of, but its presence is clearly suggested.

The concept of "will" is often considered as a Christian concept, not a Greek one. Augustine is named as being its great exponent. But what we want to say is that Augustine is still Greek, and that the *only* difference between Augustine and Plato, and hence between Catholicism and Greek thought, is a stronger accent upon the conditioning of the determinant, resulting from a more pessimistic view of human nature. The Christian knows the difficulty of leading a so-called good life more acutely than any other person. Hence, if he comes to Christianity from a Greek background, and if he tries to reconcile Christian with Greek thought, he will still move in Greek categories; but he will accent the conditioning of what he calls "will," which is precisely the aim that Plato has in mind with his educational scheme. Hence the difference between Catholicism and Platonism is a matter of degree. The first states that the "will" must be divinely conditioned; the latter asserts that enough of man's natural aspiration remains for education and illumination to achieve its end.

Section III

1. In the previous section we observed how Plato saw the falsity of saying that men do in fact seek the good, and how he insisted on a lengthy process of education as illumination to enable men to seek the good. The process of illumination may be termed a period of "exposure" to the good whereby the will is conditioned or determined or urged to return to the natural object of its desire and to the proper and perfect object of its aspiration. We also observed how Plato thought this could be done by the efforts of men and by intelligent and rational education, although there may be some question as to whether Plato did not really expect a sort of "divine" philosopher king to achieve this end.[26] Whatever may be the answer to this last question, it seems fair to say that Plato believed that man could save him-

26. See Leon, *Plato,* p. 133.

self by his own efforts and by stimulating his aspirations to the good by means of careful illumination.

2. What happens to this Platonic scheme when Augustine comes on the scene? Does he completely overturn the Greek conception? Does he really tear himself away from his earlier neo-Platonism, and if not, how does he reconcile his Catholicism with his Greek heritage? Our answer to this question is briefly as follows: (a) We believe that Augustine was always essentially Greek in his basic thought and that he accepted naturalistic ethics in that he believed that virtue was seeking a specific object by natural desire, and that men, in their perfect nature, seek this good as their proper end. (b) Augustine differs from Plato in that he lays a tremendous stress upon the conditioning of the determinant, namely, the will. Plato thought that man could save himself. Augustine denies this, and states that the will must be divinely conditioned and determined if man is to seek the object of his natural desire and hence the highest good. The above is another way of saying that the will, without grace, is a slave to sin. In the discussion that follows, we shall consider chiefly the second consideration mentioned above.

3. In the first four centuries of Christian theology, the chief problems concerned objective dogma. The relation of Christ to God, the relation among the three Persons of the Trinity, the connection between the man Jesus and the second Person of the Trinity, and similar problems held the center of theological discussion. Around the end of the fourth century, however, the tenor of dispute took a sudden turn to subjective dogma, and the main problem became the relation between grace and free will. The cause of this sudden shift lies chiefly with the appearance upon the scene of a British monk, a certain Pelagius, who taught that man could do good works and could save

himself without the aid of grace. He taught that man's nature was not corrupted by Adam's fall, he denied that there was any such thing as original sin, and he maintained firmly that the current notion of man's depravity was merely an excuse for men to remain lax. He further believed that Christ had come only to set an example, that He was not a savior in the orthodox sense, and that man by nature was fully capable of responding to the divine instructions and winning for himself the virtuous life which all Christians agreed he had lost.

Through the previous centuries there had been a great deal of hesitation concerning the above problem, but with one voice all Christians had asserted the need for grace, although their conception of grace was at times extremely confused. As a result, Pelagius created a considerable disturbance and was finally condemned along with others who agreed with him. When Augustine heard of the view of Pelagius, he immediately entered vigorously into the dispute. He saw immediately that it meant a shallow optimism and a repudiation of the whole orthodox dogma of the Incarnation. But it was chiefly Augustine's own personal experience which told him that Pelagius was wrong. Pelagius was wrong because Augustine had experienced the slavery of sin and felt that he had only been saved by an act of divine mercy. His conversion was of such a sort that he was led to believe that he was literally snatched out of the cauldron of sin without merit on his own part.[27] In reply to Pelagius, Augustine wrote a number of treatises concerning the bondage of the determinant, that is of the will, and the unconditional necessity for grace.

4. Augustine immediately answered Pelagius with a firm denial of the freedom of man's will and with expressions of the depravity and bondedness of man's present nature. He was willing to admit that

27. *Confessions,* especially bk. VIII.

Adam was made upright and perfect; but the upright nature of man had been corrupted by the fall. By disobedience Adam had thrown the whole human race into bondage, a sin for which we are responsible since we all sinned in Adam; ". . . becoming not as he desired his own master, but falling even from himself, became his slave that taught him sin, changing his sweet liberty into wretched bondage, being willingly dead in spirit, and unwillingly to die in the flesh, forsaking eternal life, and condemned to eternal death, had not God's good grace delivered him."[28] In the following passage Augustine expresses even more clearly his opinion in the matter: "Behold what damage the disobedience of the will has inflicted on man's nature! Let him be permitted to pray that he may be healed. Why need he presume so much on the capacity of nature? It is wounded, hurt, damaged, destroyed. . . . It requires the grace of God, not that it may be made but that it may be remade."[29]

The fallen state is characterized by a *vitium,* that is, a fault, which Augustine, provoked in the controversy with Julian, identified with concupiscence,[30] the war in our members, as Paul called it in his Epistle to the Romans. Over this concupiscence man's free will has no power; it rules his flesh and is rooted therein beyond his control. Men are born possessing this fallen nature. "Before Thee none is free from sin, not even the infant which has lived but a day upon the earth. . . . in the weakness of the infant's limbs, and not in its will, lies its innocency. I myself have seen and known an infant to be jealous though it could not speak."[31] Men are so bound that they are not even free from themselves; they cannot flee their own conscience since they must carry it everywhere with them. Augustine can only exclaim "Evil

---

28. *City of God,* bk. XIV, ch. 15, *P.N.F.* vol. II, p. 274.
29. *Nature and Grace,* ch. 62, *P.N.F.* vol. V, p. 142.
30. See Burnaby, *Amor Dei,* p. 191.
31. *Confessions,* bk. I, ch. 7, *P.N.F.* vol. I, p. 48.

Bondage!"[32] The paradox of the whole situation and in a sense the crowning blow is expressed in the following passage: "But that free will, whereby man corrupted his own self, was sufficient for his passing into sin; but to return to righteousness, he has need of a physician, since he is out of health."[33] By free will we lost our uprightness, that is in Adam; but by our own free will we cannot restore ourselves to our former state. It is something that has drastic effect upon our actions in the future. The will does not operate in a vacuum, but pays for its past errors. Its actions are cumulative upon itself. "But when by that liberty we have done something and the pernicious sweetness and pleasure of that deed has taken hold upon the mind, by its own habit the mind is so implicated that afterwards it cannot conquer what by sinning it has fashioned for itself."[34] The bondage is complete: "For, as a man who kills himself must, of course, be alive when he kills himself, but after he has killed himself ceases to live, and cannot restore himself to life; so when man by his own free will sinned, then sin being victorious over him, the freedom of his will was lost."[35] Such then is man's bondage. There is no possibility of his saving himself. He has sold himself into sin, and only by God's grace can he be saved from the mass of perdition.

Such, then, is our bondage. Knowledge is not enough with which to face the crisis.[36] Even the knowledge of truth must be granted to us by God. Sin has darkened our minds as well as our hearts. It is obvious that we have traveled a considerable way since Plato. No longer can the sick be doctored merely by education and by illumination. For who could doctor them, all men being sick? Who could show

---

32. *Homilies on the Gospel of John,* Tractate XLI, 4, *P.N.F.* vol. VII, p. 231.

33. *Nature and Grace,* ch. 25, *P.N.F.* vol. V, p. 129.

34. *Disputation Against Fortunatus,* sec. 22, *P.N.F.* vol. IV, p. 121.

35. *Enchiridion,* ch. 30, *P.N.F.* vol. III, p. 247.

36. See Warfield, *Studies in Tertullian and Augustine,* pp. 135–225.

them the good, and how could they bring good near enough to men to raise them out of the mire of sin?

5. Augustine's genius comes in marvelously at this point. Faced with the above problem, he had at his ready disposal the doctrine of the Incarnation. God Himself is the one who comes near us and so determines us. God is that good which makes His presence felt upon the soul and so draws it from sin. The process is analogous to Plato's theory of education, only here it takes place by divine action. For Plato, the soul is led to the good by catching the eye of the soul by proper illumination—putting proper "goods" before its vision so as to make it aspire upwards. In Augustine, it is God who descends and by His action either comes near us and so determines us, or places goods He knows we will accept before us, and so draws us to Him, to that good for which we all should aspire, and which will fully satisfy all our desires and longings.

Augustine's view of grace thus fits neatly into the natural relations scheme of ethics which he inherited from Plato.[37] For Augustine, as with Plato, all love is acquisitive love. It is the seeking of some object which will satisfy its longings. Man by sin has turned away from that highest good and has turned to himself and to lower things. By falling away from the good, man cannot return; he neither knows the good, nor can his will resist the attraction of temporal objects. The Highest Good, if it is aloof in the other world, cannot possibly determine our will to seek it. Hence that good itself must come near us and determine us. As Nygren puts it, "Gratia [grace] is the motor which alone can set our heavenly Eros in motion."[38]

The problem is, then, as it was for Plato, to turn our desires *(caritas)* to their proper object. *Cupiditas* is love going the wrong way, that

37. See Nygren, *Agape and Eros,* vol. II, pp. 312–313 [pp. 530–531 in the one-volume edition]. (I am very much indebted to this book.)
38. Ibid.

is, love seeking below itself in the order of being instead of above. Augustine writes as follows: "but if that love [of the creature] is referred to the Creator, then it will not be desire *(cupiditas)* but love *(caritas)*. For it is desire when the creature is loved for itself. And then it does not help a man through making use of it, but corrupts him in enjoying it. . . . For as thou oughtest enjoy thyself, not in thyself, but in Him who made thee, so also him whom thou lovest as thyself. Let us enjoy, therefore, both ourselves and our brethren in the Lord."[39] (That is, by loving God as object instead of lower objects, we are made happy, and only when we desire God do we desire properly.)

Thus Augustine can reasonably exclaim, "God, our journey's end . . .,"[40] and by adherence to God we become blessed and share in His beatitude. Or the following statement: "If, therefore, God gave to thee grace, because He gave freely, love freely. Do not for the sake of reward love God; let Him be the reward. Let thy soul say: 'One thing have I desired of the Lord, that I will seek after; that I may dwell in the house of the Lord all the days of my life, that I may behold the beauty of the Lord.'[41] Do not fear that thine enjoyment will fail through satiety; such will be that enjoyment of beauty that it will ever be present to thee."[42] And so, after a long and tedious journey we end up where Plato wanted to go, namely contemplating the highest good, enjoying its beauty and its truth, and being eternally blessed. It is true that we did have to resort to grace, but unless predestined to go elsewhere, we should end up good Platonists after all.

6. Earlier in Augustine's career, especially in the anti-Manichean writings, he asserted that the will was free and that sin had entered the world by an act of free will on man's part. Later he affirmed a doc-

39. *De Trinitate,* bk. IX, ch. 8, *P.N.F.* vol. III, p. 131.
40. *City of God,* bk. XI, ch. 2, *P.N.F.* vol. II, p. 206.
41. Psalm 27:4.
42. *Homilies on the Gospel of John,* Tractate III, 21, *P.N.F.* vol. VII, p. 25.

trine of grace and a view of the bondage of the will which appears to contradict his earlier view. Augustine, however, emphatically declares that such is not the case. "Do we, then, by grace make void free will? God forbid! Nay, rather we establish free will. For even as the law by faith, so free will by grace, is not made void but established."[43] Or again: "Now we do not when we make mention of these things, take away freedom from the will, but we [do] preach the grace of God."[44] Man is also pictured as cooperating with grace, as being a co-actor in the path to salvation.[45] For Augustine, grace in no way conflicts with free will. The two are compatible. It is usually supposed that Augustine is involved in contradiction here; but the following exposition should show that he is not.

For Augustine the will never decides without a motive, without some object being presented to it. The will may be said to freely choose objects since it determines itself, and is not forced by external physical compulsion. Grace is the presentation of certain objects to the will which God, by virtue of His foreknowledge, knows will be accepted by the will. God, like an orator, may be pictured as presenting motives to the will, but presenting them in such a way and with such skill that the will must certainly accept. Thus, "corresponding to every created will . . . there exists in the treasury of Divine knowledge the idea of an indefinite series of motives towards good which, at a given moment, would in fact, though freely, be rejected by that will: as also the idea of another series of motives which in fact, though always with perfect liberty, would be accepted by it."[46] Objects which God knows we will not accept have been termed sufficient grace, the other sort of objects are called efficacious grace. The term "sufficient" ap-

43. *The Spirit and the Letter*, ch. 52, *P.N.F.* vol. V, p. 106.
44. *Nature and Grace*, ch. 36, *P.N.F.* vol. V, p. 134.
45. *Man's Perfection in Righteousness*, ch. 20, *P.N.F.* vol. V, p. 175.
46. N. P. Williams, *Grace of God*, p. 32. (I am indebted to Williams's account.)

pears as a misnomer, but in theory it means that the grace would be sufficient if the will were not in bondage. If man were not a sinner he would accept it; it would then be sufficient.

We can, therefore, never understand Augustine's reconciliation of grace and free will if we imagine grace as something which comes down and grasps the will and turns or forces it to the good. Rather, grace is action by which God draws the elect toward him by determining their wills, not by force, but by presenting objects which He is certain they will choose and which will lead them to the good. As Williams puts it: "God gently leads the elect to desire and pursue goodness by presenting the idea of virtue to them under the most beautiful and seductive guise, and by revealing Himself in some measure, albeit imperfect, of His eternal loveliness and glory."[47] Grace might be termed *"vis a fronte,"* a pull from the front, exciting the will to follow in its full and perfect spontaneity.

7. We must now briefly recapitulate the ground we have covered. We began by uncovering the presuppositions of the view presented in the *Protagoras,* namely that virtue is the seeking of some object, and that men do seek that object although often in a misguided way. We agreed that if such were the case, then knowledge would be virtue. Both Plato and Augustine, however, have denied the second presupposition. They both agree in saying that men do not seek the Good, but seek lesser goods. Plato resorts to education and illumination, Augustine to divine habituation, to enable the will to seek its proper object. Both processes are a conditioning of the determinant; and this conditioning is necessary. To be virtuous requires not merely knowing the good, but action on the part of the will.

We have undertaken this exposition of Plato and Augustine to il-

---

47. Ibid., p. 33.

lustrate what we mean by the natural cosmos. The same could have been done by examining Aristotle and Aquinas. We have shown that the natural cosmos is possible within the context of different views, pagan as well as Christian. The natural cosmos is marked by the following characteristics: (a) all relations are relations to objects; even God may be treated as an object; (b) appetitional desires are the energies of all relations, and all love is acquisitive, hence not love in the Christian sense; (c) grace (when the system is Christian) is likewise spoken of in terms of an object presented to the will as an object of desire; and (d) all natural systems lose communality, personality, and the true nature of God, and are therefore not really Christian but individualistic.

chapter four

The Meaning of Sin

Section I

1. So far we have tried to do three things: (a) We have vindicated the natural cosmos, attempting to show that the natural cosmos is good and not bad, and that the evil of the world does not derive from nature as such. (b) We have seen how with Plato and Augustine the entire cosmos was spoken of in terms of natural relations, and therefore how easy it is to fall into this error. (c) The first point has led us to suggest that we will have to look for the meaning of sin in a region of experience which is not natural, while the second has exposed us to the natural cosmos, has shown us what it means, and thereby supplies us with a contrasting backdrop for our own view.

2. In the first and introductory chapter, we gave a list of criteria which distinguish personal and natural relations. Personal relations were described as relations between two persons, natural relations as between a person and an object. If the characteristics of the two types of relations listed in the first chapter have been partly forgotten by the reader, it will be advisable to turn back and refresh them in his mind. What we have to say will depend on a clear understanding of what the difference is.

It must be affirmed once again that natural relations are totally distinct from personal relations. They must never be confused. In the following sections we shall use these definitions: (a) Natural relations mark off that sphere of experience in which a person desires, strives for, wants, or needs an object or a concrete process. The activity may be described as desiring, wanting, or striving for. (b) Personal relations mark off that sphere of experience in which one person seeks to establish a definite relation or a definite rapport between another person and himself. The activity cannot be described as desire or wanting or needing in the appetitional sense. The activity is not an urge or an impulse, but something different. It is the sharing of fellowship, of communion, of mutual presence; or it is giving, loving, and sharing; or it may be, as it most usually is, hating, envying, despising, priding oneself over the other and so on. The rest of this chapter will try to clarify the above distinction, and will attempt to show that sin involves personal relations.

3. The word "appetition" in its common usage does not have the wide meaning that we are going to give it. By "appetites" people most often mean bodily impulses and needs; an appetite is considered as belonging to a purely physical nature. Appetite for us means the impulse or the striving for *any* object whatsoever. The criterion of appetition is that it seeks some *object*, something which is impersonal, objective, and self-revealing by nature. The object of an appetition can be adequately considered or disclosed by the examination of sense-data alone. Appetitions fall into four main categories:

(a) Appetitions which are bodily and which belong to our physical nature. Such appetites may be called "concrete." An example of such an appetition is, of course, any physical desire such as hunger or thirst. Also, one can include desire for exercise, craving for fresh air, sexual needs and so forth. In short, any desire or impulse which seeks an object, or any desire which relates to a change of the present physical condition of the body, may be termed a "concrete" appetition.

(b) The second sort of appetitions are "rational" appetitions: the desire and longing for truth, for coherence, or for necessity in the interpretation of experience. Their object may be considered as Truth, with a capital "T." It makes no difference, however, whether the above type of appetition exists or not. If the situation is as the pragmatist says it is, then pure "rational" appetitions do not exist. Pragmatists, if I understand them, consider the process of thought as a means to action, or a means to satisfying some desire. Thought is often considered as an instrument of the desires. If the pragmatist is right, then there are no "rational" appetitions as such. I do not believe, however, that the pragmatist is right. My own opinion is that there is such a thing as wanting to know the truth for its own sake, such a thing as the desire to know for the sake of knowing. Thought, then, may have its *own* object,[1] as well as serving as an intelligent instrument for other types of appetition. When thought seeks its own object, there is a pure "rational" appetition.

(c) There is also the "aesthetic" appetition or the desire to enjoy an object of beauty. When we see a beautiful object we do, I believe, enjoy it for its own sake; particularly in those sensitive to beauty, there is the longing for a beautiful object. Kant's dictum that a work of art is "purposive but without purpose" expresses a good part of the truth. We appreciate and desire beauty for its own sake. It is not advantageous to continue this discussion since it would involve us in the subject of aesthetics, about which I know nothing. Further, if someone wanted to deny that there were "aesthetic" appetitions, he would not

---

1. See Blanshard's criticism of pragmatism, *The Nature of Thought,* vol. I, ch. 10.

upset us in the least. It would merely mean that there was one class less of appetitions.

(d) Lastly, there is the sort of appetition which we might call the "religious" appetition. An example of such an appetition may be found in the works of Plato, Aristotle, Augustine, and Aquinas. It is that appetition which is the coping-stone of the natural cosmos. In short, it is the appetition which seeks God as its object, or the Form of the Good, the Alone and so forth. It is the appetition directed to the highest object, to the source of all Beauty, Truth, and Goodness. The existence of this appetition has been attested to by many mystics, by many great philosophers, and by the two greatest doctors of the church.

Whether such an appetition exists, I do not know; but if it does exist, it should not be allowed to exist. To have such an appetition is to sin. To the writer it is sheer impiety to desire God as an object. It is a return to paganism in a subtle and even more dangerous form. To speak of God as the most beautiful object, the most satisfying object, the most desired of all objects is to sin, because one of the forms of sin, as we shall see, is to turn a personal relation into a natural relation, and to do this misdeed in relation to God is surely sin. If one cannot have faith in God because He is our Heavenly Father, because out of His unspeakable mercy He came into the world to save us, because His forgiveness and charity exceed our fullest expectations—in short, if one cannot have faith in God just because He is what He is, but has to add that He is most satisfying in His beauty[2] and such an *object* that we shall never crave anything else—then perhaps it is better not to be a Christian at all.

Natural relations exist in a sphere which is good, not bad, as we

2. See Kierkegaard for much the same point of view, *Concluding Unscientific Postscript*, pp. 221–222.

have previously stated. They are, however, limited to that sphere, and if we imagine the realm beyond them as a natural realm, then we err. A man should seek for truth, he should enjoy beauty, he should treat his body well. But he also should realize that when he comes before God he is not dealing with an object, nor with an ordinary person, but with God, and that he is thereby obligated to act in a way which only God Himself can show him, and which in no fashion resembles the proper attitude toward objects. Our polemic on this point is another step toward our repudiation of the natural cosmos.

We have completed our list of appetitions. Only two comments are in order: (a) We accept the first three as being legitimate, as being proper for man, and as forming the substance of natural activity in the natural sphere of our experience. The fourth kind of appetition was rejected as constituting the sinful extension of natural relations to a sphere where they do not apply. Such an appetition is an abuse of the relation between man and God. (b) Appetitions are the relations between the human person in his natural aspect and nature as a creation or gift of God. It is proper and necessary for us to want the bodily goods of nature. It is proper and right for man to seek the truth about nature and to appreciate the beauties of nature and of man's own created art. Rational and aesthetic appetitions complete the development of the natural man.

4. We have now to show two things: (a) that there is nothing in appetitions of any sort which gives rise to egotism and therefore to sin; (b) that there is likewise nothing in appetitions to give rise to community and that therefore in a natural cosmos there could be no community and hence no sin.

(a) In an earlier chapter[3] we quoted Leon as saying that there is

---

3. Chapter Two, Section III, Subsection 3 (iv).

nothing in appetition itself to lead to egotism. This statement cannot be proved absolutely by empirical facts. It cannot be proved because all of our experience involves us as persons. Even if no other persons are around, we often are doing things which are preparations to meet persons. We study because we know that sometime we shall be able to show off our knowledge. We practice the piano hours on end for the same reason. We eat food to build up our bodies so that we may astonish our fellows with our athletic prowess. In short, even our natural activities are so closely bound up with our personal relations that we never find in our experience a *pure* appetition. As Niebuhr puts it, man's creatureliness is always mixed up with and involved in his spirituality. Therefore, it will be difficult for us to find pure appetitions. What we shall try to do is to single out instances in which we approach nearest to pure appetitions, and then ask ourselves, "Does this state of consciousness lead to egotism, and could it *ever* lead to egotism?"

(i) A pure appetition would be characterized by the concentration of the activity of consciousness upon the object of the desire and upon the expected state of relief once the object was acquired. The whole focus of a pure appetition would thus revolve around the object and the state of satisfaction expected. Let us take to begin with a bodily appetition. Imagine a man who has been sailing a boat all night. The night has been cold and damp. The wind has blown fairly hard, and he has become tired from holding the tiller. In a short while it is his turn to go below to the warm cabin to get a cup of coffee and to go to sleep. Let us imagine him with his whole consciousness concentrated on this blissful future state. He is now cold, he hopes to be warm; he is now tired, he wants to rest. He has approached a state of pure appetition. He is simply a bundle of desires, for warmth, for sleep. He is a miserable creature, a bit of dust from dust, tired, cold and exhausted. Assuming this state has been reached, will he think of being proud, will he boast, will he be envious? Will he not rather rush down into the cabin as soon as he is relieved, hurriedly warm up his coffee and crawl into bed without a word, looking forward to nothing but the warm blankets around him and the warm coffee within him? Would not this person call off boasting and vainglorious bragging for the time being? Would his state of pure appetition allow for such things? I do not believe it would.

In the morning, perhaps, this person, satisfied in his desires, would resume his boasting which no doubt has filled his life as it fills all our lives. He would chide his companions for being sissies. He would brag about how he stood the cold. He would exclaim in pride how tough he was. But while he was in the state of pure appetition, he would not do so. Thus, we are led to the conclusion that the more we approach the point of pure appetition, the more the sinful activities of personality fall into the background. Consciousness is transformed into a dynamic state of pure appetitional egoism. Innumerable other examples could be given which would tend to verify our conclusion.

(ii) In the instance of an aesthetic appetition or of a rational appetition, the same situation applies. A person deeply engrossed in watching a beautiful or awe-inspiring phenomenon of nature is, for the time being, not an egotist. Likewise, a person immersed in metaphysical speculation is not simultaneously indulging in self-glory. Insofar as he is concentrating upon his problem, he is not an egotist. The more he concentrates, the less possibility there is that he will be proud of himself at the same time.

Thus we conclude that insofar as we seek objects for their own sake, that is, insofar as we are engaged in pure appetition, we are not egotists. Our natures are such that we seldom, if ever, are in a state of pure appetition. But when we examine this appetitional activity in us, we find nothing that could lead to pride. In appetitions we are dealing with objects, with things, with "others" which are impersonal. Hence, the whole activity is egoistic, not egotistic. The entire process is objective and merely a question of expectations and satisfactions in terms of needs and desires. In a world which was purely appetitional there would be no such thing as egotism.

(iii) That appetitions as such are not in any way involved in sin is testified by our use of words. We do not call a man of strong appetition a sinner. When a man is extremely hungry or thirsty he is committing no sin, nor do we give the artist or the metaphysician such a title; nor do we call a person a sinner who cannot appreciate beauty, nor a person of slow intellect. Almost instinctively we reserve the word "sin" for the willful perversity which abuses or destroys personal relations.[4]

(b) We now come to our second point: appetitions in no way lead to egotism (so much has been shown), and it is likewise true therefore that appetitions cannot lead to community. Community is a personal relation based upon fellowship, sharing, "giveness." Since appetitions do not lead to egotism which breaks up community, neither can they lead to fellowship which is the basis of community. The second statement in the preceding sentence is not a necessary logical deduction from the first. It is perfectly conceivable that the world could be such that appetition did not lead to egotism but nevertheless did lead to fellowship and community. Such, however, is not the case. Both premises are true, although not deducible from one another. Community cannot be based upon appetitions. To base community on appetitions is to attempt the impossible. Just as there is nothing anti-social about appetitions as such, there is likewise nothing pro-social about them. Something's power for the good can often be judged by its power for evil. If appetitions do not lead to evil, then we can presume

4. Section II will define sin in these terms.

that they do not lead to good. The following considerations will try to support this statement.

(i) Let us return to the case of the man who has been sailing all night, and let us ask the question, "In what way would another person enter into his consciousness?" or, "What would the presence of another person mean to him, and to what extent would he be interested in other people?" Being in the state he is in, he might ask a number of favors of his companions. He might ask one of them to warm the coffee before he came down into the cabin; he might ask one of them to lend him a sweater; or he might ask one of them to hurry and relieve him. In each case, the request is made in regard to some aspect of his own appetition. The actions of the other people are considered as so many successions of sense-data which he knows will lead to the satisfaction of and to the expected end of the appetition. The movements of his companions will be judged "good" or "bad" according to how they result in the satisfaction of the desire. In short, other people can only enter into his consciousness as means to the achievement of the desired end. The other persons do not enter as persons at all, but purely as means. Such a person will as readily let one person do the requested action as another. Who does it is a matter of indifference. What counts is the result, the efficiency of the person's actions in achieving the end. Thus, in this state of appetition, a man is in no way pro-social. He is not interested in persons as such, and he uses people as means only. Hence, no community can be based on egoism, because egoism is indifferent to community, either for or against.

(ii) In no region of experience does the indifference of appetition to personality and community express itself more clearly than in sexual relations. To understand this point we must realize that the sexual appetition is a peculiar one. It is utterly unique because the object of the appetition is intimately bound up with another *person.*

No other appetitions have this characteristic; they have for the end objects as objects. It is because the sexual appetition is so intimately bound up with persons as well as objects that it is subject to all of the abuses and disturbances that always accompany it. The uniqueness of this desire is what makes it the subject of so much childish and smirking laughter, of so much over-serious and pathological sincerity. Sex is absolutely unique because involved in it is the whole gamut of communal and personal relations of egotism, pride, envy, jealousy and so forth. Not until we understand this complexity can we understand sex.[5]

Our point then consists in the following observation: nowhere in experience is the contrast between appetition and personality shown more clearly than in sex. The contrast is immediately suggested because of the confusion into which such relations fall. If there were no personality in the world, then we could expect sexual appetitions to find as easy a satisfaction as appetitions for food and drink. That such is not the case immediately leads us to expect that another factor has entered the situation. The indifference of appetition to personality is seen by the way people treat each other in such relations. The everlasting phenomenon of prostitution shows that for pure appetition one woman is as good as another, and that for appetition, personality is a matter of indifference. The response of personality to the purely egoistic situation will be treated later;[6] but we can anticipate here that the response is a feeling of aloneness, closedness, of being used. The self is cut off, isolated; it can find no community in such a world, and hence it is alone. This aloneness is the result of sin and is the state in which all sinners live.

(iii)   In closing this section we might briefly suggest the impli-

5. Freudianism knows the amazing complexity of sex, but it gives a false explanation. It fails to distinguish the personal from the appetitional.

6. Section III.

cations of our conclusions: (a) No community can be based upon mutual egoism or mutual advantage. The idea of justice expressed in the political theories of Hobbes and Locke, the view of Adam Smith that we best serve our fellow men by enlightened self-interest, are all false views of community. Any society which explains itself in terms of mutual egoism is heading for certain destruction. All "contract" theories of society suffer from this fundamental defect. (b) Further, we may suggest that to use community for the sake of egoistic advantage is one of the chief forms of sin. (c) Finally, we may ask Augustine and Aquinas on what basis community can be established in their proper-act natural cosmos. That they are both at loss to understand and to give a satisfactory explanation of community has been pointed out by Nygren.[7] The commandment to love our neighbor causes both of them considerable difficulty. In a natural cosmos, how could we expect otherwise?

Section II

1. We have examined the nature of appetitions and have found that there was nothing in them either for or against community as such. What our view states is that the corruption and destruction of community, which we are going to define as sin, is not caused by any factor which is not communal in its essence. In short, man's potentialities for community corrupt themselves and are not corrupted by anything outside themselves. Throughout the centuries man has exercised his ingenuity in blaming something outside himself. Man seems reluctant to admit that it is he himself and not some external factor which is responsible for sin.

A brief list of four such views will serve to clarify our meaning: (a)

---

7. *Agape and Eros,* Part II, vol. II, pp. 331–337, 423–427 [pp. 549–555, 641–645 in the one-volume edition].

There is the view that appetitions are evil and that it is because man has a body that he is a sinner. (b) Closely related to the above view is the notion that the sensible world is evil. We have already discussed these statements, since we are concerned to vindicate the natural cosmos and then to concentrate our efforts on the personal community. (c) History shows numerous examples of times when the stars were believed to control man's fate. What men did could not be otherwise, and the evil they committed could in no way be attributed to intentional malice. Augustine had to repudiate these notions along with many others in his long career.[8] (d) There is also the temptation to blame objective institutions for the evil in the world. It was an 18th-century idea that bad institutions were one of the great barriers to a fully good mankind. Individuals cannot, however, be separated from institutions. Institutions are merely the objective rules and methods which men set up to deal with social problems. Bad institutions are a sure sign of sinful men. There would be no oppressive institutions were there not greed and malice to reinforce them. Even Rousseau admits that such is the case.[9] Augustine refuted the charge in another way. For him, institutions were the means by which God controlled sin. Man by sin made institutions necessary. Laws were to preserve the order of nature and to limit the extent of man's rebellion.[10]

The above examples are sufficient to indicate the manner in which man has tried to put the blame on some factor outside himself. The ever-present perverseness in human nature to act in this fashion expresses itself in what we are going to call the Manichean heresy. The Manicheans were an Oriental dualistic sect which penetrated Christendom in the early centuries. They blamed evil upon the force of

8. See *Confessions*, bk. VII, ch. 6; also *Homilies on the Gospel of John*, Tractate VIII, 10–11, *P.N.F.* vol. I, pp. 105–106; vol. VII, pp. 61–62.

9. *Discourse on the Origin of Inequality*, pp. 222–223.

10. *City of God*, bk. XIV, ch. 15, *P.N.F.* vol. II, p. 274.

darkness in the world which captured the good souls and held them in captivity. Thus insofar as any theory of sin finds the cause of evil as something external, we shall call that view Manichean. Even Hegel falls into this category. For him, sin is one stage in the necessary logical development of the Spirit.[11] Insofar as sin is regarded as a necessary stage and as necessarily leading to virtue, sin is made into something external or beyond the limits of the personality as such.

We can even call Manichean any attempt to derive sin from man's position in the cosmos. Niebuhr, for example, wants to argue that man, being both bound and free, both limited and unlimited, is in a state of anxiety. Although anxiety is not sin, it is the precondition of sin. Man sins when by pride he tries to deny his contingency and when by sensuality he tries to escape from his own freedom.[12] This view of sin is highly sophisticated and does not accord with the facts. The egotism of little children who have never contemplated such matters cannot be explained in this way. Further, as we shall attempt to show later,[13] anxiety is the result of sin. It is the state of the sinner in the cosmos he creates for himself, namely, the cosmos of aloneness. We have to admit that the spirit simply corrupts itself. Personality depraves itself for no reason that can be found external to it. There is nothing in the natural cosmos, nothing in man's nature as such to explain egotism, envy, vanity, pride and so forth. We must say, no matter how mysterious it may seem, that the spirit depraved itself by itself; that it turned in upon itself to love itself from no external suggestion. The apparent inevitable tendency to do this we may term, if we care to, Original Sin. The beginning of sin must be conceived as taking place in this unfathomable "causeless" way. Only realizing this truth can we properly be prepared to face the subtle perversity of per-

11. Mackintosh, *Types of Modern Theology,* pp. 115–116.
12. *The Nature and Destiny of Man,* pp. 182–186.
13. Section III.

sonality as we now find it. Hence, we must agree with Augustine that the "evil of mutable spirits, which depraves the good of nature, arises from itself."[14] Shakespeare, likewise, has expressed our meaning:

> But jealous souls will not be answered so;
> They are not ever jealous for the cause,
> But jealous for they are jealous: 'tis a monster
> Begot upon itself, born on itself.[15]

If this view of personality seems queer, then personality is a queer thing.

Thus we reject any Manichean tendency to blame evil or sin on something outside the spirit. Christianity, as I understand it, has asserted what we have asserted. It has stated that the spirit depraves itself. "Nothing that goes into a man from the outside can pollute him. It is what comes out of a man that pollutes him."[16]

2. Having stated that it is the spirit itself which depraves itself, we have now to ask in what way the spirit acts in its depravity. That is, what is sin, what does it mean, and what does it involve? What sin is may be defined in relation to what man is. As we stated in our introductory chapter, the distinctive thing about man is not that he is rational, not that he can appreciate beauty, but that he is a responsible being, a being made for community and fellowship with his fellow men, with all the company of heaven, and finally with God Himself. All of man's gifts, which he possesses above the animals, are for the realization of this end. As Brunner puts it: "The distinctively human element is not freedom, nor intellectual creative power, nor reason. These are rather the conditions of realization of man's real human existence, which consists in love. They do not contain their own

---

14. *City of God*, bk. XII, ch. 9, *P.N.F.* vol. II, p. 231.
15. *Othello*, Act III, Scene iv, lines 158–161.
16. Mark 7:15; see also A. E. Taylor, *Problem of Evil*.

meaning, but their meaning is love, true community."[17] Thus man is a being made to live in and to live for community. His gifts are means to this end.

Man's capacity to live in and for community is the Image of God. That pattern in man's nature is the reflection in man of God Himself, who is perfect community within Himself, being three persons in one as the Doctrine of the Trinity states. The perfect obedience and love of the Son for the Father and the Father for the Son gives us the model for any community.

Since man is a creature made for community, and since the perfect expression of his being is responding to God's givenness, living nourished in divine grace, it seems that sin must be some repudiation of man's true end. Sin, then, must be the abuse, the aberration, and the destruction of community, and that which sunders all responsible relations with one's fellow men. Sin destroys the foundation-ground of community. It throws one into the abyss of isolation and separation in which man ceases to be man. Sin destroys all that is human; it makes man not into a mere beast, but into something far more sinister—namely, it converts man into a satanic spirit, only held in check by the gift of creatureliness. The potentialities of man for the good are rooted in the *Imago Dei;* the potentialities of man for evil are rooted in the possibility of destruction of that image. Because man is person and thereby spirit, he can be evil to a degree far exceeding the purely appetitional egoism of nature.

Sin manifests itself in two forms: (a) egotism and (b) egoism. Under the first category lie all the great sins. The egotist is the sinner par excellence. Egotism is that perverse desire for height and that sinister craving for self-worship. It shows itself in the most subtle ways as well as in the most obvious. The open egotist is the man of conceit, pride,

---

17. Brunner, *Man in Revolt*, p. 74.

vainglory; he is self-esteeming, boastful, malicious, deceitful, and so forth. The subtle egotist is the man of self-sensitivity, of pretending modesty, of timid and cautious manners, of complacent self-satisfaction. The latter is what Leon calls the "Uranian" egotist. He is content to worship himself and does not seek the worship of others. The former is the domineering egotist; he is the man who ramps and raves, who seeks openly to command others so as to show his power. Egotism, which expresses itself in unlimited ways, is the great sin. It is in itself sin and the cause of sin. Egotism per se is the destruction of community. It is that apparent ineradicable perversity which infects human relations. It is always present. There are none free from it. It is sin because it is the repudiation of all that man should be and must be. It destroys responsibility and thereby community; it scorns givenness and is henceforth the negation of love. It means the annihilation of grace.

There follows in the wake of egotism all the host of other sins. Egoism, which seeks to use people, is justified in the mind of the sinner by a previous self-worship, a self-worship which seeks to abuse people. Egoism merely uses the other, the "thou"; egotism abuses the "thou." Egotism seeks to set the "thou" below itself, to turn the "thou" into an admirer or into an object of admiration. Once the other has been abused, the other can be used.

For example: the capitalist seems merely to use his employees. He treats them as so many cogs in the machine which piles up wealth for him. Hence, he seems merely to be an egoist; he seems to want nothing more than concrete wealth, bodily comfort, to which end those he hires are means. But all the time this use of persons is justified by a tacit abuse of them. In the mind of the capitalist those persons are inferior, while he is superior. Further, the employees are not being used as means to concrete egoism, that is, to help amass large properties and estates; no, the end is not purely appetitional, but is spiritual.

The capitalist takes great pride in his wealth; he loves to show it off. He likes to walk about his estate inwardly praising himself on his success. He likes to imagine his estate as a kingdom in which he is the most important figure. He keeps a host of servants not to serve his needs, but to swell the ranks of those who must obey him. All of his activities go to build up this petty kingdom by virtue of which his consuming vanity can congratulate itself. The entire activity of his life, all the feverish rushing in and out of town, all the unending worries of business, all these efforts which exhaust body, mind, and soul are aimed at this indeterminate end of silent, self-congratulatory self-worship. Underlying all this sinful striving is the egotist lie, namely, that he is a person distinct and superior.[18] The purely egoistic sin of using other people, of turning personal relations into natural relations, is justified by the deepest of all sins, the egotist's lie.

Concerning the above description of the capitalist, we should remark that we have no particular dislike for capitalism. We are not spreading Marxist propaganda. The sin of using people as means only, as Kant would say, can be found in all regions of experience. It infects those in the lowest walks of life as well as those in the higher. Sin is not reserved for one group of people, but is universal.

3. Keeping in mind that egotism is sin because it repudiates community, we shall examine a few characteristics of egotism to show how sin does negate community.

(i) The first thing to be noticed about the egotist is that he refuses to share anything. He wants to reserve everything for himself, not because he needs everything, not because his appetitions require such selfishness, but because he wants to possess everything as a badge of his superiority. If other people possess what he possesses, then his

18. See Niebuhr, *Nature and Destiny of Man*, pp. 203–207.

distinctiveness is lost. There exists no longer the sign of his superiority. Augustine has an acute argument to this effect. He explains the murder of Remus by Romulus as follows: "But they both could not have that glory, that if they had been but one, they might have had. For he that glories in dominion must needs see his glory diminished when he has a partner to share with him. Therefore, the one, to have all, killed his partner."[19]

The refusal to share manifests itself everywhere. The culture of the Italian Renaissance, which is now receiving soberer treatment after the naïve Victorian enthusiasm of the 19th century, is now recognized as being in large part a badge of class. Once the printing of the classics was made cheap and easy throughout Italy, the thirst for the classics took a decided drop.[20] What was the sense in being a humanist if everybody was going to be one? Those who followed the tradition of Poggio and Valla would have to find something besides the classics to mark off their idiosyncrasies.

(ii) As a direct consequence of the above characteristic, there develops the phenomenon of the closed group. The more closed the group is, the more pleasing it is to our pride and vanity. There is no satisfaction in being in a group which anyone can join. Hence, restrictions and qualifications are added. One has to be a scholar, a gentleman, a good sportsman, or a good drinker. Once in the group, one frowns on and tends to despise all those outside it. Those beyond the pale are termed dupes, dull-wits, blockheads, and no-accounts. In short, all without the group are inferior, all within are superior. This phenomenon manifests itself everywhere. In college clubs, in older men's clubs, in athletic organizations, in national groups, and in race

---

19. *City of God,* bk. XV, ch. 5, *P.N.F.* vol. II, p. 286.
20. Strayer and Munro, *The Middle Ages,* p. 531.

groups, the basic motive is the egotistic satisfaction of being within a superior group.

The ideal closed group is, of course, the group of one, where the egotist himself is the only member. All groups tend to this ideal closed group because every person in the group strives for it. The more "refined" the group is, the more rules and strict regulation it sets up, so as to provide excuses to throw out members, thereby making the group smaller and preserving its purity and honor. As a result, there is no better way to kill pride in belonging to a group than to let everybody into it. This latter technique is precisely what Christianity uses by asserting the universal Fatherhood of God. Once a man realizes this universal Fatherhood he realizes that there is no room for pride. There are no chosen people, "for God shows no partiality."[21]

The development of the closed group has been a distinctive factor in Western civilization. Closed groups are now tearing that civilization to pieces. The development has seen several stages: (a) the religious closed group, as exemplified by the Roman Church who called everyone outside the pale heretics; (b) the cultural closed group such as the Italian humanists already mentioned, or the phenomenon of 18th-century cultural distinctions; (c) in Marxism the determinant falls to the economic level, and a person's group is determined by his economic status; and (d) finally, the determinant is biological. In Nazism we find that what condemns us or exalts us is what sort of blood we have in our veins.[22]

This last closed group is pride in its most demonic form. It is possessive of a criterion which excludes others at will, and imposes a restriction which is beyond our control. If one was not a Catholic, one

21. Romans 2:11.

22. I owe these suggestions to Prof. Harbison [presumably E. Harris Harbison (1907–1964), a Reformation historian and a member of the Princeton history department, 1933–1964].

could become one. If one was not an educated Frenchman, one might also become one. But one cannot become an "Aryan" by wish. One is excluded or included from birth. Hence in Nazism we find the closed group idea fully developed. The group is closed with iron-bound certainty, and as a consequence the egotism of its members knows no bounds. Groups which do not have such iron-bound restrictions do not give rise to such full-blown egotism because one can never tell when those one scorns today will be members of the group tomorrow. When the group is foreordained and seen with absolute certainty,[23] then egotism knows no limits. I believe it is the absoluteness of the criterion which allows for Nazi pride. How otherwise could we explain egotism centering around the inclusion in a group, when the members of the group are not in any way responsible for their inclusion, but are given it by birth?

There has consequently developed an elaborate theology of egotism which can be clearly seen in the works of the official Nazi "philosopher," Alfred Rosenberg. His book *The Myth of the Twentieth Century* is the justification of Nazi nonsense. All history for him is the war of the race souls. Each race has its own soul, and each member of the race is an expression of that soul. The race soul is the absolute self of German idealism particularized so as to allow one such self for each race. The Aryan race soul, however, is superior to all the others. It has been the creator of all culture. Recently, it has fallen to sleep and has allowed itself to be overcome by Jews, democracy, capitalism, communism and so forth, all of which equal the same thing for the Germans. As the blurb on the cover of the book says: "'The myth of the Twentieth Century' is the myth of blood, which under the sign of the swastika unchains the racial world-revolution. It is the awakening of the race soul, which after long sleep victoriously ends the race

---

23. This may explain the tendency to pride in Calvinism.

chaos."[24] Once again the glorious Aryans from the lost island of At-
lantis shall prove their worth.

All of this stuff sounds like incredible nonsense. But because it is
nonsense, egotism believes and accepts it. The distinctiveness of the
race souls allows for the full-blown pride. It allows for the claim to
superiority. We have here in twisted form the idea of *Eigentümlichkeit*
which was stressed in German Romanticism.[25] The German tendency
to imagine a world full of noumenal selves, absolute selves, pure egos,
non-egos, world-spirits and so forth has provided human egotism
with the most remarkable theology, a theology which intellectually
attempts to justify man's cardinal sin. Each little German imagines,
no doubt, that the race soul is working in him, that he belongs to this
superior race soul and is somehow identified with it.[26] He thus justifies to himself the closed group, and he uses the group, perhaps un-
consciously, as a means to his own egotistic satisfaction. The group, as
a means to his own honor, can supply him with far greater strength
than he himself could attain alone. Closely identifying himself with
the group, he shares in its glory. Thus the closed group, as a vehicle
for egotism, is clearly expressed.[27]

(iii) Besides the ever-present phenomenon of developing the
closed group, pride likewise never admits itself at fault, and always
seeks to blame another. It thereby breaks up community by the denial
of its own guilt and by the false condemnation of others. If anything
goes wrong with the plans of the proud man, he always finds the cause

24. Quoted in Viereck's fine study *Metapolitics*, p. 229; for Rosenberg's ideas
see the last hundred pages of this book.

25. See Arthur O. Lovejoy, "The Meaning of Romanticism for the Historian of
Ideas."

26. For the tendency of idealism to identify the self with the absolute self, see
Fichte, *The Vocation of Man*, the end of bk. III.

27. See Leon, *The Ethics of Power*, pp. 144–145.

in some external event. Vainglorious generals always explain defeat as the result of bad weather, or slowness on the part of some subordinate. The German stab-in-the-back theory, by which the Wehrmacht sought to explain the defeat in the First World War, is a typical example. German invincibility had been preached up and down the land. The failure could only be explained as a stab in the back by Jews, capitalists, and communists. The Germans could not bring themselves to the realization that they had been beaten in battle. Nazi propaganda has used the theory to fan hate against convenient enemies at home and to work the German populace into a state of fury. The whole complex of feelings so aroused is based on egotism which refuses ever to admit itself at fault.

Augustine, always acute in his analysis of pride, remarks how Adam sought to lay the blame for the Fall on Eve: "... yet their pride seeks to lay their own evil upon another, the man's upon the woman, and hers upon the serpent. But this indeed does rather accuse them of worse than acquit them." The "pride, that makes man seek to color his guilt, is far more damnable than the guilt itself."[28] This refusal of pride to admit its own fault and its own guilt is one of its most destructive characteristics. To protect and to persevere in its closed self-righteousness, it must heap curses and blame upon another, thereby destroying all community whatsoever.

(iv) We should further observe the remarkable subtlety of egotism, the insidious way in which it creeps into personal relations and the stealthful manner in which it poisons the best of our efforts. Until we realize the subtlety of pride, we shall never see clearly its ever-presence and its continual poisoning of society. William Temple has written: "It is evidence how mortally deep is our self-centredness that even our deliverance from it in respect of many sides of life may be-

---

28. *City of God*, bk. XIV, ch. 14, *P.N.F.* vol. II, p. 274.

come an occasion of self-esteem. This is that demon of spiritual pride, which most of us are not nearly good enough even to encounter, but which, the saints assure us, is waiting as it were on the top rung of the ladder of perfection to catch us there and throw us down."[29] Pride extends itself into the highest reaches of the spiritual, into the best efforts of the personality. Even to cure oneself of pride is the occasion of pride. Truly, we are face to face with a demon. Therefore, we must never allow for pride. It must be the object of all our attacks. To permit a certain proper pride, to justify legitimate pride as some do, is to admit defeat before we have even begun. Against an enemy so subtle as pride there should be no compromise. Whenever we are proud, we are conversing with the devil and his angels.

This characteristic of pride should warn us where the most dangerous egotism is to be found, namely, in the best that we do and in the best of us. There is always a tendency to call the lower groups of society the worst sinners. The street-walkers, the beggars, the outcasts, the robbers, and the drunkards are the usual scapegoats. The real sinners, however, are those who pride themselves on being otherwise, those who bask in their own success and look down upon those who are not upright members of society. The Bible understands this truth clearly. Everyone knows the passage in Luke[30] which tells of the Pharisee who went into the temple and thanked God that he was not as other men were, greedy, dishonest, or adulterous. Christ tells us, however, that it is not this man but the tax collector, who was afraid to raise his eyes to God and only asked for mercy, who went back to his home with God's approval. For righteousness so easily cloaks the sin of self-righteousness, and of this greater sin was the Pharisee guilty. This kind of egotism, which is sin in the face of all that is good, is the

29. *Nature, Man and God*, pp. 389–390.
30. Luke 18:10–14.

most dangerous and the most poisonous. As Whale puts it: "There is no sin so subtly dangerous as the self-sufficiency of the morally religious man."[31] This subtlety of sin enables it to corrupt the best, as well as the worst, that is in us. Sin is not a question of some sort of a lag which has held on to drag us down; it springs from no imperfection. It is the self-corruption of pure spirit; it is the self-destruction of the best and the most perfect.

(v) The standard definition of sin throughout Christian ages has been phrased somewhat differently from our account. We have called sin the aberration, abuse, and destruction of community. The classical statement says that sin is rebellion against God. Sin is revolt from and the denial of God. Ultimately, we are in complete agreement with this definition, as we shall show in a latter division of this section.[32] Here, however, we want to point out that for us, as well as tradition, sin has the characteristic of rebellion. Nevertheless, the usual definition of sin as rebellion tends to lose the subtlety of sin. Sin may be, and often is, open defiance and therefore rebellion. But if we take the word "rebellion" in its usual meaning, all sin is not rebellion. Sin can be a more insidious kind of action such as deceit, hypocrisy, silent self-worship, indifference to God and to other men. In short, egotism may take a silent and quiet path as well as an open or violent one. Therefore, we deem it wise to note fully the instances in which sin is rebellion, but also to point out that the ingenuity of spirit is such that it finds much more subtle and insidious ways of sin. There can be no doubt, however, that egotism, in the final analysis, is rebellion in the sense that it is the denial of community, the denial and repudiation of the *Imago Dei,* and the negation of God's call.

31. Whale, *Christian Doctrine,* p. 39.
32. Division 5.

4. We should now summarize what we have said about egotism, which for us is the master sin, the root-ground of evil from which all other lesser evils flow. We have listed and discussed briefly the following characteristics: (a) Egotism refuses to share. (b) Egotism seeks to develop the closed group, the ideal closed group being one's own self. Egotism thus abuses communities for its own ends. (c) Egotism can tolerate no criticism of itself, and therefore seeks to blame others. (d) Egotism possesses a remarkable and insidious subtlety which enables the spirit to corrupt the best that is in it. (e) Egotism in the final analysis is some sort of rebellion and negation, although its technique is often silent and cautious. Our analysis of egotism has by no means been complete. We have merely scratched the surface. As Augustine remarked, "Man is a great deep,"[33] and to probe the depths is beyond our capacity. Nevertheless, the five above characteristics of sin give us a clue as to why sin is sin. All of the manifest actions of egotism and all of the inner states of sin point to one thing: namely, repudiation, destruction, and abuse of community for the sake of the self. Community is not destroyed for the sake of concrete appetition, not for the sake of egoistic satisfaction, but for the sake of egotistic satisfaction. Community is destroyed by sheer perverse self-love. The egotist simply loves himself. He seeks nothing else. He revolves completely around himself, in contented self-worship. As a result, community and fellowship are repudiated. Other persons are exterior; they become mere means or they become possible admirers, or persons to be admired.

Therefore we can say that egotism is sin because it is the negation and destruction of that spiritual community for which man was made. Man was made in God's image, which meant that man was

33. *Confessions,* bk. IV, ch. 14, *P.N.F.* vol. I, p. 75.

made as a responsible being, as a communal being, and as a being who must answer to his Creator. This capacity to answer was God's gift to man, not a law laid upon him.[34] It was part of the bounty of the creation that man should share in the heavenly community after first serving in the earthly community. Thus, repudiation of community is the repudiation of man's end and of his Creator. Egotism, therefore, is sin.

5. We have defined sin as the repudiation of community. One may ask why we call such repudiation sin. Why can it not be called simply evil? Why use the word "sin"? "Sin" is a word which we use solely in relation to God. If there were no God in the Christian sense, we would not be justified in using the word "sin." Naturalists and humanists do not like the term, and find little use for it. But we seem to have used it in a solely humanistic context. We have implied that we sin against people. Now, if we only sin against people, in what sense can we be said to sin against God? In short, in our personalistic definition of sin, what legitimate reason have we for using the word "sin" at all?

To answer this question we must recall one of the characteristics of personal relations, namely, that they form a nexus. We remarked how we could prefer one in a group of natural objects over another in the same group without disturbing the relations of the group with itself and with us. In personal relations, however, empirical facts tell us that such is not the case. We cannot like or abuse one person in a family without at the same time changing the relations between ourselves and the other members of the family. Further, by such an attachment to the outside on the part of one person in the family, the relations between members of the family itself are also changed.

All of these observations seem trivial. They are perfectly obvious to

34. Brunner, *Man in Revolt*, p. 98.

anyone. What they indicate, however, is that when we abuse one another, we sin because such an action is immediately set in some sort of a relation to God. A man cannot maltreat someone's wife without maltreating her husband. Likewise, we cannot use other people as means and tyrannize over them without immediately relating ourselves to God. Personal relations do not operate in a vacuum. A relation to one person affects the relations to others. Since it is the case that we are all related to God, by virtue of being persons in His image, it would seem to follow that an evil done to another becomes sin in our relation to God. The repudiation of another, the negation of community is therefore repudiation of God as well. Implied in the abuse of our neighbor is sin against God. If we were properly related to God, we would not sin against our neighbors. The *Imago Dei*, which allows for all our potentiality for good, makes all personal evil at once sin.

The nexus-like character of personal relations is clearly stated in the Gospels: "If therefore thou art offering thy gift at the altar, and there rememberest that thy brother hath aught against thee, leave there thy gift before the altar and go thy way, first be reconciled to thy brother and then come and offer thy gift."[35] "But if ye forgive not men their trespasses, neither will your Father forgive your trespasses."[36] "It were well for him if a millstone were hanged about his neck, and he were thrown into the sea rather than that he should cause one of these little ones to stumble."[37]

The fact that all personal relations form such a nexus makes a separation between religion and ethics impossible. What on the surface appears as an action purely in the ethical sphere possesses religious significance because God is sovereign of the community, and no ac-

35. Matthew 5:23–24.
36. Matthew 6:15.
37. Luke 17:2.

tion can be severed from relation with Him. There is no person who can escape this connection. By virtue of the Image he is claimed as belonging to community; and because God is the ultimate reference of community, all sin is sin in relation to God. Therefore, we have justified our usage of the word "sin," showing that although actions against our fellow men appear to operate solely in a humanistic context, they are in fact bound up into the relation to God. The classical definition of sin is consequently correct. All sin is rebellion against and repudiation of God, and therefore of the proper community which should exist between all persons and Him.

Section III

1. We have tried to explain what sin is. We have called it the repudiation and negation of community. The time has come for us to suggest the result of sin. We should ask ourselves, "What does sin lead to?" The answer to this question follows from our previous analysis. If man is a creature made in and for community, and if sin is the destruction of community, it follows that the consequence of sin is *aloneness.* To be alone is the most terrible, soul-racking state that the human person can fall into. This aloneness, this closedness, which shuts the individual person within himself, which isolates him from his fellows and which leaves him deserted amid the frenzied wreck of community, is the immediate result and the inevitable end of sin. If sin is destruction, the result is aloneness.

Aloneness means the death of the personality. "The soul that sinneth, it shall die."[38] Closedness is the death of spirit, because spirit is in its essence communal. It is communal by virtue of the *Imago Dei.* The *Imago Dei* is communal because God is communal, Three Persons in One, each equal with the other because that perfect commu-

38. Ezekiel 18:4.

nity is bound by that perfect love and faith, and love seeks equality with the person to whom its givenness is directed.[39] To destroy the community in which the human person is to live, is to destroy the nourishing-ground of his life. It results in a choking off of the Image in isolated aloneness and unmitigated despair.

Those scoffers at Christianity[40] who accuse it of saying that man is only weak and pitiful and therefore dependent on external help in times of need, have succeeded in missing the whole point. Man is not weak because he is man. Man as man, as an animal, is intelligent and crafty; he is master of the creation. That man is subject to nature in that he dies, needs food and shelter, is a useless truism. We all know that such is the case. The whole point of the Christian doctrine of man's dependence does not deal with his *physical* weakness at all. What it does deal with is the fact that man is dependent upon community, not because he is dust from dust, but because man is by nature a communal being. Man is dependent upon God because he is made in God's Image. Animals are not dependent on God. Man is dependent upon his brothers because his communal nature requires fellowship. Take a fish out of water and it dies; extract man from community and man dies likewise. Aloneness, to which sin leads, is that spiritual death on the border of which all of us sinful men live. This precipice is always at our side. Some of us have fallen over it; others of us sit along its side, dangling our feet over the space below.

T. S. Eliot has given us a statement of aloneness which I am tempted to quote in full:

> . . . only is here
> The white flat face of Death, God's silent servant,
> And behind the face of Death the Judgement

39. See Kierkegaard, *Philosophical Fragments,* p. 19 [revised edition, p. 31].
40. I refer to such thinkers as Nietzsche.

> And behind the Judgement the Void, more horrid than active shapes
>   of hell;
> Emptiness, absence, separation from God;
> The horror of the effortless journey, to the empty land
> Which is no land, only emptiness, absence, the Void,
> Where those who were men can no longer turn the mind
> To distraction, delusion, escape into dream, pretence
> Where the soul is no longer deceived, for there are no objects, no
>   tones,
> No colours, no forms to distract, to divert the soul
> From freeing itself, foully united forever, nothing with nothing,
> Not what we call death, but what beyond death is not death,
> We fear, we fear . . .[41]

The aloneness we speak of is spiritual aloneness; it is not something in nature. The natural man never feels aloneness.[42] We are locked up within ourselves, "foully united forever, nothing with nothing." We are bound to "nothing" because the end of egotism is to seek the self, merely to love the self. The end is indeterminate, vague, and therefore in poetic terms "nothing." The Greeks were right in saying that we were bound in a prison house. The prison house is, however, not the body, but the spirit, locked within itself by its own willful and perverse egotistic self-love.

Aloneness is the punishment of sin, the despair of closedness in the spirit reaping its own harvest. Accompanying this spiritual punishment is often pain in the form of wars, diseases, riots, murders and so forth, all of which spring from the destruction of community.

Aloneness is aloneness because the *Imago Dei* remains. God's likeness is never destroyed, merely covered up, defaced, repudiated; and yet despite this repudiation, the image remains and man is still communal. If such were not the case, then aloneness would be no punish-

---

41. *Murder in the Cathedral,* Part II, Scene I (p. 210).
42. See Kierkegaard, *The Sickness Unto Death* (Introduction), p. 14.

ment. If the Image were destroyed man would be an animal, a purely natural creature, and therefore no longer alone. Man tries to free himself from community. He drowns himself in distraction. But to no avail. Man is man; the image remains, and God still claims him from on high and will someday burst into his aloneness, shatter his closedness, and restore him to community.[43]

2. Before closing this chapter, we should note that there are two different kinds of aloneness: (a) egoistic aloneness and (b) egotistic aloneness.

(a) By egoistic aloneness we mean the aloneness of the personality in a world in which there are no personal relations, and in which all personal relations have been turned into natural relations. Such a world is the world envisaged by many thinkers varying widely in character and philosophy. The worlds of Plato, Aristotle, Epicurus, Augustine, Aquinas, Hobbes, Locke, modern evolutionism and psychological determinism are all worlds of egoistic aloneness. These are all proper-act, natural cosmos schemes of the type previously examined. The objects which are included in the systems vary. Some include such objects as God, the One, the Form of the Good; others restrict the objects to more mundane ones such as nature, beauty, food, drink, needs and so forth. For us, however, they are all the "natural cosmos," and therefore they can find no place for community, personality, and spirit. As a result the human person is alone in such a world. Community is lost, and life has lost its "meaning," since to live means to be in community.

We should all be ready to admit that the world as we know it is in practice a cosmos of egoistic aloneness. To admit this fact is to open one's eyes to the sin in the world. But to go on and say that such is the

---

43. The restoration of community is the subject of our final chapter.

"natural" and proper state of the world, and that the world will *always* be this way, is something we must never assert. Our world is a world of sin—yes; that it will forever be so—no. To accept this egoistic order of things as the normal order is to commit spiritual suicide. Personality can never live in an egoistic, natural, proper-act world. To make it live in such a world is to isolate it, choke it off, kill it.

Concerning this subject, Thomas Huxley had a number of things to say. Huxley is not a great thinker, but he saw one thing clearly, namely, that evolutionist and Darwinistic ethics had gotten off on the wrong track. In accenting the survival of the fittest, Spencer and Darwin had missed the problem of human society altogether. Huxley saw that sheer struggle was the way of nature, and that it was only by contradicting nature and only by forming societies that man had achieved what he has. "Laws and moral precepts are directed to the end of curbing the cosmic process and reminding the individual of his duty to the community, to the protection and influence of which he owes, if not existence itself, at least the life of something better than a savage. It is from neglect of these plain considerations that the fanatical individualism of our time attempts to apply the analogy of cosmic nature to society."[44]

Huxley would hardly draw the conclusions we draw; but he has clearly seen that nature is not communal, and that man lives bound into a scheme of relations of a different character from those of nature. He saw also that the world of pure nature extended to society meant the death of all that is personal, and therefore meant the death of man. To turn personal relations into natural relations is sin; in the face of a completely naturalized cosmos the human person is alone, isolated, and in despair. His own sin has created a world in which his

44. *Evolution and Ethics*, p. 82.

personality cannot find community, and therefore his existence has lost its meaning.[45]

The world of egoistic aloneness is the world in which all relations have been made natural by sin. Man never confronts persons, but only objects. In such a world he is lost, alone, out of place, unwanted. He is confused amidst the atoms, the impulses, the desires, the impersonal ends, the automatic drives of such a cosmos. Like a plant without rain, he must shrivel up and die, or else revolt.[46]

(b) The second kind of aloneness is egotistic aloneness. It is the aloneness resulting from pride, vainglory, demonic repudiation, envy, jealousy and so forth. Since egotism underlies all sin and since the turning of personal relations into natural relations is justified by pride of some sort, it follows that egoistic aloneness is accompanied by egotistic aloneness. Egoistic aloneness is the objective, external mask of egotistic aloneness.

Egotistic aloneness is aloneness in a different sort of cosmos. Egotism still preserves persons because pride makes no sense in an impersonal world. Hence egotism preserves personality in the world as a means to its own honor. There is no honor in being admired by objects. Therefore, the world of aloneness imagined by the egotist will be different from that imagined by sheer egoism. The egotist's world will be personal; it will not be natural. It will be demonic, forceful, violent perhaps, but never the automatic action of dead atoms or the natural striving of proper-acts. The egotist's world will be one of closed spiritual determination, of locked-inness. He will read the demonic out into the universe, and will thereby construct a blind and raving cosmos of aloneness. If what we have said sounds

---

45. Nazism may be considered as a revolt against the egoistic aloneness of capitalism and socialism. See Drucker, *The End of Economic Man.*

46. See note 45.

exaggerated, perhaps the following passage from Nietzsche will illustrate the point:

> And do you know what 'the universe' is to my mind? Shall I show it to you in my mirror? This universe is a monster of energy, without beginning or end ... It is energy everywhere, the play of forces and force-waves at the same time one and many, agglomerating here and diminishing there, a sea of forces, storming, staying in itself, forever changing, forever rolling back over incalculable ages to recurrence, with an ebb and flow of its forms, producing the most complicated things out of the most simple structures; producing the most ardent, most savage, and most contradictory things out of the quietest most rigid and most frozen material ... this, my Dionysian world of eternal self-destruction, this mysterious world of two-fold voluptuousness; this my 'Beyond Good and Evil,' without aim unless there is aim in the bliss of the circle, without will, unless a ring must by nature keep goodwill to itself,— would you have a name for my world? A *solution* of all your riddles? Do ye also want a light, ye most concealed, strongest and most undaunted men of the blackest midnight?—This world is the *Will to Power* and nothing else! And even ye yourselves are this will to power—and nothing besides![47]

Note first of all that this cosmos is not the cosmos of atomic movements proceeding according to the natural principle of causality. No, here we have the world of the demon, the monster, the spiritual beast. This picture of the cosmos is the egotist's ravings writ large. One finds the accent on power, force, will, rage, creative frenzy and the like. This world is one of aloneness because it is completely self-centered. It revolves around itself in a circle. It has no aims, no purpose, no goal, unless, as Nietzsche says, to move in a circle is an aim. The chain of spiritual determination is a closed one, evolving and whirling madly out of itself. The world is the gigantic monster, the Will to Power.

Nietzsche has presented us with the inner workings of the egotist

---

47. Nietzsche, *The Will to Power,* sec. 1067.

raving in his aloneness. The world he lives in is the world above, the world of the monster. Community has been destroyed, the world has become demonic, forces madly whirl themselves, and the spirit exhausts itself frantically in its self-created aloneness. This is the result of sin which is truly sin. Such a spiritual state is a prelude to death, to spiritual nihilism. The end is in sight; the shattering against the bottom of the abyss is swiftly approaching. Aloneness has ended in death.

chapter five

The Meaning of Faith

Section I

1. In this chapter we want to discuss the meaning of faith and the fruits of personality which grow out of faith. Such a discussion is the complement to the chapter on the meaning of sin. As sin is the separation from and the destruction of community and therefore of personality, so is faith the integration into and the reconstruction of community. The proper antithesis is between sin and faith. Sin is that closedness which bears the fruits of wicked actions, whereas faith is that openness which flowers into the complete fullness of communal life.

2. The problem, then, arises as to how the sinner is to be converted to the man of faith. This is the problem of salvation. When we ask "how is man to be saved," we mean simply how is man to be restored to community; how is he to be won from closedness to openness; and how is the visible human community to be incorporated into the community of all persons of which it is a part, and finally to God who is Sovereign of the Universe. In short, the problem of salvation is a communal and a personal problem, and therefore salvation is a spiritual process at its very heart.

That salvation is such a problem is a correlate to what we have said previously about man. Man is a personal and communal being, and this communality and personality constitutes the truly distinctive thing about man as opposed to the other animals which man sees in nature. Further, human nature is not personal and communal at its outer crust, but communality forms the core of man's being. Man's sociality did not come about as some measure of expediency in the process of evolution or as some further attribute to be tacked on to an already developed human nature. Communality is therefore not a by-product of natural forces or of agreements for mutual advantage, but is that which constitutes the inner essence of man's being and of all those beings to whom he is so intimately related.

Therefore the problem of salvation is a problem dealing with personality and community, not a problem dealing with man's natural aspect as such. Insofar as man possesses an appetitional nature, that nature must be integrated into the full plenitude of his personal being. But the process of salvation cannot begin from his appetitional and natural aspect. Rather, it must begin at the very root of his being, at its very core, and once this inner essence of man has been won, then the rest of his nature can be restored to order. The problem of salvation is to win the inside of personality, and then "turn it inside out."

Since the problem of salvation is a personal and communal problem, it follows that the agency of salvation must likewise be personal and communal. There is no question of strict logic in this deduction, but the more we view experience, the more we see that the deduction is true to experience. In short, if we examine our experience we can discover that the only action which can solve our personal problems is personal action, i.e., action by another person together with ourselves. We cannot solve our personal problems by natural methods and by the regulation of our impersonal natures. Personality can be restored only by personality, and community only by community. It is this truth which condemns most modern methods as superficial, since the modern way is to seek the agency of salvation in economic reform and in the education of intelligence. As useful as these methods may be, they are a long way from being sufficient. They fail to realize that the agency of salvation must be personal and communal. It will be incumbent upon us to show why the personal agency must come from another person, from the "other," and therefore show the Christian truth that man alone cannot save himself.[1]

In summary, then, we conclude that the problem of salvation is personal and communal because man is personal and communal by nature, and further that the agency of salvation must likewise be personal and communal. With these three statements always in mind, we shall be able to understand what the process of salvation and conversion really is and what is the nature of its goal.

3. Before passing on in detail to our own account, we shall discuss briefly a few other views on the matter. In this way we shall clarify what we mean by salvation.

(i) First of all, there is the view which we have already discussed at some length, namely, the view of naturalistic thinkers. For them, as we have seen, salvation is that process in which the appetitional aspirations of nature are turned to their proper objects. The good life consists in directing the desires to the right channels of impulse and action. Therefore for this view the problem of salvation is a natural problem, a problem of purifying appetitions, of seeking and guiding desires, and of fulfilling and completing the natural nature as a whole. We reject this view because it is superficial, and it is superficial because it has no place for the inner essence of man's being—his personality and communality. It makes no difference for us whether the

---

1. The argument of Section II is to show this truth.

philosopher in question is Christian or pagan. Augustine errs on this point just as severely as Plato, and Aquinas as much as Aristotle.

(ii) There is also a view of salvation prevalent in our modern world which identifies salvation with economic reform. This view has a long history. It begins definitely with Locke, however, who considered the chief aim of the social contract as the protection of private property. Thus, the chief end of society was somehow economic. This idea develops down through Adam Smith, Malthus, Ricardo, and Cobden until Marx makes everything depend upon it. In rejecting this theory, we do not want to reject many valuable insights which it has given us. Men do act for economic ends, and no one cares to deny this truth. Man is not, however, primarily an economic creature, and so all-pervasive is the non-economic element in man that it often rises up not only to overthrow the predictions of the economist, but to seep into the entire economic structure and to corrupt it with the sin of egotism.

(iii) Among the other superficial views of modern times is the view that man is a biological animal and therefore his salvation consists in making him more animal-like. The scientific theory of the survival of the fittest gave considerable support to this theory, although it was already suggested to people of the time by the economic struggle. Business literally became the survival of the fittest. Advocates of this biological theory have all sorts of methods to bring Utopia about. One of the most superficial of these is eugenics. The program is to sterilize, to discourage and to encourage according to the breeding possibilities of each person. Nazism is a combination of this method with German mental and emotional obscurantism mixed with egotism and despair. Another method to restore man to health has been suggested by the Freudians. The aim is to give all our appetitions a free play. We are told that there is no neurosis where there is a normal sex life. We reject this biological conception of man for the same reason that we have rejected the two already mentioned. The fact is that man is not biological, but communal; he is not an animal but a person.

(iv) Nazism really is a profound theory of man compared to many other modern theories. It far surpasses the theory of economic man and that of biological man in understanding human nature. Nazism and fascism understand that man is something different from the animals, something different from a pure businessman. For the other views they substitute the view that man is heroic; he is the saint, the champion, the warrior, and the soldier.[2] We reject any such theory as being one which caters to sin. Nazism thrives on the fact that there is sin in the world. Its appeal is to egotism. This fact accounts for the tremendous power of the movement. It realizes that man is somehow spirit and not an animal of pure appetition. Nazism is profound, but profound in the sense that the devil is profound. It is conscious of spirituality, but it knows only the spirituality of egotism which leads to destruction. Therefore the Nazi method of salvation is in the end self-destruction, since it bases itself upon sin which leads to aloneness and annihilation.

If we cared to, we could mention other modern theories of salvation, such as the escape to nature theory of Rousseau, the guidance by intelligence advocated by Dewey, and so forth. To do so would be to extend our argument needlessly. What we want to point out is that few modern theories are profound because they do not see the real underlying and crucial problems. They see only the difficulties that are objectively manifest in society. Economic theories like Communism clearly note the abuses rampant in our social system; Dewey ob-

---

2. A classic statement is by Mussolini, "The Political and Social Doctrine of Fascism."

serves keenly the lack of intelligent cooperation and enterprise. All these theories, however, fail to penetrate to the central core of the problem which is, as we have said, the problem of establishing community.

4. These modern methods fail to see the real difficulty because they are based on superficial anthropologies. Unless we know what man is, there is little sense in discussing the problem of his salvation. Therefore the first problem of ethical theory is to inquire into the nature of man himself. Moral philosophers would do much better if they undertook an anthropological analysis before doing anything else. Unless we understand ourselves, all discussions of the good and the right are left in the air, and hover idly detached from reality. For this reason we have stressed throughout the personality and communality of man, and have repeatedly stated, almost to the point of becoming labored, that such is man's nature. We stress this point because it is at once so simple and yet so easy to forget. Although Christianity is said by all to be a very simple religion, it is surprising how few people understand it.

5. We can now proceed to clear away some of the debris which clutters up discussions on the subject of salvation. We reject two concepts.

(i) The first concept to go, as we have already suggested, is the concept of the good as an object of desire. We maintain that objects of desire have nothing to do with salvation whatsoever except insofar as they are part of man's natural nature, which receives its due only after personality and community have been set in order. Community in the full sense, that is, the heavenly community, is the end in itself. It is the goal of creation, and while it may be true that man's natural being is fulfilled therein, such fulfillment is secondary to the community itself. Therefore, all of the terms of the natural cosmos will be banished from our discussion. Among such terms are: appetition, desire, objects, needs, wants, impulses, instincts, and so forth.

(ii) The second concept that goes by the board is the concept of will. The rejection of this concept is a difficult step to take because it has long been a favorite notion with many theologians, but we are going to reject it for the following reasons: (a) It is a concept which is identified with the natural cosmos. This identification is accidental, perhaps, but the fact remains that Aquinas explicitly defined it as that which chooses the good. For Augustine, it meant the same thing. Therefore the concept has become a favorite term of the naturalistic view. For this reason, the concept is dangerous for us. (b) Secondly, and this objection is the most serious, the concept is misleading in that it is a false representation of personal experience. Personality is not a thing that wills. It is more appropriate to say that our natural nature wills.

This point may seem obscure; hence, the following contrasts are designed to illuminate what we mean. Our natural natures are frustrated, but as persons we are disappointed; appetitions are satisfied, as persons we are happy and joyful; impulses and instincts in a sense drive us forward, but personality longs; and whereas nature hunts, personality seeks. If the above phrases capture the distinctiveness of the spiritual nature as opposed to the natural nature, then "will" is more applicable to the natural aspect of us rather than the spiritual.

The result of this recognition of the inadequacy of the concept "will" is to be cognizant of the fact that the spiritual presence is that ineffable distinctiveness of personal consciousness. As opposed to nature, the spirit is in a sense delicate, and intangible; it hopes and enjoys, sorrows and longs in an unconcrete and almost indeterminant way. Even when the spirit sins and appears powerfully demonic even to itself, it is aware of its vulnerability. The above discussion is obscure and vague, and for that reason we should not make too much of it. Nevertheless, the traditional concept of will as that which chooses the good is somewhat unfortunate. Further, the traditional discussions of the problem on the part of Augustine and Aquinas are of little value to us. They did not come to grips with the problem of "free will" as we know it today; and if the concept is employed in the naturalistic sense, it will only obscure the argument. Therefore, it seems that the best thing to do is to drop the concept altogether or to redefine it in some way suitable to the realm of personality. We have chosen the former alternative.

6. We close this section with the frank admission that our results are negative. All that has been accomplished is the statement of the problem of salvation as opposed to false statements. In addition, we have denied that certain concepts are germane to the discussion. The task now before us is to elaborate in brief detail what is the meaning of conversion and faith. The thread is once again picked up where it was temporarily dropped at the end of our last chapter. Sin, we found, leads to aloneness, and aloneness is the equivalent of death. Whatever death means to many, for us it implies separation from community. If we think about death, we see that what we really mean by it is separation. For when we imagine ourselves as dead, we at the same time picture ourselves as no longer a member of the community. Therefore, the problem is how can this "dead" man, this sinner, be restored to community, and how can it be that a group of "dead" men can be brought back to life to form a community? How can mankind, wrapped up within the closed circle of egotistical self-worship, be "torn open" and reintegrated to community? To answer this question

is now our problem, and the answer must come in those terms in which the question is stated, namely in terms of personality and community.

Section II

1. In this section we want to describe the inner state of the man who is a sinner, and the psychological obstacles which prevent him from entering, by his own efforts, into community. This state is what we want to call the period of the "barrier." When the sinner, dependent on his own efforts, tries to restore himself to community, he finds obstacles and obstructions clogging the path of his actions. He suddenly finds that he has lost his personal spontaneity of action (not to be confused with "free will"). His life is blocked up within himself, and all attempts to establish community with another end in disappointment and failure. The upshot is that he cannot save himself alone; salvation is a communal process and cannot be achieved from one side only. Since man is estranged from God as well as from himself, the personal problem of establishing community raises itself in an extremely acute form.

Assuming, therefore, that the state of the sinner is one of egotistical aloneness, and that he is locked within himself, what will be the barriers that block his efforts in restoring community? What will be those walls which cement the alienation of man from God?

2. The first barrier which alienates man from God is the inner state of tension which springs from knowledge of the offense. No matter how deep man thrusts himself into sin, and no matter how far separated he is from community, he finds himself in a state of tension once he attempts to return to community. He may have felt that he no longer possessed a conscience, he may have believed that he was strong and independent and aloof, but once he tries to return, once

he tries to re-establish genuine fellowship with another, he finds himself in what we have termed a state of tension. Such a person is uneasy in his actions, perhaps too forward or too backward; his inner state is one of confusion and uncertainty. He knows that he has offended, but he does not know the degree of his sin. Or did the other person even know of his offense? Is he not being over-sensitive in worrying about his sin? He thinks perhaps that the "other" has not noticed his offense. But then he is not sure. As a result the knowledge of the offense, which presents itself immediately to the isolated personality on attempting to return by its own efforts to community—this knowledge of offense throws the self into a state of confusion, uncertainty, and tension.

This tension is the immediate barrier between man and God, and between man and man. It accounts for many of our uneasy and hesitant actions, for many embarrassing and tense situations. In relation of man to God it becomes a primary difficulty. What does God think? Does He know sin, and if He does, what does He think? All of these questions, coupled with the inner tension, go to construct a complex of feelings which render spontaneity and fullness of action impossible. The first barrier, then, lies in the core of the sinner himself. The very root of his being is disturbed and anxious. At the very depths of his soul, he is uneasy and uncertain. He longs for community, and yet within him the knowledge of offense creates a limbo of suspicious anxiety which renders his attempts futile. He still remains locked within himself; for all his efforts, he is still alone.

Thus, man's sin which leads him to aloneness follows him on his attempt to return to community. His offense throws him into a state of anxiety and tension. This anxiety is a further result of sin. It is the way that sin roots itself into the personality and overthrows all efforts to re-establish community.

3. The second great barrier is ignorance. Imagine the person who seeks to re-establish community and who receives no response from the "other." Suppose that throughout all our efforts the "other" remains silent and makes no answer, then what can we do? If the other person makes no disclosure on his own part, then our efforts are certain to fail. Yet this condition of affairs is precisely that in which man finds himself unless God reveals Himself. Man seeks in his misguided way to restore himself to God, but not only is he anxious but he is ignorant. God does not answer his cry. The seasons come and go, the sun shines, the rain falls, the way of nature continues along its unchanging way. God has remained silent.

How ignorant is man before the silence of God! What can man do, what can he know? Added to the burden of his aloneness is the weight of his ignorance. He knocks in despair at the door of the universe; he pleads before God but he receives no answer. He is not only alone, but he lives in the unknown.

Man's intelligence cannot come to his rescue in this situation. Natural theology is helpless before the personality of God. Why? Because all knowledge of other persons is knowledge given to us by them. Personal knowledge is revealed knowledge. It comes about through communication in community. Natural objects immediately disclose their nature; but persons must consent to communicate knowledge of themselves. Therefore by reason man can know very little about God. Even assuming that some traditional arguments for God's existence are valid, they tell us nothing about His person. They can tell us perhaps that He is intelligent, that He is powerful, and that He is eternal. These arguments cannot tell us more. God still remains the great unknown, and before Him, man lies in blindness and ignorance.

Therefore, man must wait for God to speak to him. He must wait for His word. He of his own efforts cannot pry into the inexhaustible secrecy of God's own self. So man's natural knowledge ends in hunger for knowledge of God Himself. It is no cure for man's longing aloneness if he is told merely that God is, and that His majesty rules the heavens. Man wants to know something about God Himself. What does He think, how does He act? Is He angry, does He punish? Since man is personality, he must know something about God's own personality. Man seeks not to pry into His privacy, or at least he should not; but he does seek to know *something* of His person. Man must have this knowledge of God before he can be restored. If the "other" does not reveal itself, then the establishment of community must end in failure. Such knowledge of God can come only from God: "For what human being can understand a man's thoughts, except the man's own spirit within him? Just so no one understands the thoughts of God but the spirit of God."[3]

Thus added to man's anxiety is his ignorance. Before God he is not only anxious but unknowing. As he calls out to God, even the most sincere of his efforts go unheeded. Nature still presents the awful face of unchanging silence. This ignorance chains man further within his aloneness. The secret of God remains unknown, and man is still isolated and alienated. The sting of aloneness is now God's silence; man is cut off from His word. The emptiness of silence can only be filled by the Word, which only He can give.

4. As a result of the above two barriers man constructs a third barrier for himself, namely, the barrier of the false conception. Man reads his own feelings and his own sin into the secret life of God. He imagines God as angry, and he lives within himself the life of a man trembling and fearful before the God of wrath. The misfortunes in the world, which are really the result of sin, he imagines as the result of God's active punishment. Thus, the sinner imagines himself as punished,

3. 1 Corinthians 2:11.

and he imagines God as angry. He thus lives burdened by the fear of God.

The belief that God is angry is a result both of man's ignorance and of reading his own fallen nature into the nature of God. We should, therefore, never make this mistake of conceiving God as angry. Paul shows great profundity on this point. For Paul it was proper to say that God is loving, merciful, righteous, just, and so forth, but he never anywhere in his writings makes God the subject of the verb "to be angry." He makes frequent use of the theological concept of "wrath," but he uses it in a subtle and impersonal way. Wrath, for Paul, means the objective process of sin working its own retribution in the world. Wrath is the consequence and effect of human sin; it is the punishment of sin upon itself.[4] Therefore to experience the wrath of God is not to fall into His hands and to be actively punished by Him; but it is rather to fall out of His hands, and to be left within the aloneness of sin which works towards its own desolation. Wrath, as Paul uses the term, is thus the process by which sin punishes itself and brings about its own retribution. When Paul says that "God's anger is revealed from heaven against all the impiety and wickedness of those who hinder the Truth by their wickedness,"[5] he means that "God has given them up"[6] and has allowed sin to reap its own harvest. Wrath is not the attitude of God to man, but the inevitable effect of sin in the world.

The sinner, however, does not possess the wisdom of Paul. He therefore imagines that God in His person is angry. He thus constructs an insuperable barrier between himself and God. Added to the previous difficulties, this third barrier has created a desperate situation.

There is also another way in which man can read his own nature

4. C. H. Dodd, *The Epistle of Paul to the Romans*, pp. 21–23.
5. Romans 1:18.
6. Romans 1:24.

into God, and that is to imagine God as indifferent. God is not considered as angry, but He is pictured as being aloof. Such a God is that of the "Uranian" or silent and complacent egotist. A perfect example of this type of conception is to be found in Aristotle, who pictures God as a being who contemplates His own perfection with nary a squint at the rest of the world.[7] This conception likewise interjects an unconquerable barrier between man and God. Man will surely fail to establish community if he imagines God as a glorified egotist.

Therefore, the third barrier consists of a false conception of God, the conception of wrath or the conception of indifference. Added to the barrier of ignorance and that of tension is now the barrier of the false conception, which is rooted in man's fallen nature. Man imagines God in terms of himself, i.e., in the terms of sin.

5. Out of the barrier of the false conception (especially the concept of wrath) grows the barrier of the bargain basis. This manifests itself in the barrier of legalism in religion and in contract theories in politics. They both spring from a lack of trust and faith, and therefore the scheme of the bargain is a method used by the sinner to bind the "other" and to protect his own self. Bargaining springs from fear, and fear is the most self-centering of all the emotions. Thus, to use the method of legalism is to thrust us further into aloneness and separation.

To make clear what we mean we shall briefly inquire into the political theory of Hobbes, for nowhere in political thought is the fear which underlies the contract theory better exposed. Hobbes's basic assumption is a radical individualism. Society for him is atomic, an aggregate of individuals. But Hobbes goes beyond mere atomism; he gives a description of the inner nature of these "atoms." He tells us

7. *Metaphysics,* bk. XII.

that men are not born fit for society, and that men are not social as such. Men therefore do not seek society for its own sake, but for the purpose of gaining something from it, namely, honor and profit. Society is either for gain or for glory. The "atoms" of this society are not "casual" atoms, but are bundles of greed and vainglory. All men by nature desire to hunt and injure each other for reasons of vaunting oneself over another or for the sake of egoistic gain. Therefore men construct societies not from goodwill but from mutual fear. He writes: "We must therefore resolve, that the origin of all great and lasting societies consisted not in the mutual goodwill men had towards each other, but in the mutual fear they had of each other."[8]

Men, even in the best society, live in a state of suspicion: "They who go to sleep, shut their doors; they who travel, carry their swords with them, because they fear thieves. Kingdoms guard their coasts and frontiers with forts and castles; cities are compact with walls; and all for fear of neighboring kingdoms and towns."[9] Thus the natural state of man is the war of every man against every man, and life is of a "nasty, brutish"[10] sort. To end this miserable state of affairs men establish a common power to overawe them, which process is to the mutual advantage of all. Thus the contract is established on the bargain basis. "The final cause, end, or design of men, who naturally love liberty, and dominion over others, in the introduction of that restraint upon themselves, in which we see them live in commonwealths, is the foresight of their own preservation, and of a more contented life thereby. . . . [and the overawing power is to] tie them by fear of punishment to the performance of their covenants, and the observation of . . . [the] laws of nature."[11]

8. Thomas Hobbes, *De Cive,* ch. I, sec. 2.
9. Ibid.
10. Thomas Hobbes, *Leviathan,* ch. XIII.
11. Ibid., ch. XVII.

Thus we arrive at the bargain-contract society, but we should note that it is no community at all for the following reasons: (a) first and most obvious, it is a scheme of mutual advantage which uses society as means only; (b) second and most important, the members of this society live in fear and suspicion of one another. But fear, as William Temple remarks, is the most self-centering of all the emotions,[12] and consequently no community is established at all. For nothing perhaps will disrupt society quicker than mutual fear. If men cannot trust one another, then community immediately dissolves. To attempt to establish community by fear is therefore self-defeating.

The same bargain process can be carried over into religion. Men try to placate the God of Wrath which they have constructed in their darkened minds. By doing good works, they hope to escape His punishment. They try to bind Him and attempt to bargain with Him. Thus there is in any "merit" scheme of salvation a manifest lack of faith. This point has been seldom noted. Pelagianism and its "semi" varieties are usually interpreted as man's attempt to claim his freedom and to assert his ability to act virtuously. Although this interpretation contains some truth which is not to be denied, the real core of Pelagian falsity is a lack of faith and trust. Man wants to flaunt some merit before the decisions of the divine election; he wants to control that election by merit because he does not trust the elector. He shudders when he hears other men speak of election; he is afraid because he lacks faith. Little does he know that the elector is most just and merciful; but picturing to himself the God of Wrath, he tries to determine his destiny, he tries to seek reward by some merit or by some indulgence. When the indulgence complex is examined, it will reveal a lack of faith and an inner state of fear.

Therefore Christians should not seek to bind election by merit.

12. *Nature, Man and God*, p. 460.

Why? Because, as we shall see later, merit is beside the point in establishing community. Faith bears the fruit of good deeds and fellowship; but you can never establish faith by claiming good deeds beforehand. We must accept the absolute preveniency of God's election; we can accept it without fear because we have heard His Word. We know that His election will be just. We have no fear because His love has driven out fear.

Thus the reward-merit scheme is just another barrier which man constructs between himself and God, and between himself and other men. Even in the face of God's Word manifest in the Cross, man insists on holding on to his vain conceptions. So great is his error that he can even construct the Cross as a new law and as a new rule to be obeyed and rewarded. Man falls into these errors because he is alone and alienated. He does not yet understand the real nature of community. As we shall see later, the errors which infect traditional doctrines of election arise by attacking the problem from the standpoint of individualism. Misunderstandings of election proceed therefore from the barriers constructed by sin.

6. Lying beneath all these barriers, there still remains the sin of egotism. Man has not escaped his closedness, and therefore pride is still with him. He is not yet open but is closed up within himself. Thus sin continues to infect all his efforts, and dooms his strivings to failure.

The best example of the infection of sin in man's efforts to save himself is the pride of those who think they have been successful at the bargain scheme of redemption. In the Epistle to the Romans, Paul speaks severely of those who pride themselves on being upholders of the law. He attacks those who pride themselves on their good works, and he criticizes the Jews as strongly as the Gentiles. The Jew finds compensation in bearing the name of Jew; he relies upon the law, considers himself a "guide to the blind" and "a light to darkened souls."[13] Paul himself had experienced the pride of the Jew in his pre-Christian days. He tells us how he strived to be "immaculate by the standard of legal righteousness."[14] Paul after his conversion came to realize that the ideal of his religious endeavors had been at bottom the sinful attitude of boastful self-confidence.[15] The Apostle knew how easily legal righteousness comes to be infected by pride. He knew that the best efforts in Judaism were so corrupted—not the worst, but the best. So, even in the most intense religious endeavor we find the sin of pride casting us once again back into aloneness. The same can be said for legal righteousness wherever it is found, and unfortunately it is still with us. Man cannot allow any merit for himself. If Pelagianism is marked by a lack of faith, it is also condemned by its pride.

Therefore the sin of pride and silent self-satisfaction inheres in all efforts on man's part to save himself. The sinner not only has to contend against the barriers between him and the "other," but at every point his egotism comes in and destroys his efforts. Sin constructs the barriers; sin corrupts all attempts to overcome them. Man is locked off from without and bound from within.

7. As a result we conclude that man alone cannot save himself. He cannot save himself because all salvation implies community, and after sin, community can only be reestablished by God. The sinner himself is helpless, as we have tried to show. Therefore, salvation depends on God. If He holds back His word, then man must continue in his blindness and in his aloneness. Man lies at the mercy of God, although in his egotistical closedness he does not know that he lies at His mercy. His pride tells him that he possesses power on his own

13. Romans 2:19.
14. Philippians 3:6.
15. See Dodd, *Epistle of Paul to the Romans*, p. 62.

part. Therein is the source of his pride and the cause of his failure. This false fabrication of sin is weak, however, and before the penetratingness of the Word, it dissolves.

Before closing this section we should remark on the nature of our analysis. We have examined the problem in terms of community and personality, not in terms of the bondage of the will to wrong objects, or in terms of improper desires. Man's natural nature is not bound; there is no loss of freedom in the will in regard to its choice of objects. The approach of the natural cosmos is false; it misses the heart of the matter. Where freedom is lost is in the sphere of personal relations. Man is no longer free before God in the sense that he is open to God. But this loss of freedom does not spring from some peculiar physical defect such as concupiscence, but arises from the character of personal relations. Natural freedom remains, but spiritual freedom has been destroyed. No longer does man have the spontaneous openness of the community. Man is bound, yes—but not by nature, but by the closedness of his spirit.

Section III

1. Christianity has asserted that there are times when something very peculiar happens to the sinner, and this experience has been termed by theologians "conversion." In this section we want to inquire into the meaning of conversion and to try to uncover its basic rationale. To most people the word "conversion" signifies some odd type of experience, and they are inclined to say that "converts" are mystics. We think that the identification of conversion with mysticism is unfortunate, and that there is nothing mystical about conversion. Although it is an intense experience, it is not one which defies reason. On the contrary, it can be explained in terms of community; it yields itself to analysis and in fact it gives full intelligible meaning to experience. It does not defy the mind, but clarifies it.

2. What is the experience of conversion? Conversion is that intense experience of lying in exposure before the Word of God. Revelation is the Word of God speaking to us;[16] conversion is that experience in which the Word of God breaks into the closedness of sin and bends back its walls. Revelation is God's action; it is His coming to us and speaking to us; it is His presence bursting into the aloneness of sin. Conversion experience is the experience of sin during this bursting in on the part of God. Thus there is a dialectical quality about conversion. In a sense it represents a double action—a bursting in and a bending back, a being burst in upon and being bent back. God is above, man is below; God shows His power, man manifests his weakness; God reveals His love, man exposes his sin; God acts in His justice, man is torn open in his perfidy. Thus, conversion experience is the intense experience of contrast. The openness of God and the closedness of man are set side by side, and before the contrast sin dissolves into flatness.

Before presenting a more detailed analysis of the experience of lying in exposure, or conversion, we should make a few remarks about the importance and nature of this step in Christian experience.

(i) It is undoubtedly true that a full understanding of conversion is absolutely essential for the understanding of Christianity. This experience has been the true source of the doctrine of election, and all such doctrines which do not spring straight from it are purely academic. Therefore conversion is crucial because its character constitutes the womb of Christian theology. It is in this experience that Revelation, Sin, and Faith achieve their full meaning and contrast.

(ii) Conversion therefore constitutes the synthesis of Christian experience. The real unity of the New Testament lies not in the Gospels, nor in the Epistles of Paul, but in the book of Acts. The Gospels repre-

16. See Brunner, *Theology of Crisis,* p. 32.

sent the Word; Christ is the Revelation of the Word; and the Cross is the symbol of the Word. The Epistles of Paul and of the other Apostles represent the answer to the Word, the acceptance of the Word and the life of Word in the hearts of the new community. In Acts, however, we are presented with the double action at its climax—the Word as it converts, the Word as it bursts into the aloneness of sin of the world and restores it. Generalize the story of Paul on the road to Damascus, and therein lies the crux of the New Testament. On the road to Damascus the double action was united. The Cross dissolved sin and restored faith. The missions, the establishment of new churches, and the spread of the "good news" by the Apostles represent the Word accomplishing its task of restoration and fulfilling its intention, which is the re-establishment of that community which is ultimately to be present with Him throughout all ages.

(iii) Further, we should note that there is a certain difficulty in examining conversion experience. Although it possesses a certain dialectic, i.e., the dialectic of contrast, conversion is at the same time a formless and indeterminate kind of experience. Everything dissolves, so to speak, and there results a quality of flatness or what we have called lying in exposure. The experience is difficult to describe from the outside, and often its meaning can be best explained by what has gone before and by what is to follow. Wherever necessary we shall speak of conversion in terms of what it follows and what it precedes.

(iv) Conversion is not necessarily a sudden experience. It need not take place so quickly, as in the case of Paul. We must remember that Paul's election was of a most marvelous sort, since Paul was given special authority and called for an important task. Therefore his conversion was of a sudden and instant-like character. But others of us are converted over a much longer space of time. We live in the dim presence of lying in exposure; the Word lies on the border-consciousness of our actions. Therefore the process may be gradual, as it usually is; or it may be sudden. In either case, conversion experience has the same quality. Whereas for Paul the contrast was immediate and compelling, for us it is hesitant and groping. Whereas the Apostle "dissolved" all at once, we live for many months with the uneasy awareness of being "dissolved." Therefore there should be no sharp contrast between the once-born and the twice-born, if by the latter we mean those marvelously chosen like the Apostles. If any of us examine our experience, and if that experience is genuinely Christian, then we should all agree. Although we may have never experienced a sudden conversion like Paul's, we can nevertheless understand Paul and agree with him.

3. The first characteristic to be noted about conversion experience is its flatness. Conversion is the experience of being spread out and bent open. It has the quality of complete exposure before the other "from whom no secrets are hid." Conversion has this quality of being dissolved, of being shattered and of being made weak. It is a time when the spirit is made helpless before the other. It is a time of sobbing, of bowed heads, of the arms hanging loosely alongside the body; of inner remorse and acute pangs of conscience. Before God the spirit is simply lying open, bowed down and exposed. The spirit has nothing to say; it can offer no complaint. There is no loud wailing, no shouting, no crying. The person is simply ripped open; he is exposed, naked. There is nothing more to be said.

The Bible is marvelously clear on this point. Take for example the denial of Peter. The Lord has told him that he would deny Him three times. Peter denied that he would ever deny his Lord, but true to prophecy Peter was wrong. After the trial one of the maids of the high priest, seeing Peter, said to him that he was one of Jesus' disciples, but Peter denied the accusation. She said the same twice again but still Peter denied the charge, "and straightway the second time the cock crew. And Peter called to mind the word, how that Jesus said unto him, Before the cock crow twice, thou shall deny me thrice. And when he thought thereon, he wept."[17] Peter makes no complaint, for he knows that he can say nothing. Christ's words have been revealed to him in all their fullness, and the contrast with himself leaves him speechless.

The conversion of Paul is a perfect example of being "struck dumb." "But on his journey, as he was approaching Damascus, a sudden light flashed around him from heaven and he fell to the ground. Then he heard a voice saying to him, 'Saul! Saul! Why do you persecute me?' 'Who are you sir?' he asked. 'I am Jesus, whom you are persecuting,' said the voice. 'But get up and go into the city, and there you will be told what you ought to do.' Saul's fellow travelers stood speechless, for they heard the voice but could not see anyone. When he got up from the ground and opened his eyes he could see nothing. They had to take him by the hand and lead him into Damascus, and for three days he could not see, and neither ate nor drank."[18]

Note the wording of the last sentence of the passage and how clearly it expresses the whole tenor of Paul's feelings. Paul says nothing; he has no answer. There is no shouting, no wailing. Paul goes to Damascus for three days and does not touch food or drink. His eyes are darkened, he can see nothing. This description of lying in exposure is perfect. It conveys what Paul felt—his complete abjection, his acute remorse, his sorrow, his repentance, his exposure before the mercy of God. These are the three most crucially important days in Paul's life, and about them we are told nothing except that Paul did not eat or drink, and that he was blind. The sparsity of description represents the depth and fullness of the experience. There are no fit descriptions

17. Mark 14:72.
18. Acts 9:3–9.

to describe Paul's state, but "by their fruits you shall know them," and no experience bore greater fruit than the Apostle's three days in Damascus.

Thus "flatness" is the first characteristic of the conversion experience to be noted. It is marked by a certain bending-backness, as a penetrating feeling of exposure, a sensitive perception of lying before the "other" and being bowed down in remorse.

4. The conversion experience is marked by an acutely intense contrast between the wickedness of the self and the bounteous mercy of God. The gracious love of God works itself into the egotistical self-love of sin. Absolute goodness and absolute evil, so to speak, rest side by side; and the good is working to redeem and to call back the bad. Mercy meets sin, and overcomes it; and in the heart of the sinner the contrast between the goodness of God and the wickedness of the self is overwhelming. God's bounteous mercy is staked against Paul's consuming wickedness. For Paul was "still breathing murderous threats against the Lord's disciples,"[19] and he was still the proud Pharisee priding himself on his own righteousness in obeying the law, and therefore he was not deserving of the Lord's mercy. But, nevertheless, God elected him in the moment of his rebellion against Him. Christ was true to His word: "For if ye love them that love you, what reward have ye? do not even the publicans the same? And if ye salute your brethren only, what do ye more than others? do not even the Gentiles do the same?"[20] Thus the principle of the Sermon on the Mount, which is at its core the principle of acting on the analogy of God's free and bounteous grace, is incarnate in the election of Paul. God seeks those who do not love Him, and He elects those who breathe fire and

19. Acts 9:1.
20. Matthew 5:46–47.

anger against Him. Paul himself perceived this contrast in all its clarity—the contrast between God's mercy as against his own iniquity; and from this perception follows the dissolution of his own sin. The obstructions and the barriers of sin and the whole fabrication of egotism crumble into the flatness of exposure. Before the mercy of God, and in stinging contrast to his sin, Paul is broken and helpless, speechless even before himself.

5. Although Paul is "dissolved," Paul still lives. Paul struck dumbfounded, bowed down before God, is nevertheless still Paul. His person notwithstanding its brokenness continues to hang together; and the existence of his spirit seems to be carried along by support from outside himself. No doubt in his remorse Paul wishes to die, to pass out of existence, to escape, even if it be by death, from his shame. Yet he still lives, he is still borne along. It is perhaps this continuance of the self amidst its dissolution that makes the sinner aware of his dependence upon community and upon God. For the first time the scales of sin have been broken away, and the self perceives that every thing in heaven and on earth is a gift of God and that every minute of its own life is likewise given. Thus, the self is prepared to see givenness wherever it is found. The human person recognizes that every thing he has received is a gift and that he has nothing that had not been given to him. His parents have raised him, his friends have helped him; the land provides him with food and nature succors his life. Behind all these earthly gifts he can now see that the totality of what he has possessed and enjoyed has been the gift of God. He now understands his communal nature, and he perceives that the sin of pride is to destroy community. Out of the feeling of being dissolved there thus grows this perception of givenness, of the bounteous mercy and love of God which gives even in the face of denial, and the understanding of dependence upon God.

It is in this way that the Word in breaking down the fabrications of sin reveals itself. It reveals itself in contrast to the sin it dissolves, and thus presents to the broken self the bounteous mercy of God in all its overflowing spontaneity and in all the plenitude of its givenness. Sin cannot help but be destroyed before the grace of the Word. The lie of independence and the spirit of repudiation are shattered to pieces. The in-coming of the Word has so exposed the sins of the self that they have no longer a hiding place. The barriers are gone, and the givenness of God is everywhere manifest.

6. Thus far the totality of the conversion experience has led to a condemnation of the self. The Revelation of the Word judges the self. The spirit perceives with penetrating clarity its own sinfulness, and likewise perceives the everlasting goodness of God. It is the love and mercy of God which judges by being put in contrast with the depravity of the self. God does not actively condemn in the form of punishment, but He speaks to us in such a way that our own sin judges us. It is the presence of our own sin in contrast to the mercy of God which condemns. God, by showing Himself to us in His perfect goodness, forces our own sin to judge us within ourself. It is the presentation of love and mercy that constitutes this most stinging of all judgments. Thus it is that judgment and mercy are closely interwoven. It is mercy and not wrath which is the most powerful condemnation of all. Therefore God forces us to judge ourselves by His own judgment of love and mercy. The Word of God symbolized by the Cross is at once the most severe judgment and the most perfect expression of His mercy. Justice and mercy are not disparate, but bound together. The givenness of God's love judges, redeems, and binds together.

The human person, once perceiving that the Revelation of the Word is a condemnation of the self, casts away all thoughts of his own merit. He sees that the givenness of God is everywhere prevenient, and that he possesses nothing that has not been given. He knows that what he has received has been given by some "other," and that ultimately all good things are gifts of God. Therefore in the face of this givenness of God, in the face of His perfect and righteous mercy, he knows that he has no merit. Never again can he hope to boast of his good deeds, of his skill, of his prowess, for he knows that they are gifts.

The more he examines his life, the more he looks into himself with complete honesty, the more clearly he perceives that what he has is a gift. Suppose he was an upright man in the eyes of society, then he will now say to himself: "So you were an educated man, yes, but who paid for your education; so you were a good man and upright, yes, but who taught you your good manners and so provided you with good fortune that you did not need to steal; so you were a man of a loving disposition and not like the hard-hearted, yes, but who raised you in a good family, who showed you care and affection when you were young so that you would grow up to appreciate kindness—must you not admit that what you have, you have received? Then be thankful and cease your boasting." Thus there is no man so upright that the Word of God beside his goodness will not condemn. There is no goodness that beside God's goodness does not become a "filthy rag." There are none who before God can escape the judgment of His mercy. Before His givenness, there is not one who can be too thankful.

Thus it is that "we love because He loved us first."[21] All goodness, all kindness, all righteousness are given by God. Because He acted first, we can act; because He gives to us, we can give; because He cares, we can care. Hence it is that community must be established by the "other" coming to us, in giving to us, and only then can we be drawn

21. 1 John 4:19.

out of closedness into openness. Therefore no man can claim good deeds as his own, since the very possibility of his goodness presupposes someone's giving to him.

The spirit now perceives that it was through no merit that God loved him. "Christ died for us while we were still sinners."[22] Thus we reach the heart of the matter—God gave when we were undeserving. Even when we have desert it is because He first gives it to us; but further, should that desert be lost, He still comes to us. Mercy would not be mercy were this not so. God then does not want merit that He can reward. He does not want us to enter into a contest or amassing good works as a bargain for future blessings. He wants to establish a community which will last through all ages, a community not torn apart by those boasting of their good deeds. He wants a community bound together in faith and rejoicing in thanksgiving. Achieving good deeds as merits serves only the demon of spiritual pride. Goodness must grow out of faith and thanksgiving. Goodness must be giving as God gives. It must seek to restore the lost ones by giving to them first as God gave to us first. To be in community means to live in this way, and for the establishing of such a community Christ came into the world. Thus sin is melted down and cast away, and along with it the source of spiritual pride, merit. There is no merit before God. Nor should there be merit before Him. True community does not count the merits of its members. Merit is a concept rooted in sin, and well disposed of.

Therefore before God merit is cast aside along with the other errors of pride. To hold on to the concept of merit is to turn Christianity upside down. God came when man most needed Him. Christ did not come to confer honors upon merit, but to destroy sin. To receive

22. Romans 5:8.

the Word is not to be rewarded, but to be condemned. God's call is not a call to praise, but a call to repentance.

7. The spirit thus comes to realize the true majesty and goodness of God. All of the fear, all the false conceptions of God are swept away. God has spoken; and although His Word constitutes a terrible judgment in its presence to us, it also calls us to repentance. The Word calls, it does not merely condemn; it manifests God's forgiveness as well as His insisting righteousness. Thus out of the presence of the Word of God grows the source of new life. The spirit laid low can now raise itself up again in confidence and trust. The fabrication of sin has been dissolved, and His forgiveness calls us back once again to community. The self is now open. It knows God and walks in faith and thanksgiving.

From the conversion experience grows also the true conception of God. Take for example the Doctrine of Creation. It means primarily two things: first, that man is dependent on God, and second, that everything is a gift of God. These two truths are learned during the experience of His Word. The Creation is no necessary emanation from God. He was not bound to create the world, but created the world from His own bounteous love. The Creation was an act of grace; its gift of God is like His Word, undeserved and uncaused. It has its roots in His free and spontaneous givenness. We learn the ever-present givenness of God by the presence of His Word. At the same time do we learn our inseparable dependence on Him.

Therefore, "rational theology" cannot separate itself from the Revelation of the Word. Reason cannot tell us whether God is Creator, Eternal, all-powerful and so forth. But He himself can tell us. By knowing His Word in its presence to us we perceive His givenness behind everything, sustaining the world, seeking the world, and we know therefrom that He is over and above the world, independent of it for His being and therefore eternal. The nature of God, insofar as it is intelligible to us, is not discovered by playing with metaphysical categories, but is rather presented to us unmistakably in the experience of His Word. If God speaks to one out of the heavens as He spoke to Paul, one will know more about Him than reason can say. Not that we want to disparage reason, but reason, unless guided by faith, is a poor leader.

8. Thus the conversion experience is summed up by the perception of the majesty and glory of God, of His bounteous mercy, and perfect justice. The false conceptions have melted away; pride has been destroyed along with the falsity of claiming merit. But although the trials of the spirit have been great, although the judgment has stung and the old sinful self has been dissolved, there is a new life which begins. The Word not only shatters, but it restores. God also calls, for His speaking is a calling. Thus the spirit, perceiving the call and knowing His forgiveness, picks itself up in faith. A newness of life has flowed into it, and it lives once again, open to God and to men. In raising itself up, the spirit returns to community in faith.

Section IV

1. The spirit returns to the community in faith—so we ended our discussion of the conversion experience. But what do we mean by faith? We must now inquire into the full meaning of the return by faith and the fruits of faith. If the reader will bear in mind the discussion of sin, he will perceive the contrast between sin as closedness and faith as openness. Sin is separation from community; faith is integration into community. Egotism bears the fruit which separates man from God and from man. Faith is the openness out of which grows Christian love, which binds the community together under God.

2. Being presented the Word, being judged by the Word, the self is struck down, as we have stated. There is more than pure judgment, however, for God's Word is also a call to return. The conversion experience is negative in that it dissolves the fabric of sin, positive in that it is an election into community. God comes to us and by His Word restores us to community and calls us back to community. The self is once again rooted in that power which sustains it,[23] and apart from which it is dead and alone. Thus conversion results in being restored as a son of God. All men have God as Father, but not all men are His sons. They are not His sons because they have turned away, and not until the Word penetrates their closedness are they reinstated as sons. Conversion thus results in the restoration of sonship before God. Man is justified by faith, he is re-opened before God. Thus the first aspect of election is to be open to God, to be set in proper relation to Him. The barriers have been dissolved and man's sin has been judged. The personal relation has been re-established by the Word, and the self is open in faith. To be restored to God is thus the first aspect of election.

The second aspect of election is to be restored to one's fellow men and to work for their restoration. It must always be borne in mind that election possesses this dialectical character. It changes relations both vertically and horizontally, both to God and to men. The man who is elected and restored to sonship before God is not thereby lifted out of the earthly community; he is not abstracted from his fellow men and assumed into heaven. Rather, he is planted more firmly into that earthly community. He has been elected not for his own sake but for the sake of others. He has been chosen to spread the "good news" and to tell others of the mercy of God. The elect are not those arbitrarily chosen by God to manifest His mercy. Rather, they are those

23. See Kierkegaard's definition of faith in *The Sickness Unto Death.*

chosen for the task of restoring the community. They are to work and endure for the Lord.

Witness how He spoke to Ananias concerning Paul: "This man is the means I have chosen for carrying my name among the heathen and their kings, and among the descendants of Israel. For I am going to show him what he will have to endure for my sake."[24] Paul himself knew of this dialectical character of election: "For, as I see it, living means Christ and dying something even better. But if living on here means having my labor bear fruit, I cannot tell which to choose. I am undecided between the two, for I long to depart and be with Christ, for that is far, far better, and yet your needs make it very necessary for me to stay on here. I am convinced of this, and so I know that I shall stay on and serve you all, to help you to develop and be glad in your faith. So you will find in me fresh cause for Christian exultation, through having me with you again."[25]

Thus Paul knows that his election does not mean that he can run off and depart from the earthly community. It means just the opposite, namely, that he must work in that community for the establishment of God's community. He is chosen to preach the Word; God will use him as a means for further election. "And He said to them, go ye into all the world, and preach the Gospel to the whole creation."[26] Thus election possesses this double axis. When we lose sight of this double nature of election and of the dialectic uniting the two, then the Word of God is made into a purely escapist and individual doctrine or else into a secular social gospel.

We should further remark on the rationale of election. The purpose behind election, the end which the coming of the Word has in view, is the reestablishment of community, and ultimately the forma-

24. Acts 9:15–16.
25. Philippians 1:21–26.
26. Mark 16:15.

tion of the heavenly community which is to endure throughout all ages. In short, the process of election is guided by the goal towards which creation moves, namely, the Kingdom of Heaven. Therefore the penetration of the Word is not some arbitrary phenomenon making itself known to some and concealing itself from others. Rather, the Word works to restore community and to bring men together under God. Therefore the guiding motive of election on God's part is not God seeking His own glory. To make God's motive His own honor is to make Him into an egotist. God works rather to establish His community, which is the Kingdom of Heaven. Surely His community will manifest His glory, but to see His own glory is not His motive. Therefore the rationale, the end, and the purpose of election is the heavenly community which at the end of all ages will burst in to complete and fulfill the world as we know it. Thus election is a communal process moving towards a communal end. It seeks to restore openness, to destroy sin, and to bind men together by faith.

3. We should now mention three false notions which have cluttered up and confused many traditional discussions of election.

(i) If one combines the New Testament concept of election, which we have accepted in its full sense, with the Greek notion of God as a completely static being, then it is difficult to avoid many harsh predestinarian conclusions. These two conceptions are combined for the first time in Augustine, with results well known to all. To avoid the difficulty one has simply to get rid of the Greek notion, which is foreign to Christianity. If the Platonic contrast between the changing and the changeless is allowed to enter Christian theology, there results a view of election which is as false as Pelagianism. If Pelagius rendered the Cross of Christ to no effect, so did Augustine.

(ii) Further, traditional theories of predestination are infected by a radical individualism. We have already seen how the natural cosmos of Augustine and Aquinas is necessarily individualistic, although verbally the conclusion is avoided. Because of this individualism, salvation is imagined as choosing one individual here and another there. Society is merely an aggregate of separate units from which God arbitrarily chooses some to show His justice and some to show His mercy. Only a theology infected with individualism could imagine election working in this way.

(iii) The third error has been to misunderstand the purpose of election. It is either conceived as an attempt to save individuals, or as God working to seek His own glory. But the Biblical view, if I understand it, is that God is working to establish a community. Creation is moving toward the Kingdom of Heaven, and for that reason God came into the world. Thus, the purpose and intention of His electing is not to save an isolated person here and there, but is to restore and to gather together a community of His created ones, which is not merely an aggregate, but a community in the full sense bound together by faith and love.

Therefore, we do not believe that the doctrine of election leads to the deterministic predestinarianism of Augustine and Aquinas. Their views are mixed up with Greek staticism and individualism, and hence they are not correct. The refuge from this type of theology is not semi-Pelagianism but a proper understanding of the Biblical doctrine of grace. If one understands the communal dialectic of election, then one can avoid the traditional difficulties.

4. The elect are chosen to re-establish the community. To restore the community is their prime intention, or should be. They are to go to the "heathen" and tell them the "good news." Thus there immediately begins the reconstruction of community. God's Word was not primarily the revelation of some eternal truth (that is a Greek notion). God's Word is something active. It penetrates into some, saves them,

elects them, and then moves forward by their action into the rest of the community. The Word is essentially a message, a "tidings of great joy," to be spread about to all. The Word is the call of return to community. Therefore it is the duty of the elect to see that the Word is preached far and wide that all may hear it. It is the task of the elect, working together with the Holy Spirit, to re-establish and to reconstruct the community which has been destroyed by sin.

The Word is not an ethical precept. As we have seen, it is the Word of God Himself speaking to us which destroys sin and which converts the inner spirit and immediately sets it open to and into community. Thus, the fundamental principle of Christian "ethics" is as follows: man cannot be saved by teaching; community cannot be restored by talking about it. To restore community, man must be brought into community and restored first. This statement may sound like a paradox, but this is precisely what happens to God's chosen. They are those immediately converted and thereby set into community, and by their efforts, together with the Holy Spirit, others can be brought into community. Man cannot be enticed into community by ethical precepts. He must be first opened up and set into community by the "other." The principle of Jesus' teachings is this very point. He begins not with the ethical precept, but rather with bringing men into the Kingdom of God. Out of the family life of God spring the right relations. Precepts are present in Jesus' and Paul's teachings, but they grow out of a deeper source, namely, the life of God in us, or His Word coming to us.

Since the conversion experience has brought the sinner into the family life of God, it follows that he now leads his life in right relations to others. He knows his full communal obligations to men as well as to God. Therefore, there grow from the conversion experience those actions which restore and reconstruct community. Thus obligations are now fulfilled. The givenness of God has carried over into action with others, and the principle of conduct becomes the analogy of grace. As Luther puts it:

> Therefore, if we recognize the great and precious things which are given us, as Paul says, there will be shed abroad in our hearts by the Holy Ghost the love which makes us free, joyful, almighty workers and conquerors over all tribulations, servants of our neighbors and yet lords of all. But for those who do not recognize the gifts bestowed upon them through Christ, Christ has been born in vain; they go their way with their works, and shall never come to taste or to feel those things. Just as our neighbor is in need and lacks that in which we abound, so we also have been in need before God and have lacked His mercy. Hence, as our heavenly Father has in Christ freely come to our help, we also ought freely to help our neighbor through our body and its works, and each should become as it were a Christ to the other, that we may be Christs to one another and Christ may be the same in all; that is, that we may be truly Christians.[27]

Thus it is that the example of the givenness and mercy of God should guide us in our communal life, and it is because we have actually experienced the Word and have been actually accepted by God into the proper relation of sonship with Him, that we can carry out our obligations. The experience of His Word leads, then, to the reconstruction of community with others as well, and we act, or try to, according to the analogy of His grace. Thus it is that a Christian man is not only open and therefore free, but he is a servant of all. Community involves responsibility and obligations, and now being restored to community, he is responsible. As God gave to him, he gives to others. As God called him to community, so he calls others. In this way the community which the Word seeks to gather is formed in the hearts of the faithful and in those whom they seek to win back to God with His help.

---

27. *Treatise on Christian Liberty,* in vol. II of *Works,* p. 338.

5. Openness, which we have called faith, is the fundamental attitude of those in community. To be open to some, one presupposes faith which is openness. Persons in community are thus open to one another. But faith grows into stronger bonds; its fruits are charity, kindness, sacrifice, and love. The greatest of these, as Paul says, is love. Since there has been much confusion concerning the question of Christian love, we should make a few remarks about it.

(i) To begin with, it is not to be confused with appetition and desire, which deal with objects and which seek concrete impersonal processes. Desire, as we have seen, is neither anti-social nor pro-social. Christian love, however, is primarily communal. It refers to another person. Christian love therefore is a purely spiritual thing.

(ii) Desire is egoistic; it seeks some object for the self. It is controlled by an attitude of seeking and of getting. Desire leads us to acquire something. Christian love, on the other hand, seeks not its own; it manifests the spirit of giving. While there is, to be sure, affection in love, love gives. Its end is to give something to the other person as person. Like grace, it overflows in its bestowal of gifts upon the other.

(iii) Christian love includes the whole person in its giving. Desire includes but a "part" of the person, so to speak, i.e., it does not deal with personality except as being joined to it. But love includes the totality of the person in its giving, and it aims at the full personality of the other as well. In short, love is an intense and full personal contact. It does not merely touch the border of the person involved. Like faith from which it grows, it is expressive of the very center of the spirit. Therefore love, although it is giving, does not overlook the personality of the giver. The self is not destroyed when it gives, but it is completed. It is completed, however, not in an appetitional sense nor, of course, in an egotistical sense, i.e., by being glorified. The spirit completes itself in faith and love because it is communal by nature, and faith and love in all their intensity are proper to it.

(iv) The best way to understand Christian love, however, is to view it against its background of the conversion experience. To distinguish love from desire is to distinguish one simple feeling from another. But Christian love is a tremendously complex affair. It is complex because it grows out of a complex experience, namely that of conversion wherein judgment and mercy are contrasted yet bound together, and wherein the bounteous goodness of God exposes the iniquity of the self, and so on. In brief, Christian love cannot be understood apart from the Word. It is knowing and being judged by the Word that gives love its character. For Christian love is a fruit of faith which is given to us by the Word bursting in upon us. Therefore, love cannot be understood apart from the totality of the experience which precedes it. It knows all the trials of the spirit—sin, aloneness, closedness, the barriers, lying in exposure, judgment, and finally faith. Once Christian love is separated from its background, it becomes something purely sentimental. It is no longer the same thing at all, but is immature, formless sentimentality.

But Christian love, in all its fullness and tempered by the context from which it grows, is firm, mature, sober, and yet genuine and complete in its givenness. Thus, if one views Christian love in its proper experiential, rational, and theological context, then one will see that it is not what many people think it is. It possesses a character peculiarly Christian because it grows out of Christian experience. To discuss it apart from its background is to lose its meaning completely. To examine Christian love in light of its entire context is the best way we know to defend it against charges of sentimentality. There is nothing sentimental about Paul, and who would say that there is anything sentimental about grace?

Thus, it is this peculiarly Christian love which, growing from faith, binds the Christian community together under God. It is this love which looks up to God in faithful thanksgiving, which knows the full structure of its obligations and its duties, which has accepted the complete responsibility of its communal nature, and which gives itself to others in the way in which the Son of God gave Himself to suffer on the Cross—it is *this* love, which draws its richness from the totality of Christian experience, that binds together the restored community under God in faithful thanksgiving.

6. We now reach the conclusion of our exposition. Discarding the categories of the natural cosmos, we have gone on to explain sin and faith in terms of community, using such phrases as openness, closedness, aloneness, togetherness and so forth. Sin is that which separates one from community. Faith and love bind community together. It only remains to say that faith and love have not only a temporal significance but a significance which is to endure for all ages. To have faith means to be elected and restored before God, and it therefore means that the elect are pilgrims on their way to Him. But on the way they are to gather together with His aid all those who still remain behind, and are to help bring the totality of the creation before Him. Creation moves toward that great day, burdened by the stubbornness of man's sin to be sure, but then all things are possible with God.

That day may not be so far off as we think. Who knows how soon it will be that God gathers together His elect under Him? Is it not written that "the Day of the Lord is to come like a thief in the night"?[28] Therefore, we may look forward to the day, which may not be far off, when Christ will appear in His glory and when the heavenly community will be established under God. At that time sin will have been destroyed, and men will be open to one another, looking up to God in rejoicing and thanksgiving. The whole creation will be bound together and all the creatures of God will kneel at His feet. This community joining all together under God is the goal toward which God moves His creation. This community is another of His bounteous gifts, and the most perfect and gracious of all.

28. Thessalonians 5:2.

Bibliography

Rawls divides his bibliography into three parts: "Naturalism," "Our Own View," and "Miscellaneous." Titles in the first and second categories are listed below, followed by fuller bibliographical information on them and all other works referred to.

Part 1: Chief Sources for Naturalism

    1. Plato:
       Phaedrus
       Symposium
       Republic
       Protagoras

    2. Aristotle:
       Nicomachean Ethics
       Politics
       Metaphysics

    3. Augustine: (all works listed are found in *P.N.F.*)
       Confessions
       The City of God
       Homilies on the Gospel of John
       Enchiridion
       On the Trinity
       Morals of the Catholic Church
       The Spirit and the Letter
       Nature and Grace
       On Grace and Free-Will
       Man's Perfection in Righteousness

> *Disputation Against Fortunatus the Manichean*
> *Reply to Faustus the Manichean*
> *On the Good of Marriage*
> *Marriage and Concupiscence*

  4. Aquinas:
     Summa Theologica: Treatise on God, Treatise on the Last End
     Summa Contra Gentiles: Book III

Part 2: Chief Sources for Our Own View

  1. The Bible (always the last word in matters of religion)
  2. Luther:
     Babylonian Captivity of the Church
     On Christian Liberty
  3. Brunner, Emil:
     Man in Revolt
     The Mediator
     The Theology of Crisis
  4. Leon, Philip:
     The Ethics of Power
  5. Niebuhr, Reinhold:
     The Nature and Destiny of Man
  6. Nygren, Anders:
     Agape and Eros

Below is a complete bibliography of works referred to.

Abingdon Bible Commentary. Edited by Frederick C. Eiselen, Edwin
  Lewis, and David G. Downey. New York: The Abingdon Press, 1929.
Aeschylus. *The Suppliant Maidens, the Persians, the Seven against Thebes
  of Aeschylus.* Translated by E. D. A. Morshead. London: Macmillan,
  1908.
[*A.N.F.*] *The Ante-Nicene Fathers: Translations of the Writings of the
  Fathers Down to* A.D. *325.* Edited by Alexander Roberts and James
  Donaldson. Edinburgh, 1884. Reprinted: Grand Rapids, Michigan,
  Wm. B. Eerdmans, 1951.

Aquinas. *Summa Contra Gentiles.* Translated by English Dominican Fathers. London: Burns, Oates & Washbourne, 1923–1940.

———— *Summa Theologica.* Translated by English Dominican Fathers. London: Burns, Oates, & Washbourne, 1920–1943.

Aristotle. *The Basic Works of Aristotle.* Edited by Richard McKeon. New York: Random House, 1941.

Augustine. *The City of God.* Translated by John Healy. Edinburgh: John Grant, 1909. Later this was the basis of the Everyman edition of 1945.

Barker, Ernest. *The Political Thought of Plato and Aristotle.* London: Methuen, 1906. Reprinted: Dover, 1959.

Berdyaev, Nicolas. *Freedom and Spirit.* London: Centenary Press, 1935.

Blanshard, Brand. *The Nature of Thought.* New York: Macmillan, 1940.

Brunner, Emil. *Man in Revolt.* Published in German in 1937. English translation by Olive Wyon. New York: Charles Scribner's Sons, 1937.

———— *The Mediator: A Study of the Central Doctrine of the Christian Faith.* London: Lutterworth Press, 1934.

———— *The Theology of Crisis.* New York: Charles Scribner's Sons, 1929.

Burnaby, J. *Amor Dei: A Study of the Religion of St. Augustine.* London: Hodder and Stoughton, 1938.

Demos, Raphael. *The Philosophy of Plato.* New York: Charles Scribner's Sons, 1939.

Dodd, C. H. *The Epistle of Paul to the Romans.* New York: Harper and Row, 1932.

Drucker, Peter F. *The End of Economic Man.* New York: John Day, 1939.

Eliot, T. S. *Murder in the Cathedral,* in *The Complete Poems and Plays.* New York: Harcourt, Brace and World, 1958.

Fichte, Johann Gottlieb. *The Vocation of Man* [1800]. Open Court, 1940.

Fortescue, A. Article on Docetism, in Hastings, ed., *Encyclopaedia of Religion and Ethics.*

Gilson, Etienne. *The Spirit of Medieval Philosophy.* Translated by A. H. C. Downes. New York: Charles Scribner's Sons, 1940.

Hastings, James, ed. *The Encyclopaedia of Religion and Ethics.* New York: Charles Scribner's Sons, 1908–1927.

Hobbes, Thomas. *De Cive* [1642]. Translated into English as *Philosophical Rudiments Concerning Government and Society* [1651].

———— *Leviathan* [1651].

Howard, W. F. Article on First Corinthians, in *Abingdon Bible Commentary.*

Huxley, Thomas Henry. *Evolution and Ethics and Other Essays.* New York: D. Appleton and Co., 1895.

Irenaeus. *Against Heresies,* in *A.N.F.*

Kierkegaard, Søren. *Concluding Unscientific Postscript.* Translated by David F. Swenson and Walter Lowrie. Princeton: Princeton University Press, 1941.

———— *Philosophical Fragments.* Translated by David Swenson. Princeton: Princeton University Press, 1936. Revised edition by Howard V. Hong, 1962.

———— *The Sickness Unto Death.* Translated by Walter Lowrie. Princeton: Princeton University Press, 1941.

Leon, Philip. *The Ethics of Power.* London: George Allen and Unwin, 1935.

———— *Plato.* New York: Thomas Nelson and Sons, 1940.

Lovejoy, Arthur O. "The Meaning of Romanticism for the Historian of Ideas." *Journal of the History of Ideas,* vol. 2, no. 3 (June 1941).

Luther, Martin. *Treatise on Christian Liberty.* In *Works.* Philadelphia: A. J. Holman, 1915.

Mackintosh, H. R. *Types of Modern Theology.* London: Nisbet and Co., 1937.

McGiffert, Arthur Cushman. *A History of Christian Thought.* New York: Charles Scribner's Sons, 1933.

Mussolini, Benito. "The Political and Social Doctrine of Fascism," in *Contemporary Civilization Source Books.* New York: Columbia University Press, 1941. Reissued as *Introduction to Contemporary Civilization in the West,* Columbia University Press, 1946. Vol. II, pp. 1115–1125.

Nettleship, Richard Lewis. *Lectures on the Republic of Plato.* London: MacMillan, 1937.

Niebuhr, Reinhold. *The Nature and Destiny of Man.* New York: Charles Scribner's Sons, 1941.

Nietzsche, Friedrich. *The Will to Power.* Translation by Anthony M.
     Ludovici in *Complete Works,* ed. O. Levy. Edinburgh: T. N. Foulis,
     1909–1923.

Nygren, Anders. *Agape and Eros.* Originally published in Swedish,
     1930–1936. English translation by A. G. Herbert and Philip S.
     Watson, first published in three volumes by the Society for the
     Promotion of Christian Knowledge, 1932–1939. Revised English
     translation by Philip S. Watson, published in one volume by
     Westminster Press, Philadelphia, 1953. Reprinted: Harper & Row,
     1969; University of Chicago Press, 1982.

Origen. *De Principiis,* in *A.N.F.*

Plato. *Phaedrus, Ion, Gorgias, and Symposium, with passages from the
     Republic and Laws.* Translated by Lane Cooper. New York: Oxford
     University Press, 1938.

———— *Laches, Protagoras, Meno, Euthydemus.* Translated by W. R. M.
     Lamb. Loeb Classical Library. London: Heinemann, 1924.

———— *The Republic.* Translated by F. M. Cornford. Oxford: Oxford
     University Press, 1941.

[*P.N.F.*] *A Select Library of the Nicene and Post-Nicene Fathers of the
     Christian Church,* Series I. Edited by Philip Schaff et al. Buffalo,
     New York, 1887. Reprinted: Grand Rapids, Michigan, Wm. B.
     Eerdmans, 1978–1979.

Rosenberg, Alfred. *The Myth of the Twentieth Century* [1930].

Rousseau, Jean-Jacques. *Discourse on the Origin of Inequality,* in *The
     Social Contract and Discourses.* Translated by G. D. H. Cole.
     London: Everyman Library, J. M. Dent, 1915.

Schopenhauer, Arthur. *The World as Will and Idea* [1818]. Translated by
     R. B. Haldane and J. Kemp. London: Routledge and Kegan Paul, 1883.

Scott, E. F. Article on Gnosticism, in Hastings, ed., *Encyclopaedia of
     Religion and Ethics.*

Strayer, Joseph R., and Munro, Dana C. *The Middle Ages, 395–1500.* New
     York: Appleton-Century-Crofts, 1942.

Taylor, A. E. *Plato, the Man and His Work.* Dial Press, 1936.

———— *The Problem of Evil.* London: E. Benn, 1929.

Temple, William. *Nature, Man and God.* London: Macmillan, 1934.

Tertullian. *Against Marcion,* in *A.N.F.*

———— *On the Resurrection of the Flesh,* in *A.N.F.*

Viereck, Peter. *Metapolitics.* New York: Alfred A. Knopf, 1941.

Warfield, Benjamin Breckenridge. *Studies in Tertullian and Augustine.* New York and London: Oxford University Press, 1930.

Whale, John S. *Christian Doctrine.* Cambridge: The University Press, 1941.

Williams, N. P. *The Grace of God.* New York: Longmans, Green, 1930.

ON MY RELIGION

(1997)

1. My religion is of interest only to me, as its various phases and how they followed one another are not unusual or especially instructive. I was born into a conventionally religious family. My mother was an Episcopalian, my father a Southern Methodist, but my two parents went to the same Episcopal Church in Baltimore. I never had any sense that either had other than a conventional religion. I too was only conventionally religious until my last two years at Princeton.

Then things changed. I became deeply concerned about theology and its doctrines—for example, the different ways of conceiving of the Trinity and how such an apparently dark conception could express distinct forms of Christianity. I even thought about going to the seminary but decided to wait until the war was over: I could not convince myself that my motives were sincere, and anyway I felt I should serve in the armed services as so many of my friends and classmates were doing. This period lasted during most of the war, but all that changed in the last year or so of the war. And since then I have thought of myself as no longer orthodox, as I put it, which expresses it vaguely enough, as my views have not always remained the same.

I have often wondered why my religious beliefs changed, particularly during the war. I started as a believing orthodox Episcopalian Christian, and abandoned it entirely by June of 1945. I don't profess to understand at all why my beliefs changed, or believe it is possible fully to comprehend such changes. We can record what happened, tell stories and make guesses, but they must be taken as such. There may be something in them, but probably not.

Three incidents stand out in my memory: Kilei Ridge; Deacon's death; hearing and thinking about the Holocaust. The first occurred about the middle of December, 1944. The struggle of F Company of the 128th Infantry Regiment of the 32nd Division to take the ridge overlooking the town of Limon on Leyte was over, and the company simply held its ground. One day a Lutheran Pastor came up and during his service gave a brief sermon in which he said that God aimed our bullets at the Japanese while God protected us from theirs. I don't know why this made me so angry, but it certainly did. I upbraided the Pastor (who was a First Lieutenant) for saying what I assumed he knew perfectly well—Lutheran that he was—were simply falsehoods about divine providence. What reason could he possibly have had but his trying to comfort the troops? Christian doctrine ought not to be used for that, though I knew perfectly well it was.

The second incident—Deacon's death—occurred in May, 1945, high up on the Villa Verde trail on Luzon. Deacon was a splendid man; we became friends and shared a tent at Regiment. One day the First Sergeant came to us looking for two volunteers, one to go with the Colonel to where he could look at the Japanese positions, the other to give blood badly needed for a wounded soldier in the small field hospital nearby. We both agreed, and the outcome depended on who had the right blood type. Since I did and Deacon didn't, he went with the Colonel. They must have been spotted by the Japanese, because soon 150 mortar shells were falling in their direction. They jumped into a foxhole and were immediately killed when a mortar shell also landed in it. I was quite disconsolate and couldn't get the incident out of my mind. I don't know why this incident so affected me, other than my fondness for Deacon, as death was a common occurrence. But I think it did, in ways I will mention in a moment.

The third incident is really more than an incident, as it lasted over a long period of time. It started, as I recall, at Asingan in April, where the Regiment was taking a rest from the line and getting replace-ments. We went to the Army movies shown in the evening, and they also had news reports of the Army information service. It was, I believe, here that I first heard about the Holocaust, as the very first reports of American troops coming upon the concentration camps were made known. Of course much had been known long before that, but it had not been open knowledge to soldiers in the field.

These incidents, and especially the third as it became widely known, affected me in the same way. This took the form of questioning whether prayer was possible. How could I pray and ask God to help me, or my family, or my country, or any other cherished thing I cared about, when God would not save millions of Jews from Hitler? When Lincoln interprets the Civil War as God's punishment for the sin of slavery, deserved equally by North and South, God is seen as acting justly. But the Holocaust can't be interpreted in that way, and all at-tempts to do so that I have read of are hideous and evil. To interpret history as expressing God's will, God's will must accord with the most basic ideas of justice as we know them. For what else can the most basic justice be? Thus, I soon came to reject the idea of the supremacy of the divine will as also hideous and evil.

2. The following months and years led to an increasing rejection of many of the main doctrines of Christianity, and it became more and more alien to me. My difficulties were always moral ones, since my fideism remained firm against all worries about the existence of God. The so-called proofs of God's existence in St. Thomas and others proved nothing of religious significance in any case. That seemed clear. Yet the ideas of right and justice expressed in Christian doc-trines are a different matter.

I came to think many of them morally wrong, in some cases even repugnant. Among these were the doctrines of original sin, of heaven and hell, of salvation by true belief and based on accepting priestly authority. Unless one made an exception of oneself and assumed one would be saved, I came to feel the doctrine of predestination as terrifying once one thought it through and realized what it meant. Double predestination as expressed in its rigorous way by St. Augustine and Calvin seemed especially terrifying, though I had to admit it was present in St. Thomas and Luther also, and actually only a consequence of predestination itself. These doctrines all became impossible for me to take seriously, not in the sense that the evidence for them was weak or doubtful. Rather, they depict God as a monster moved solely by God's own power and glory. As if such miserable and distorted puppets as humans were described could glorify anything! I also came to think that few people really accept these doctrines or even understand them. For them, religion is purely conventional and gives them comfort and solace in difficult times.

In the early years after the war I took much interest in the history of the Inquisition and how it had developed. I read various books about it, including parts of Henry Lea's history of the Inquisition in the Middle Ages, and Lord Acton's review of it and Acton's own views on the corruptions of the power of priests as much as political power. I came to feel that the great curse of Christianity was to persecute dissenters as heretics from the early days of Irenaeus and Tertullian. This seemed to be something new: Greek and Roman religion was civic religion, and it served to instill loyalty to the *polis* or the Emperor especially in time of war and crisis. They insisted on this, but beyond that civil society could be largely free and many different religions flourished in the *polis* and Empire. The history of the Church includes a story of its long historical ties to the state and its use of political power to establish its hegemony and to oppress other religions.

Being a religion of eternal salvation requiring true belief, the

Church saw itself as having justification for its repression of heresy. Thus I have come to think of the denial of religious freedom and liberty of conscience as a very great evil, and for me it makes the claims of the Popes to infallibility impossible to accept. True, the Church claims infallibility only in questions of faith and morals; the doctrine is not that the Pope as a man is infallible but that God will see to it that the man who is the Pope does not speak falsely. Yet if freedom of religion and liberty of conscience are not questions of faith and morals, what are? These freedoms and liberties became fixed points of my moral and political opinions. Eventually they also became basic political elements of my view of constitutional democracy, realized in institutions by the separation of church and state.

To the extent that Christianity is taken seriously, I came to think it could have deleterious effects on one's character. Christianity is a solitary religion: each is saved or damned individually, and we naturally focus on our own salvation to the point where nothing else might seem to matter. Whereas actually, while it is impossible not to be concerned with ourselves, at least to some degree—and we should—our own individual soul and its salvation are hardly important for the larger picture of civilized life, and often we have to recognize this. Thus, how important is it that I be saved compared to risking my life to assassinate Hitler, had I the chance? It's not important at all. Surely one ought to take that chance, and one could do so, although as Kant said, no one would be confident ahead of time that he would. I mention this case of assassinating Hitler: I have thought a lot about those times and wondered whether I would have had the courage and guts to do it. Certainly such acts are not easy. It seemed to me a grave fault in the German resistance that they were so much bothered by scruples against assassination, or against killing as such, or against attacking the head of state. Stauffenberg was right: these concerns were so far outweighed by the enormous evil Hitler perpetuated that it is difficult to give credit to their reasoning and to think that they weren't moved by other concerns they did not want to mention.

3. Of the many texts I have read on religion, few have struck me as much as Bodin's views as expressed in his *Colloquium of the Seven.*[1] Three things especially are striking about Bodin. The first is that he was all his life, so far as we know, a believing Catholic. He asked for a Catholic burial, and he had been a leading member of the *Politiques.* He was not someone who, like Spinoza, came to toleration after rejecting or changing his religious faith. For him, toleration is an aspect and consequence of the harmony of nature as expressed in God's creation. Although he recognized the political importance of toleration, and held that the state should always uphold it, his belief in toleration was religious and not only political.

Another feature of Bodin's thought was that it was wrong to attack a person's religion, especially if one did not try at the same time to present a better one to put in its place. At the end of the *Colloquium,* the seven speakers agree to abandon their attempts to refute one another's religious opinions, and instead to encourage one another to describe their religious views so that all may learn what others think and be able to understand what their beliefs are in their best light. Thus, while friendly and sympathetic discussion of our beliefs is accepted as an important part of religious life, argument and controversy are not. In view of the harmony and multiplicity of religions, what point would argument and controversy serve?

Finally, Bodin surely recognizes some bounds on what religions are admissible. He does not discuss these bounds as clearly as he might, but one of them obviously is an affirming toleration as part of a reli-

1. Jean Bodin, *Colloquium of the Seven about Secrets of the Sublime,* trans. Marion Leathers Daniels Kuntz (Princeton: Princeton University Press, 1975).

gious doctrine and distinct from political ideas. And from there we might take the steps of political liberalism and say that the religions of the seven are each reasonable, and accept the idea of public reason and its idea of the domain of the political. Part of the significance of this is that a person's religion is often no better or worse than they are as persons, and the idea of the reasonable, or some analogous idea, must always be presupposed.

4. It is clear that atheism is the one view Bodin cannot abide. He understands it not only as the view that God does not exist but also as rejecting the principles of right and justice. To deny the existence of God, he thinks, is to reject those principles. For he believes that people will honor right and justice only when they believe in God and fear divine punishments. The denial of God leads, he thinks, to a hideous social world in which no one acknowledges any limits on self-interest beyond what tactics and strategy may suggest. Once we question Bodin's assumptions—common to his age—then nonvoluntarist theism (as opposed to atheism) need not involve such consequences and is compatible with faith in God. If we say that God's will is the source of all being, and of moral and political values, then the denial of God's existence entails the denial of those values also. But if we say that the ground and content of those values is God's reason, or else known to God's reason, then God's will serves only a subordinate role of sanctioning the divine intentions now seen as grounded on reason. In this case the denial of God's existence leads only to the denial of the divine sanctions but not to the denial of values.

We need to consider how the relation between God's reason and moral and political values may be conceived. Perhaps we can say this: God's reason and our reason are in some ways similar and in some ways different. God's reason is different in that its powers far surpass ours: it comprehends all possible information and it can see all possible inferences; for example, it grasps at once all the relations between and facts about numbers. God knows straightway that Fermat's theorem is true and need not labor to work out new mathematics as we do in order to establish it. Yet God's reason, I believe, is the same as ours in that it recognizes the same inferences as valid and the same facts as true that we recognize as valid and true. Beyond that we may suppose that God's reason is consistent with ours: so far as we can comprehend a case, God's idea of reasonableness and ours yield the same judgment.

Let's accept these remarks as sound enough. Now if we deny the existence of God, we do deny the existence of a reason with divine powers, but do we deny the soundness of reason's content? There is a great divide on this point. For my part, I don't see how it is possible that the content and validity of reason should be affected by whether God exists or not, thinking of God as a being with will. We cannot deny the validity of those inferences or the truth of the facts recognized as true. If we do this, we undercut our reasoning about anything and might as well babble at random.

Suppose, then, that reasoning in its most basic forms is invariant with respect to the various kinds of beings that exercise it. Hence God's being, however great the divine powers, does not determine the essential canons of reason. Moreover, the content of the judgments of practical reason depends on social facts about how human beings are related in society and to one another. The divine practical reason will also connect with these facts, just as ours does; and this is so even if these facts are themselves the outcome of God's creation. Given these facts as they undeniably are in our social world, the basic judgments of reasonableness must be the same, whether made by God's reason or by ours. This invariant content of reasonableness—without which our thought collapses—doesn't allow otherwise, however pious it might seem to attribute everything to the divine will.

So I go along with Bodin this far: atheism (as he understands it) is a disaster, but nontheism need not be feared, politically speaking. Nontheism is compatible with religious faith; and even atheism is to be tolerated, for what is punishable in religion is not beliefs but deeds.

General Index

Index of Biblical Passages